also by Tony Checko, "The Striped Bass 60 + Pound Club"
published in 2007, IUniverse, 224 pages.

The Striped Bass

60++

Pound Club

Tony Checko

also published: *The Striped Bass 60+ Pound Club*

iUniverse, Inc.
New York   Bloomington

The Striped Bass 60++ Pound Club

iUniverse books may be ordered through booksellers or by contacting:

iUniverse
1663 Liberty Drive
Bloomington, IN 47403
www.iuniverse.com
1-800-Authors (1-800-288-4677)

Because of the dynamic nature of the Internet, any Web addresses or links contained in this book may have changed since publication and may no longer be valid. The views expressed in this work are solely those of the author and do not necessarily reflect the views of the publisher, and the publisher hereby disclaims any responsibility for them.

ISBN: 978-1-4502-5799-2 (sc)
ISBN: 978-1-4502-5800-5 (dj)
ISBN: 978-1-4502-5801-2 (ebook)

Printed in the United States of America

iUniverse rev. date: 10/26/2010

Dedicated to those fishermen and women of all ages who did battle with this magnificent fish in sunlit days and moonless nights, in calm and storm tossed waters in spite of continuous changing weather conditions. May all their battles be successful either by surf or by boat.

Catching a 60+ pound Striped Bass is a rare event

Book I, "The Striped Bass 60+ Pound Club" contained stories written by anglers who caught these giant fish. Book II (++) continues the same theme with new stories, new chapters, new tips, effect of governmental intrusions into ocean fishing and many photos of 60+ pound stripers from the present and years ago.

The chapter about **Striped Bass Vision** has been updated by the guru of fish vision, **60+ Pound Register** has added members, does ten 60+ pound bass caught in one place in one year mean a **"Southern Shift", Surveys** of the popular saltwater fishing equipment, where has all the menhaden and eels gone, **More Controversy and Problems** and saltwater licenses and 'catch shares' restrictions. **Five hundred + fish** species to be government regulated including...........

Contents

List of Images

1
Introduction

Whether with symbols or script the written word intends to inform people of their history and culture so that future generations can evaluate the quality of their civilization. The lives of people are contained in stories. Biblical stories recall historical events and contain a time- line for many nations. Each culture had scribed ways to tell their off- springs of their heritage.

Stories contain the knowledge of civilization. Knowledge at one time traveled by horse- back hence so did the progress of man. Today information, both knowledge and clutter, travel at the speed of light and possibly beyond the wisdom of man to use intelligently. The "how to" is now available worldwide from weapons of mass destruction to miracles of robotic surgery transmitted miles apart. Is the planting of a potato crop with mule and tiller too low tech and time consuming? Sitting behind a $250K tractor robs your body of vital exercise for longer life and loses it to the mono- minded tractor. So we have our choices. The balance between idle time and productive work is one we must choose day by day. As we schedule our time in pursuit of other activities, much of our daily script is governed by family, school and the products of production, yet stories of other worlds around us stimulate our imagination. Adventures by others are often the basis of exciting stories that we are very willing to share with others, especially kids.

As kids our parents told us stories based on their experience. School encouraged the reading of a variety of books. Books were replacements for stories our parents told us. In libraries you found stories you liked as well as those you had to read but never liked. They were not like Mom's and Dad's experiences that explored subjects unknown even to our imagination.

Fictional stories excite the mind to a point where one may fear to go but hoped for a close encounter. No fear, no danger, yet one could perhaps experience part of the adventure. Time, space and beyond could be met with anticipated danger, yet still on your warm and comfortable sofa. Grand adventures could be traveled in the space of a few pages, yet one knew they were extensions of the mind and safely explored.

Are true stories stranger than fiction? History has shown this to be true. Man cannot manufacture stories that cannot be superseded by stories of actual events that are very strange and unexpected. From true stories of man's spirit and man's will to endure, we all admire the individuals as they confront and succeed in their true adventure.

Today there are 2-3 million striped bass anglers seeking this magnificent fish, yet less than 150 bass over 60 pounds are known to be caught by rod and reel since records have been kept. The catch of a 60-pound striped bass is a rare event. Such stories need to be written in script and preserved. Many of these wonderful stories have been lost forever due to the passing of the fishermen and women. These stories are found in the crevices of rock piles along the coast, along the sandy surf line of eastern beaches or in the wheel- houses or center consoles of Striper Speed Serpents with twin V-8s.

The stories are about men and women who confronted the soul of the striped bass in it's realm and won. Strength, endurance, persistence, confrontation and environmental adversities, all clashed between man and fish.

This clash was a summation of years of strife for both man and fish, several decades for the fish and maybe longer for the man. While the fish struggled to survive in its environment, plagued with its problems of pollution run -off, red tides and limited food supply; the angler faced an array of unregulated and uncoordinated regulations from state to state.

While the fish may spend 30 years enduring the above problems, the fishermen may have spent many years in the surf, jetty or in their boat, during daylight, twilight, moonlight, and darkness waiting for this great battle to commence between two giants. Maybe the same age for fish and man, maybe not. Each one in its own arena, each one like gladiators waiting for the first strike, each one skilled with its own weapons of experience, intelligence and spirit. The bass armed with strength and keenness and its adversary with rod and reel, each combatant measuring how to gain an advantage. Forces of tide and wind create the background for the struggle. It favored one, then the other and then both;...... then none.

What epic stories. The true stories you are about to read were <u>written by the anglers</u>, who challenged the uncertainty of tide and wind as well as their own personal, physical and mental weakness. They won with their weapons of skill, intelligence and....... luck.

It is more likely that fewer big bass will be swimming the Atlantic Coast in the future. With 2-3 million striped bass anglers, scores of commercial netters after them and their food supply, the big bass in the future may only be written about in fictional stories. "The way it was" may be just around the corner or after the last wave. A passing of an era, a passing of an opportunity to battle with the giants; the passing of hope that one day it could have been your true story in the record books. One or two of these stories may give you the feeling that the glory days of big bass fishing has passed. Let us hope not but it is like two lifelines going in opposite directions. The effect of the commercial netters with improved technology, reduced quantity of the food supply and the chemical run-off or dumping, tend to limit their life's span.

Since striped bass are migratory throughout the year, states would rather wash their hands of regulations since they are "passing" fish. Yet it is what the states do or refuse to do that affect the life of these migratory fish. A harvest of one species in one state may be offset by protection in another state. Does the harvest of food fish in one state affect the survival of the species in another state?

These are not unrelated problems. These problems have known relationships among them. The argument between states is how much is this relationship. Those fishing for a livelihood would rather maximize their catch in the present age while shifting the problems to future generations. Those fishing for sport would like to maximize their chance to have a successful catch in the present age and expect or hope the future will stay the same.

You will find stories by boaters were shorter and the experience by the anglers less rigorous. The boaters may have had considerable help from friends on board and the expert handling by the captain may have moderated the excitement during the moment of the battle; but not afterwards. The joy and excitement may have been heightened for the angler after the boarding of the big fish. If anything was lacking during the battle of man-woman versus fish, the celebration amongst the boaters' fraternity was still the same. Information concerning the bait, rod, reel, location of the catch, make of boat, motor etc, etc prolonged the story for months afterwards in the media.

The surf fishermen more likely fought a multi- faceted battle; big bass, tall waves, strong tides, high winds, pelting rains, dangerous jetty rocks, total darkness etc. His was a lonely battle; the outcome always in doubt. His joy shared by others of a similar bent. Others realized how all the factors in landing a big bass had to be in tune with the wind and tide, even with rod, reel, line, terminal tackle and plain good luck.

In neither case the battle is mostly a fair one; the fish in it's environment and the fishermen in theirs. Luck may have been evenly distributed between fish and angler whether in the surf or in the boat.

When all is said and done in these stories; as they proclaim in the boxing ring " May the best man win." So it was done by these men and women.

2
Preface

The theme of Book II of the book "**The Striped Bass 60++ Pound Club**" is the same as the first book: *to save and preserve the rare stories from those who have caught Striped Bass of 60+ pounds or more.*

The striped bass is a moving target figuratively and literally. Most anglers are after them for only sport, less Massachusetts and Rhode Island, for two. The eastern coastal states monitor the catch of the commercial fishermen while the Federal Government also checks that they are not harvested beyond 3 miles. All others are only by- standers who read the headlines about the never ending battle between the recreational and commercial fishermen and the Government.

Even though the fishing laws and regulations are partially based on data gathered by scientific means or approximated through statistical calculations, the data may not be perfect and even if perfect, the statistical results have errors which when applied may lead to inaccurate conclusions. Political pressures can also distort the intent of the scientific data.

Included in this book is data from federal agencies. This was used along with other historical information to develop the laws, regulations, quotas, size, length of seasons, days to fish, time to fish, license fees, gear allowed to harvest fish, pounds harvested per day, week and season etc. and to a lesser degree, the food the striped bass prefers- the menhaden.

Throughout the chapters you will find data located in the appropriate places which you may find boring. If you have little interest in reviewing what the states and feds use to make the decisions that affect your sport, you can move on to the next chapter. I thought it necessary to have the reader realize that the groups that issue these controls use information that is imperfect. They even give the error rates for many of their calculations including those of the by-catch and the poachers. **In** goes scientific data with statistical errors and **out** comes all the laws, regulations, quotas etc. etc. ect. The easy job may be to do the calculations but then you have the political influences of the local and state officials. If only the striped bass could read and write so it could speak on its behalf and tell us what is really going on along the waters of the east and west coasts.

Data can be boring and contain errors but it also establishes the limits of where, when and how much is for you and how much is left for the striped bass.

3
Acknowledgements

Without the stories from the fishermen and women, there would be no book, no stories, and no memories for future big bass anglers to read and dream about.

I am sure these big bass anglers would like to thank their families for all the times they left their routine chores unfinished, in pursuit of their passion. Hours, days, months, years stealing an hour here and there while their wives and kids were waiting at the clock for the telltale sounds of rod, reel, boots and tackle box being deposited in the garage.

Some striped bass fishermen and women may be missing from their homestead due to their passing but are duly registered as members of the 'Club' and are therefore acknowledged. Their stories have been recalled by family members or uncovered by investigative reporting. Others are out there but their locations are unknown and their stories still yet to be published for all of us to enjoy.

This book contains the stories from:

Alfred Anuszewski	Alfred Mc Reynolds
George Cheshire	Ted Nimiroski
Richard Colagiovanni	Mark Sherer
Bill Gavitt	Joe Szabo
Ray Jobin	Peter Vican
Sherwood Lincoln	

Acknowledgements would not be complete without the help from those at the Philadelphia Free Library who helped locate all the issues of Field and Stream Magazines from 1950 to 1970. What a wealth of information is contained in these issues written by the old masters. Likewise to Tommy Needham, although a two -time 60+ pound bass angler, he decided to supply me with data, pictures and news articles of other 60+ pound class anglers and not write about his own catch. His reputation is already well known and respected by his peers.

Critical reviews of the book prior to release by experienced fishermen gave me the confidence to proceed further. Thanks to; JD Muller, Karl Motter, Les Tollier and David Martin. The last and best review is always best from the ones closest to you like; my daughter, Barbara Nolen. She told me what she liked and didn't like. She chose better descriptive words, separated multi-layered sentences; added short pointed phrases etc. all amounted to a better " word picture" in the book.

The stories were not altered in order to create a legend. It wasn't necessary. Landing a 60+ pound striped bass is a rare event. There is little doubt that its weight puts it into the class of 'Big Bass', a true legend in itself. One's mind or witnesses may not be totally clear of the details of the day's battle, but the scales registered the fish for what it was- a 'Big Bass' over 60 pounds- no illusion, no further witnesses required.

Thanks to the tackle shops that weighed these fish. Without them we would not have a verified weight of the fish and hence a story about a true 60+ pound bass.

Thanks also to the IGFA who are ready to record the catch and certify the scales at the weighing stations. Their 300 plus committee members worldwide monitor the record catches in their region as well as conformation to the rules and regulations of the catch.

Other stories of 60 + pounds striped bass are yet to be found while others are lost due to the passing of the anglers. Some of their families and friends have kept the news stories of these fishermen; some with pictures. News groups have been found that highlighted the tussle between man and fish.

Finally, thanks to my fishing buddies Fred Gockley, Harry Weber, David Martin, Herb Davies, Tom Atkins, Alex Field and my brother Stash as they shared with me the struggles to fish for stripers up and down the New Jersey coast. Not all trips were successful, if one were to look into the refrigerator, but our friendship was always enhanced as we tried to outwit, outguess and out 'luck' the bass. We also fought the surf, wind, rain, riptides, and seaweeds just like the 'big bass' fishermen and women did. When the surf temperature is warmer than the air temperature you know its 'big bass' time. We all have been there.

Likewise, to my wife Eileen who put up with those fishing trips, interviewing schedules, reading and rewriting the script, organizing the multitudes of pictures, stories, and miscellaneous data into a final product. While I wrote for content, she read and looked for details that made for interesting and easy reading. Our friend, Kathleen Hoynes Malfi, spent days reading the stories for errors in grammar and suggested changes. Thanks again to all that pointed out my errors and those in a few of the fishermen's stories.

I hope the reader finds the final product as exciting as when I heard the stories directly from the ones who caught these "big bass."

I am the one blessed by meeting and listening to them recall the battle between themselves and their 60+ pound bass. I hope you also feel blessed by reading their stories.

Thanks to the Lord above for giving me the burning passion and sufficient health to complete books I and I I. The projects started in 2005 and now it is 2010.

4
Again, Who Are They?

In the book " The Striped Bass 60+ Pound Club" you read various stories of men and women who caught 60+ pound striped bass and most of these were introduced with a short bio about the anglers. I tried to categorize these men and women but I could determine only that it was their spirit that drove them to accomplish the feat of seeking, hooking and landing the big prize. Their varied backgrounds had little to do with success. They, as you may recall, were policemen, engineers, lawyers, chemists, housewives etc. You would never pick them out of a crowd as successful members of the "Striped Bass 60+ Pound Club." I had the opportunity to meet many of them face to face in their homes, office or café and try to understand what made them strive to catch the rarest of Striped Bass- the 60+ pounder.

How can one uncover the soul of these men and women? You can't. Try to paint a verbal picture, a picture of them in their realm, with rod and reel, scanning the horizon for diving birds, searching for deeper waters along the shoreline, spotting the tell-tale clods of pods of bait fish cruising along the sandbar, spying the angry, swirling rip off the jetty, squinting at the foggy horizon to find other fishing seafarers, trudging along the sandy shore seeking some evidence of previous scars in the sand of other surf jockeys who were itching for a battle with their favorite foe. Only by their actions you could identify them, words being only a forecast of their intentions.

All fishermen are optimists. If the world will ever get better, perhaps we ought to pray for fishermen to lead the world out of its problems. As he strolls the beaches or gunnels of his boat, the eyes, mind and spirit seek the gifts the water will offer. Hopefully he or she is at the prescribed place and time to be the recipient of these gifts. Not seeking to maim or destroy but to humbly accept the gifts as offered. No wars, no threats, no hatred; just seeking the same peace as the gentle waves lap softly along the seashore. The sound of peace is also found in the hiss of receding waves as they hurriedly flee from the shoreline and fade to a mere whisper.

There are generally two kinds of fishermen, not including the spear-gun guys, commercial and recreational i.e.; fish for a living, fish for sport. The commercial fishermen's aim is to support their families with goods and services commonly found in the community they reside in. It's not a 9 to 5 job but an occupation most likely ingrained in the family heritage. Can a fisherman or woman be born, probably not but in the family environment; if a net can snag a fish, then a family tradition can direct an off -spring towards a deck.

You will probably find the most successful striped bass fishermen to be on the commercial side of the pier. It's their livelihood. They know the haunts of the bass, day and night. They know their appetite from season to season. They know not to give their secrets away that were accumulated by sweat and tears. Some have lost their lives and their secrets are still secrets.

Recreational anglers seem to fall into two separate but related groups: those with nearly uncontrolled passions that require continuous fishing activities and those who seek spiritually motivated ideals. The former needs a never- ending adrenalin rush, like a cup of caffeinated coffee each morning or a puff of a cigarette. It's like taking a drug with a never- ending supply. It's a passion like no other that continually waits for that twinge of the rod that produces an injection of euphoria. A wonderful feeling, needed and necessary. The more the merrier, the more the intoxication. Better than residing at the local tavern, better than talking about the one that got away, better than trying to solve the world problems while strolling the beaches of the world or bobbing the boat in the bay or in the basin.

The surfcaster has his lightweight full waders, salt stained plug bag strung over his shoulder, half gloves with exposed fingers gripping his 11 foot Lamiglas rod married to a 750SS Penn reel loaded with 350 yards of 20 pound braided line. Jiggling from the rod tip is his yellow 2 ½ oz. weighted Bomber tied directly to a 50-pound fluorocarbon leader. The well-worn wide brim cap is tucked low on his forehead due to the early October 25 knot winds. The 10-foot waves dance over the sandbar looking like angry and sweaty 7-foot tall basketball players ready to slam- dunk and scatter both imbedded clams and frighten mullet.

He is alone as he plods through the soft sand looking ahead and glancing left towards the potential action just inside the sandbar. He is an optimist.

He must be. Who else would meander the sandy shores like Race Point, MA. Montauk Point, N.Y., Sandy Hook, N.J., Outer Banks, N.C., and the likes or speed full throttle with his 26 foot Boston Whaler towards the screaming birds ½ mile south and just off the sand- filled groin. The storm with its onshore winds push the mullet pod towards the shoreline favoring the surf jockeys but threatening the Whaler. The captain gauges the length and strength of the stormed- tossed waves vs. the bass swirling around the scattered seaweed laden rocks. It's Risk and Reward time.

Golfers need company in order to enjoy the laughs produced by their hooks and slices. The pain and punishment of a solo duffer wailing his clubs at that little white ball is too much if it dives left or slices right. But in a group it can be the spark that ignites great laughter shared by the golfer and his companions. The warm sun of mid-spring or mid-summer warms the body, mind and spirit. Come fall and winter the golfer may bag his clubs and retire to the Lazy Boy sofa while the bass angler loads his lure bag with the tools for the late fall and early winter season.

The off-shore boater, an optimist, checks the fall tide charts and long-range weather forecasts looking for that Nor'easter which will test his boating and fishing skills. The tavern captains have docked their boats and now mull over the catch of the summer season, while the bass optimist checks the fall hours of the bait boats in the bay. Checking and rechecking the compass headings of the navigation buoys to and from the inlet is essential to lead him home after a midnight striper search. He too may be a solo adventurer just like the surf jockey both betting their skill and knowledge against the unpredictable striped bass.

There is another side to the commercial activity, the "comrecreational" angler. He fishes for dollars while being basically a recreational fisherman with a commercial interest. He purchases a commercial license at the appropriate time, uses it and then after the quota is met reverts to recreational fishing. In some states they are also permitted to sell their recreational catch to license dealers. This was a popular way to pay for your weekend fishing trip back in the 1950s and continues today. Some things never change.

When anglers wear different fishing hats at different times, they walk among similar comrades. These are unique anglers- part commercial, part recreational. They aren't much different from the weekend fishermen who close the office door on the weekend and head to the beach or to the dock. The competitive business activities are left at home but the competitive fishing juices slowly rise as they approach the saltwater environment. Weekend bragging rights may arise among close friends but it is subdued quickly as the office door opens on Monday morning.

The multi-hat anglers have a rating among their peers. There are no votes taken, no badges worn, no reserved seats at the local café but their accomplishments are like an unexplained presence that surrounds them no matter where they go. A handshake, a nod of the head, a tip of the hat are exchanged between these fishermen of similar accomplishments. Silent they may be yet their actions speak loudly as demonstrated by the honors they receive from social, fraternal and fishing associations.

Their crafts are deployed among the rocks and in the dense fog at midnight of a new moon. If you look for them, they can't be found, can't be seen, can't be heard, less the low throbbing sound of a trolling motor or the lapping waters against the bow of a drifting 20'craft. By the early AM, they are gone. Work finished, they are at the fish warehouse with the catch. The catch hangs from the certified scales. Dollars for fish are merely the visible rewards of their labor. A successful night's fishing trip, like an unexplained presence, is spread throughout the docks and the seafood warehouse. A nod of the head, a handshake, a tip of the cap confirms the " man knows how to fish." It will be repeated in the early AM hours tomorrow, then another nod of the head, handshake and tip of the cap. He did it again. His presence grows bigger and follows the fisherman wherever he goes.

These are the best bass fishermen with the most accomplishments of the 2-3 million striped bass anglers along the coastal states. Tip your cap and nod your head if you are lucky to know one of them. A 60+ pound bass is a rare catch and so is finding one of these 'big bass' fishermen.

Optimists they are. Their part of the world may try them during the daily 9 to 5 routine but their inner spirit may lift the whole world to a higher level. Optimists they must be. Within the clan, they never met another optimist they didn't like – especially a striped bass angler. They are all optimists.

Unfortunately there are only a couple of million of them searching for the striped bass along the East Coast from Maine to North Carolina. These sportsmen and women support the numerous bait and tackle shops, boating facilities, fishing clubs and the rules governing "the catching of the striped bass." Sportsmen seek to have the states and Federal Government designate the striped bass as a game fish. Around 40% of the bass served as table fare in restaurants are caught wild by commercial fishing vessels or sold by anglers from their catch. Probably more bass may have been killed as by-catch than caught for eating fare by commercial ground fishing boats. Fish farms supply almost 60 % of the public need for this table fare. Is it a strong case to make the striped bass a game fish?

Essentially the striped bass is a game fish in name because it is illegal to catch striped bass in Federal waters or between 3 to 200 miles off the beach. The Feds consider the striped bass and the channel bass game fish per the Oct.7, 2007 law signed by President Bush (see attached letter).

It is unlikely that the states would allow the Government to designate the striped bass a game fish because of its affect on the commercial fishing industry. Loss of control of one natural resource by the states, leads to other losses. License fees, quotas, law enforcement, management staffing, lends to political control. There is no guarantee that control by the Federal Government would be cost effective or the wisdom at the federal level would be more enlightening. One fact that would be true is that we will know where the problem will be debated and a solution negotiated. The bass may or may not get the best solution at the federal level because the more powerful states will influence the outcome. With competent commercial boaters and concerned recreational sportsmen working together, the best of both efforts might be better than have the Feds tell both what to do.

President Bush Signs Executive Or4der to Protect Striped Bass and Red Drum Fish Populati...Page 1 of 4

THE WHITE H011⁷SE

Home > News & Policies > October 2007

For Immediate Release Office of the Press Secretary October 20, 2007

President Bush Signs Executive Order to Protect Striped Bass and Red Drum Fish Populations

The Chesapeake Bay Maritime Museum St. Michael's, Maryland

M Executive Order: Protection of Striped Bass and Red Drum Fish Populations

L9= Fact Sheet: Guarding Against Over-Fishing 'Through Cooperative Conservation 9 In Focus: Environment

10:12 A.M. EDT

THE PRESIDENT: Thank you all. Stuart, thanks for the introduction. Thanks for the invitation here to the Maritime Museum. It's a beautiful site you got here. I can see why people want to live in St. Michael's, and I do want to thank the good citizens of this community for coming out and greeting me and Laura. $y the way, Laura is not here -- she's headed over to the Vice President's house. They've kindly invited us for lunch. l guess you could say she's the taster. (Laughter.)

The Vice President tells me there's a lot of fine fishing here, and I'm looking forward to going out and trying to catch some. I love to fish. And the good news there's a lot of good fishing here is because the Secret Service won't let me go hunting with him. (Laughter.)

I'm going to sign an executive order today to protect our striped bass and red drum fish populations, that's what I'm here to do. The executive order is part of our commitment to end over-fishing in America and to replenish our nation's fish stocks and to advance cooperative conservation and responsible stewardship. And this is a good place to come and sign the executive order. I thank you all for coming up and letting me say hello to you and witness this presidential act.

I want to thank the Secretary of the Interior, Dirk Kempthorne, for joining us today. He cares about our waters and our fish stocks just like I do. And I appreciate Carlos Gutierrez, he's the Secretary of Commerce, for joining us as well. He's in charge of NOAA, as is Conrad Lautenbacher -- run NOAA -- you've got a fancy title, Under Secretary of Commerce for Oceans and Atmosphere. That means he runs NOAA. (Laughter.) And I appreciate your concern about our waters, Conrad, and I want to thank you for your service to the country.

I appreciate Wayne Gilchrest, he's the congressman from this district. Mr. Congressman, fm honored you're here; thank for taking time, appreciate you welcoming us. I want to thank all the

http://www.whitehouse.gov/news/releases/2007/10/20071020-3.html
11/28/2008

President Bush Signs Executive Order to Protect Striped Bass and Red Drum Fish Populati...Page 2 of 4

state and local folks who've joined us. Particularly I want to thank people who care about fishing, and thank you for being here. I want to thank the different groups represented here. I want to say one -- there's a fellow up here named Walter Fondren, he's a fellow Texan. He had a lot to do with making sure conservation *efforts* on the Texas Gulf Coast worked. He proved, as have others here, that if you get together with responsible officials you can help get these fishing stocks back to robust. We were losing our red fish in Texas, and he, along with other concerned citizens, came together and said let's do something about it. And as a result, red fishing is good again. But we want to make it as good as possible all throughout the country, because fishing is important to the country.

Listen, it's important to be a commercial fisherman; I understand that. But the commercial fishermen and the sport fishermen don't have to be antagonistic. It's not a zero-sum game. Good policy will help our commercial fishermen and good policy will help our sport fishermen. And that's what we're here to talk about. And it's important to recognize here in America that sport fishing is a important industry; a lot of people make a living because o sport fishing. I don't know if people know this, but millions of Americans are spending about $40 billion a year on sport fishing. I know in our state, a ter, ere's a lot of people, a lot of entrepreneurs making a good living -they're fishing guides. A lot of bait shops and small business owners are doing well as a result of good sport fishing policy.

And so we're here today to talk about sport fishing. As a matter of fact, fm fixing to go do some sport fishing. I can't guarantee I'm going to catch anything. I hope that frogman out there does his job. (Laughter.)

I want to talk about a little bit of the comprehensive strategy we've put in place. In 2004, our administration released an Ocean Action Plan, the whole purpose of which was to make the oceans and the Great Lakes and the coast cleaner and healthier and more productive. The plan is producing some positive results. On one of the results of the plan was the -- the Marine National Monument in the northwestern Hawaiian Islands that I declared. The action created the largest single conservation area in the history of the nation. It is the largest protected marine area in the world. It is a visible sign that we care about conservation and good water policy.

I also signed the bipartisan Magnuson-Stevens Fishery Conservation and Management Reauthorization Act. It's a good piece of legislation. Many here worked on it and I want to thank you for working the halls of Congress to get this bill to my desk. The legislation closes loopholes in the law by setting a firm deadline to end over-fishing in America by 2011. The law puts in place market-based incentives to help replenish our fish stocks by granting fisherman the right to catch a designated amount of fish during a specified season. The law increases enforcement and raises penalties for those who break our fishing laws. This law improves data collection to help ensure our decisions are based on sound science. It is an important piece of legislation. And I want to thank the authors of the bill for getting it done. I think it's going to help a lot when it comes to managing our fish stocks in a constructive, smart way.

In addition to the Magnuson-Stevenson [sic] Act, over the last couple of years we've made a strong commitment to improve, restore and replace our wetlands. I set out the goal that during my presidency we would restore -- improve, restore and replace 3 million acres of wetlands. The reason I did that is because wetlands act as what we call nature's nurseries by helping small fish

http://www.whitehouse.gov/news/releases/2007/10/20071020-3.html
11/28/2008

President Bush Signs Executive Order to Protect Striped Bass and Red Drum Fish Populati...Page 3 of 4

survive before they head into deeper waters. We're going to make that goal. We will have replaced, improved and restored over 3 million acres of wetlands during my presidency.

Another significant problem is marine debris. And 1 was talking to Dirk Kempthorne, and he's going to host a symposium on the Gulf Coast to call our nation's attention to this issue. Our strategy is going to be to work with the private sector to help clean up the debris. I don't know if you understand -- it is a significant problem. Out there in the Hawaiian Island area that I set aside, Laura went out there and a lot of birds are eating this stuff that gets washed up as a result of people just dumping whatever they want to in the ocean. It's like a -- people kind of view it as, I guess, a giant garbage heap. And part of making sure that doesn't happen is to make it clear to our public the consequences of people just getting on our waters and just dumping whatever they feel like dumping out there.

And we're also going to work with the international community. A lot of the nets we're picking up out of that beautiful sanctuary in the -- or the monument in Hawaii of -- wash ashore because some trawler decides they don't want to mend the net or store the net or take care of the net -- they just cut it and let her go, and the currents wash all that stuff ashore. We literally pulled out tons of material off these islands. And so we're going to develop a comprehensive strategy to deal with this and call people to account, and ask them to join in protecting our oceans and waterways.

We're also talking about today to make sure that [we] not only protect the waters, we're going to protect the marine life in the waters. And so I want to talk today about two of the most popular recreational fish: the striped bass and the red drum. The striped bass -- I don't know if our citizens follow the striped bass, but it's a good fish to catch. It's a lot of fun. It's also a good fish to eat. We've got to make sure we've got enough to catch as well as enough to eat, and we can do both in a smart way.

Striped bass range from the St. Lawrence River in Canada to the St. John's River in Florida. They inhabit parts of the Pacific and the Gulf of Mexico. Some people call them stripers or rockfish. I guess we're going to call them rockfish today. (Laughter.) They can live up to be 30 years old. In the old days you could catch them up to 55 to 70 pounds pretty easily. And what we're trying to do is to make sure that the old days come back; that the striper is plentiful and that you can catch some good-sized ones, too -- nothing like catching a big striper.

They were once so plentiful back in 1614, that Captain John Smith wrote this, he said, a man could cross over the water "dryshod" by walking on the backs of all the fish. What's interesting is the striped bass was also one of the first species to be protected by the American people. In 1639, Massachusetts forbade the use of striped bass as fertilizer. By the early 1980s, striped bass were significantly depleted by poor water quality and over-fishing.

Over the years since that time, there's been some progress made to protect the striped bass. But not enough has been made, so today we're going to try to make some more progress.

Red drum is another popular fish that has experienced over-fishing. These fish are called reds, or redfish, or channel bass or spottail. What happened to this particular fish was that it became popular to eat. The restaurants found it to be good food and it became a popular dish and they got over-fished.

Now, we put protections in place both at state and federal level to protect the red drum. Unfortunately, the red drum species is still trying to recover. That's why I'm going to take this additional step today, because the recovery is not complete. In the waters from North Carolina to the tip of Florida, the numbers are still too low. And in parts of our Gulf, we're not sure of their

http://www.whitehouse.gov/news/releases/2007/10/20071020-3.html
11,/28/2008

President Bush Signs Executive Order to Protect Striped Bass and Red Drum Fish Populati...Page 4 of 4

status. So if you're not sure of the status, we ought to be taking special precaution. It's important that our fish stocks be full and robust and healthy.

And so I'm about to sign an executive order all aimed to help the federal government conserve striped bass and red drum in three key ways. First, the executive order directs the Commerce and Interior Departments -- that's why the two Secretaries are standing here -- to work with our fishery management councils and commissions to protect -- to prohibit the sale of striped bass and red drum caught in federal waters.

Second, this executive order encourages the periodic review of the status of the striped bass and red drum populations. This will ensure we have the most up to date information for determining whether breeding stocks are attaining healthy numbers and size in federal waters. Data is important when it comes to managing the fishing stocks. To improve the quality of our data we're building a recreational saltwater registry that will collect information from sportsmen about local fish stocks, which will help us better protect striped bass, red drum and all our fisheries. We're going to count on the people who really care about the fish stocks to get good, solid, sound information so we can do a better job not only today, but tomorrow, in making sure our fisheries are strong.

And finally, the executive order encourages states to take a look at their own management of the fish stocks. See, we believe in cooperative conservation. That means cooperation at the federal, state and local levels. We believe in a collaborative approach. The federal government ought to work with all stakeholders to achieve common consensus. And I respect the state's role in the management of the natural resources under their care. So I'm directing federal agencies to work with state officials to find innovative ways to help conserve striped bass and red drum.

And one such way is to use the state designation of "gamefish" where appropriate. I hope the state officials take a serious look at gamefish designation; it is an effective tool to protect endangered or dwindling species. See, it prohibits commercial sales, which removes the incentive to catch the fish for anything other than recreational purposes. State designations of gamefish have helped the recovery of species such as trout and large-mouth bass and tarpon and snook. People need to take a look at this tool to make sure that the fisheries are robust. Strong fisheries mean local sales. Local sales means better local economy.

And so the executive order shows our commitment to conserving our nation's resources. Our hope, everybody -- the hope of everyone here is that decades from now our children and grandchildren will see oceans, lakes and rivers teeming with fish and sea life. I can't guarantee they're going to be able to walk across their backs -- (laughter) -- like John Smith observed. But I can guarantee that we're committed to taking care of that which we have been given. My hope is people look back at our oceans' policies and our record of conservation and say, we're grateful that concerned citizens came together to protect our heritage.

And so I want to thank you all for coming and giving me a chance to visit with you about a vision that is a hopeful vision and an important vision. And I thank you for witnessing the signing of the Executive Order to Protect the Striped Bass and Red Drum Fish Populations.

God bless. (Applause.)

(The executive order was signed.) (Applause.) END 10:28 A.M. EDT

http://www.whitehouse.gov/news/releases/2007/10/20071020-3.html
11/28/2008

5
The 60+ Pound Striped Bass Club Registration

Weight	Angler	Date	Place	Misc.
78.5 lbs	Albert R. McReynolds	9/21/1982	Atlantic City, NJ	Surf-p
76.9 lbs	Peter Vican	7/18/2008	Block Island, RI	Boat-e
76.0 lbs	Robert A. Rocchetta	7/17/1981	Montauk Pt., NY	boat -e
75.4 lbs	Steven Franco	5/25/1992	New Haven, CT	
73.0 lbs	Fred Barnes	1/23/2008	Fisherman's Island, VA	l
73.0 lbs	Charles B. Church	8/17/1913	Cuttyhunk, MA	boat-e
73.0 lbs	Charles E. Cinto	6/16/1967	Cuttyhunk, MA	boat-e
73.0 lbs	Tony Stezko	11/2/1981	Nauset, MA	surf-l
72.0 lbs	Emil Cherski	1926	San Joaquin Delta, CA	
72.0 lbs	Edward J. Kirker	10/10/1969	Cuttyhunk, MA	
71.0 lbs	John Baldino	7/14/1980	Norwalk, CT	boat e

70.5 lbs	Joe Szabo	11/1984	Block Island, RI	surf e
70.0 lbs	Chester A. Berry	9/5/1987	Orient Pt., NY	
69.5 lbs	Steven Petri Jr.	10/15/1981	Nauset, MA	surf-e
69.2 lbs	John Alberda	7/23/1983	Montauk Pt., NY	boat-e
69.0 lbs	Joe Alexander	----------	Montauk Pt., NY	
69.0 lbs	Thomas J. Russell	11/18/1982	Sandy Hook, NJ	surf
68.8 lbs	Syl Karminski	1978	Chatham Inlet, MA	
68.8 lbs	John J. Solonis	8/5/1967	North Truro, MA	
68.5 lbs	Ralph Gray	10/1/1958	North Truro, MA	l
68.5 lbs	James Patterson	1962		
68.08 lbs	Clay Armstrong	4/4/ 2006	Virginia Beach, VA	boat
68.0 lbs	Wilfred Fontaine	10/3/1965	Green Hill, RI	surf e
67.6 lbs	Harold Hussey	6/8/1963	Cuttyhunk, MA	
67.5 lbs	Donald Riesgraf	2007	Virginia, Beach, VA	boat- e
67.5 lbs	O'Neil Forebay	5/1998	Merced County, CA	
67.5 lbs	Donald Riesgraf	12/ 2007	VA Saltwater Tour.	boat
67.5 lbs	Devin Nolan	5/13/1985	Bloody Point, MD	boat-l
67.2 lbs	Harry Hussey	6/8/1962	Chttyhunk, MA	
67.0 lbs	Tim Coleman	11/18/1985	Block Island, RI	surf
67.0 lbs	Doug Dodge	9/27/1978	Georgetown, ME	
67.0 lbs	Jack Ryan	5/31/1963	Block Island, RI	
66.8 lbs	Ronald A. Braun	6/27/1960	Gay Head, MA	l
66.8 lbs	Michael De Barros	8/21/ 1968	Cuttyhunk, MA	
66.75 lbs	Steven R. Thomas	11/1/1979	Bradley Beach, NJ	surf e

66.5 lbs	Tom Parker	6/29/1963	Nauset, MA	
66.5 lbs	Donald Nee	6/14/1962	Gay Head, MA	
66.5 lbs	Dennis Kelly	7/9/1982	Orient Pt., NY	
66.25 lbs	Frank Mularczyk	6/4/1954	Gay Head, MA	
66.25 lbs	Jim Paterson	7/14/1964	Narragansett, RI	
66.0 lbs	Harold Slater	10/15/1964	Weekapague, RI	
66.0 lbs	Frank Hunsinger	11/12/1960	Montauk Pt., NY	eel skin
66.0 lbs	Dennis Kelly	7/17/1981	Orient Pt., NY	
65.4 lbs	Paul G. Cook	6/20/1960	Cuttyhunk, MA Russelure	
65.25 lbs	Roger S. Tisdale	12/ 2007	VA Saltwater Tour.	boat
65.10 lbs	Neil J. Cordeiro	9/28/1961	Race Point, MA	p
65.10 lbs	Don De Benandino	9/6/1971	Charlestown, RI	eel
65.0 lbs	Jarret Binz	11/1/1985	Long Beach, NY	surf
65.0 lbs	Authur S. Clark	10/22/1936	Jamestown, RI	e
65.0 lbs	Maurice Levesque	9/19/60	Charleston, RI	boat-e
65.0 lbs	Wendell Olson	5/9/1951	San Joaquir Rv., CA	
65.0 lbs	James Patterson	1960s	Point Judith, RI	e
64.8 lbs	Louis Katine	11/4/1958	Atlantic Beach, NY	surf- p
64.8 lbs	David Webb	8/21/1960	North Truro, MA	boat- m
64.75 lbs	Tom Rinaldi	11/18/1990	Southampton, NY	surf
64.70 lbs	Allan Sosslau	5/14/1992	Chesapeake, MD	boat- l
64.5 lbs	George T. Cheshire	11/ 14/ 2007	Virginia Beach, VA	boat -e
64.5 lbs	Joseph Eliso	11/ 1974	Seaside, NJ	surf
64.5 lbs	Anthony A. Sirianni	6/25/1964	Cuttyhunk, MA	
64.5 lbs	Rosa O. Webb	8/14/1960	North Truro, MA	boat- m

64.4 lbs	Louis J. Ammen	4/21/1956	Long Island, NY	b-worms
64.4 lbs	Lare Lare	11/8/1958	Montauk, NY	boat
64.4 lbs	W.H. Quay	6/25/1966	Orleans, MA	b
64.3 lbs	Herbert Dickerson	6/20/1964	Cuttyhunk, MA	
64.25 lbs	Jason Colby	10/14/1978	Jones Beach, NY	surf
64.1 lbs	Robert Blackwell	12/ 2007	Virginia Beach, VA	boat- e
64.0 lbs	Mike Abdow	11/-/1985	Block Island, RI	surf
64.0 lbs	Asie Espenak	6/27/1971	Sea Bright, NJ	
64.0 lbs	Bill Deforest	8/20/1959	North Truro, MA	surf- p
64.0 lbs	Glen Dennis	6/6/1980	Orient Point, NY	
64.0 lbs	Mark Malenovsky	11/25/1992	Montauk Pt.,NY	surf-p
64.0 lbs	Steve Smith	11/-/1984	Block Island, RI	surf
64.0 lbs	Peter Sparuk	1960s	Cuttyhauk, MA	
63.8 lbs	Bill Gavitt	1970s	Block Island, RI	e
63.6 lbs	Morrie Upperman	8/5/1959	Island Beach, NJ	boat-l
63.5 lbs	Kay Townsend	8/14/1960	North Truro, MA	boat- b
63.4 lbs	R.E. Couture	7/6/1954	Brenton Reef, RI	boat-e
63.4 lbs	Frank Machadd	6/24/1956	Cape Cod Canal, MA	p
63.3 lbs	Nick Smith	12/ 2007	Virginia Beach, VA	boat-e
63.12 lbs	Joseph Donoa	6/13/1958	Middletown, RI	surf- b
63.0 lbs	Carolyn Brown	1/30/2004	Virginia Beach, VA	boat-l
63.0 lbs	Bill Claar	12/ 2007	Virginia Beach, VA	boat- e
63.0 lbs	Sherwood Lincoln	11/ 1983	Fishers Island, NY	m
63.0 lbs	James Mitchell	1960s	Point Judith, RI	e
62.8 lbs	Wayne J. Bellinger	9/29/1970	Cape Cod Bay, MA	b

62.5 lbs	Frank J. Scarpo	7/9/1969	Newport, RI	
62.5 lbs	Mark Sherer	7/2008	Block Island, RI	e
62.5 lbs	Stan Nabrezny	6/26/1988	Shinnecock Inlet, NY	surf
62.4 lbs	Stephen Sonnett	7/9/1959	Cuttyhunk, MA	eel skin
62.1 lbs	Wayne Rickman	2007	Virginia Beach, VA	boat- e
62.0 lbs	Nathaniel Gifford	6/10/1959	Cuttyhunk, MA	Russelure
62.0 lbs	David Hiebert	12/29/2004	Avon, NC	boat-l
62.0 lbs	Joe Sanfrantello Spring	1970s	Montauk Pt., NY	surf
62.0 lbs	Bob Smith	6/30/1957	Boston Harbor, MA	eel
62.0 lbs	Anton Van Breemen	7/8/1959	Cuttyhunk, MA	ecl skin
61.8 lbs	Louis J. Ammen	6/18/1956	Lloyds Neck, NY	lure
61.8 lbs	Ted Nimiroski	8/3/1959	Pt. Judith, RI	eel
61.8 lbs	Wayne Rickman	12/ 2007	VA Saltwater Tour.	boat
61.5 lbs	Jay Bechtel	12/ 2007	Virginia Beach, VA	boat -e
61.5 lbs	Leo A Garceau	1956	Block Island, RI	e
61.5 lbs	Nicholas Lobasso	11/17/1957	Montauk, NY	bucktail
61.5 lbs	Ace Lombard	7/ 1965		
61.5 lbs	Paul R.Moulton	1964		
61.5 lbs	Tom Needham	11/19/1983	Narragansett, RI	e
61.4 lbs	Herbert H. Stone	6/14/1959	Cuttyhunk, MA	Russelure
61.5 lbs	Matthew Fine	Dec 2007	Virginia Beach, VA	boat- e
61.16 lbs	David Wilson	Dec 2007	Virginia Beach, VA	boat- e
61.0 lbs	Alfred Anuszewski	11/22/1984	Block Island, RI	Redfin

61.0 lbs	Wifford F. Hilton	7/1/1956	Pasque Isle, MA	eelskin
61.0 lbs	Robert G. Kraft	6/12/1954	Long Beach, NY	lure
61.0 lbs	Albert Moss	6/14/1956	Cuttyhunk, MA	Russelure
61.0 lbs	Al Ristori	7/25/1966	Cape Cod, MA	
60.9 lbs	William Snyder	9/6/1969	Montauk, NY	eel
60.8 lbs	Jack Biderman	6/28/1958	Jamestown, RI	p
60.8 lbs	Richard Fucci	10/20/1959	Hull, MA	Atom plug
60.8 lbs	Ray Jobin	8/19/1974	Watch Hill Reef, CT	bunker
60.5 lbs	Jack Biderman	6/28/1958	Jamestown, RI	Atom Pg
60.5 lbs	Oscar B. Flanders	7/2/1956	Squilnochet, MA	Atom Pg
60.5 lbs	Thaddeus Folcik	1960s	New Bedford, MA	eel
60.5 lbs	Peter Millara	1960s	Race Point, MA	
60.5 lbs	Benard O'Demers	1960s	Cuttyhunk, MA	
60.4 lbs	Joseph Lanak	10/29/1960	Montauk, NY	eel rig
60.2 lbs	Tony Lymneos	6/24/1964	Cuttyhunk, MA	l
60.0 lbs	Charles Van Atta	11/15/1957	Sandy Hook, NJ	spoon
60.0 lbs	Richard Colagiovanni	10/1954	Watch Hill, RI	
60 lbs	H.K. Bramhall	6/17/1958	Cuttyhunk, MA	Russelure
60.0 lbs	Vincent G.B. Casscio	6/29/1958	Provincetown, MA	eel rig
60.0 lbs	George E. Dietz	11/12/1960	Montauk, NY	eel rig
60.0 lbs	G.S. Hulten Jr.	9/4/1960	Truro, Cape Cod, MA	b
60.0 lbs	Robert Lindholm	6/ 1980	Great Bay, Dover, NH	
60 lbs	Ted Nimiroski	8/13/1958	Narragansett, RI	eel skin
60 lbs	Denny O Connell	11/22/1986	Montauk Pt, NY	surf

60 lbs	Bernard O'Demers	1960s	Cuttyhunk, MA	
60 lbs	Jim Patterson	1960s	RI	
60.0 lbs	A.E. Peterson Jr.	7/19/1960	Truro, Cape Cod, MA	
60.0 lbs	Polly Rosen	7/6/1956	Cuttyhunk, MA	Russelure
60.0 lbs	Louis J. Smitten	10/29/1960	Sandy Hook, NJ	l
60 lbs	Sherman E. Whiting	6/12/1955	Montauk, NY	sea worms

Legend: e-eel
         p-plug
         b-bait
         m-mackerel
         l-lure or name of lure

Other big bass in the 60+ class have been caught but not registered with the IGFA or some other recognized organization. The Ashaway Line and Twine Company held fishing tournaments in the 1950s and 60s. Here are some of their results.

125 lbs.	Unknown		Edenton, N. C.
61 lbs. 12 oz.	G. Newell Hurd	1965	Cuttyhunk, MA.
61.5 lbs	G. Newell Hurd	?	?
60 lbs. 8 oz.	David Simons	1965	re: Nifty Fifty Striper News
60 lbs. 1 oz.	Walt Pietruska		re: Nifty Fifty Striper News

Field and Stream Magazine awarded prizes for the heaviest fish per year per species during this same time period. Striped bass of 60 pounds or more are listed in the main body of the register above.

In the 1950s Harnell Rods, Penn Reels and Ashaway Line would be a common setup for striped bass fishing. Bass fishermen were always looking for an advantage hence other equipment was available as: Assinppi Line, Montauk Line, Golden Dot Line, Gladding Line, Garcia Line, Cortland Line, Rain-Beau Line. Not to be out done, other reel manufacturers introduced reels as: Pfluger, Centaure, Delfino.

As equipment improved and cost more so did the Field and Stream Magazine Individual copy from $0.25 to $0.35.

Although braided line has become popular in recent years due to its small diameter, steel —like strength, no stretch, braided line was available in 1956.

State Record Striped Bass

State	Date	Angler	Weight	Length	Girth	Location	Caught On
Maine	Sept 20, 1978	Douglas Dodge	67 lbs			Sheepscot River	
New Hampshire	June 1980	Robert Lindholm	60lbs 0oz	51"	n/a	Great Bay, Dover	
Massachusetts	August 17, 1913	Charles Church	73 lbs	60"	30 1/2 "	Elizabeth Islands	Live Eel
Massachusetts	1967	Charlie Cinto	73 lbs			Sow & Pigs Reef	
Massachusetts	Nov 11, 1981	Anton "Tony" Stetzko	73 lbs			Nauset Beach	Eel / Teaser
Rhode Island	Nov 1984	J Szabo	70 lbs	55 1/2"		Block Island	
Connecticut	1992	Steven Franco	75lbs 6oz			New Haven Harbor	Menhaden
New York	July 17, 1981	Bob Rocchetta	76 lbs				
New Jersey	Sept 21, 1982	Al McReynolds	78 lbs 8 oz	53 "	35 1/2"	Altantic City	Rebel Minnow
Delaware	Dec, 1978	Betty Roseu	51 lbs 8 oz			Indian River Inlet	
Maryland (surf)	May 6, 2006	Gary Smith	57 lbs 2 oz			Assateague Island	
Maryland (Chesapeake Bay)	May 13, 1995	Devin Nolan	67 lbs 8 oz			Bloody Point	
North Carolina	Dec 30, 2005	David Hiebert	62 lbs 0 oz			Oregon Inlet	Custom Mojo Lure
Virginia	March 4, 2006	Clay Armstrong	68 lbs 1 oz	52 "	33 1/2 "	Virginia Beach	
California	May 1992	O'Neill Forebay	67lbs 8 oz			Merced County	

6

The Battlegrounds

The following pages describe some of the environmental elements the striped bass anglers may have encountered from surf or boat. While the bass dallied in their comfort zone, the bass angler had to accept unconditionally the elements around him. Words can only hint of the excitement generated by the physical confrontation between the angler and the object of his passion, the striped bass. "Bring it on," he mutters as he mentally prepares himself for the challenges awaiting him.

The 60+ Pound Club members had some if not all these elements in their arena when they battled their record striped bass. Whether from the Nor'easter of the northern striped bass range to the rolling waves of the southern Outer Banks, they dwelled in the realm of the bass for days, weeks or even years. Putting your time in probably meant putting a lot of time in before the big one hit.

Bass and white waters have always been cohabitants even though the bass would prefer the hidden recesses in gentle lapping waters. The white water exposed clams, mussels, crabs etc. therefore made easy meals for the lazy marauding bass. But put a pod of menhaden in the same environment, the bass will show a new personality. Whether from the surf or boat, their actions indicate they have an aggressive side. The lazy hours of lounging around waiting for the menhaden residue caused by bluefish forays around groins, jetties or other rock piles, indicate they know the sounds and smells of lunch- time.

Read on and you may recall some of these events yourself whether from the surf or boat. If you haven't, put in more time!

A

by Surf

The past summer surf fishing was somewhat a bust. We had numerous coastal storms that continually changed the contour of the beaches. The old holes were sanded over and new ones had to be scouted. It seemed I spent more time in the scouting mode with binoculars than rod and reel. The waves also carved out much of the beach where the slope of the shore was minimum therefore giving the breakers full access to the sand dunes that acted as barriers. But there was one storm that absolutely frightened the most experienced surf casters. In mid summer a mighty eastern storm growled menacing towards the coast. Low purple clouds danced to a rhythm I had not seen before. The waves were not the usual ones that deposited themselves more on the ocean side of the sandbars about 300-400 yards off the beach. There were angry, ugly, mighty solders lined up in attack formation and threw their weight around by crashing through the outer sandbars and steam rolled to the beach. I never saw such an angry ocean. No waders could keep you dry and safe from the dangers of the crashing waters. The converging head- high waves from the east, from the north, from the south made the sound of booming brass drums beating a battle hymn as they vocally expired on what was left of the beach. It sounded like they were looking for more recompense in sand and gravel than past storms. It was death to challenge them and stand in their way. Twenty minutes of flaying away with a 3 ounce tin was enough to realize who was the boss of the day. It took several days for the storm to subside and months for the beaches to be restored. Our machines took our sand back which I'm sure angered the waves hence another battle loomed in the near future yet I looked forward to the Fall run that would again test man, nature and the striped bass.

It was early fall as I paste the last of the wax on the 4x4 SUV while my mind wondered about when the fall run will start or just pass by like last year. I look up and see in the eastern sky a little dark cloud formation far off just above the horizon. No excitement, it's probably a flock of geese heading south for the winter. Ten minutes later I hear the quacking noise from the dark cloud now visible as an enormous flock of Canadian geese. These guys and gals have got the right idea about heading south even though the striper season isn't on their calendar.

Polishing the last fender, I put the whole kit away, still mentally thinking about other things- like striped bass time. A few days later the weatherman said a Nor'easter could be in the forecast. Interesting but he has been wrong more often about these storms when he forecasts a week ahead. The next day he forecasts the same thing during the AM and PM news. This may be getting serious. I head to the garage to check my gear. It's all there ready to go. In early September during the warm evenings I went through all the tackle leaving nothing for chance. I knew when it was time to go "gettum" I couldn't waste time looking for that gaff I repaired and hung on one of the nails to dry. No time for "which nail."

After four days of "the storms coming," I decide to pack up the gear. I calculate that 8 hours before the storm hits, I'll head east to my favorite beach. I wander around the house the next day, almost all day, waiting for the confirmation about the storm's arrival. At 4 PM I finally decide it's a go and I head east trying to keep within the speed limits. Not much traffic. All the sugarplums must be in their cozy couches cuddling close to a hot toddy. Not me. It's that passion time of the year. In springtime a young man's fancy turns to love but now in autumn, a not so young man, finds his love in his passion. I finally arrive at the beach.

I see the fleet of 20-25 bass boats trying to right themselves in the early stages of a Nor'easter. It's twilight and getting darker. The 20- knot winds are ramping up, moving the chilly, dark clouds along at a good clip. Most are trolling but the wave action must make it a stomach -aching ride. The birds have been working all day, just about 400 yards off the beach. I've seen some big bass hauled in but nothing from the surf. I arrived with my 11-foot Lamiglas rod, Penn 706Z loaded with 30-pound mono line looking for a fight. After 1-½ hours my arms ache from hurling the Gibbs Swimmer without a hit.

It's October and I can count 10-12 surf jockeys to the right of me for about ½ mile. They are wailing away with similar gear. All seem to have full waders on, wool pullover ski masks with a standard brim baseball type cap.

They are casting right at the water's edge but scamper back with the occasional 6-8 foot angry wave.

The boats start to thin out heading towards the inlet with its converging and diverging currents a mile away. Getting in before you can't see is the wise choice. The birds do the same.

With the early darkness being driven by low, rolling clouds, we surf jockeys hope the bunker will seek the safety of the shallow waters along the surf line with its sand bars about 50 to 100 yards off the beach. The bass will then be in range of our gear. A crashing surf, high quartering wind, and reduced visibility will still keep the odds in favor of the bass. With the water temperature in the mid- forties, wind in the mid- gale range, the sting of salt water droplets feel like a cold rasp on the exposed face. The hands and the shoulders get numb and aching from working the beach with rod and reel but it's the best of seasons. It makes your blood boil like the thrashing waves as your eyes pierce the choppy horizon for the sign of the bass and bunker.

To my left I see flying fish, flying fish; no but bunker being hurled skywards trying to escape the bass. I snap the Gibbs towards the action but the wind now approaching a gale, barely gets me halfway there. There is an old, broken mostly sanded -over jetty about 100 yards further up the beach. It extends about 50 yards out but it is dangerous. If I climb out on it with my spike-less waders, carefully circumvent the seaweed and strewed rocks; I could get within casting distance of the action now taking place just over the sandbar. It's getting dark, the tide is running in, the wind could push me around on the slippery rocks while the waves would beat on me. It's a striper run. It's late in the season. If I don't do it now, I'll have to wait for next year. "It's a go," I say to myself as I shuffle towards the rocks like an over- stuffed penguin. My heart's pounding. I'm committed.

Some of my surf jockeys see the same thing. Three or four start towards me. It's a massacre. I'm in a high-speed trot towards it. I can't go much faster with all the surf gear hanging on me from head to foot. The bass are driving the bunker over the sandbar towards the beach. " Forget the rocks," I mutter to myself.

It's really getting dark now as I squint to locate the fray now about 50 yards off the beach. More surf guys are rushing towards me. I have about a 40-yard lead on them as I wing my Gibbs towards the foaming waters. It hits the water just as a wave crashes me waist high. The rod snaps forward as I struggle backwards to regain my balance. The bass is on. The cold waters of the fall season has just heated up.

B
by Boat

I am at the marina tinkering around the boat in later October. Looking around I notice the number of bare boat slips. In mid- summer I recall how you could walk on water by stepping from boat to boat. Labor Day has come and gone; the families traded summertime for school time and summer's hot, high sun for autumn's cool, low sun just above the horizon. Where has all the noise gone? No thrashing propellers, no creaking of loose wooden planks dancing with the rise and fall of the tide. It's quiet time, too quiet. Most boats have been encased in their plastic cocoons waiting for their winter's icy cover. I feel for my trusty boat hesitant to retire her for the winter sleep after she so successfully motored me around the whole summer in complete safety.

It's not cocoon time for her. I know the best fishing is yet to come. There is time to mothball the boat as well hurry me off to the local marine shop to discuss the usual boat maintenance for the next season.

It's 5 AM as I stir restlessly but quietly in order not to wake my wife and the kids. I quickly but silently peek out the window to gauge the weather. It's late October and the striped bass run is full on. What I see is not good. The few brown, dry and crumbled oak leaves are being whisked away from their summer stations on their branches. The wind is up, up and away. About 20-25 knots, I guess scanning the neighbor's weather vane. Not the best boating weather but its striper time. It will not last long, maybe a week, a week and a half at the most depending on the water temperature. The massive migrations of menhaden I know tend to move in rhythm with the seasonal temperatures. Sixty degrees is a comfortable number for them, so they say. They will speed up to find that number but it can take time for all those masses to move in the same direction, at the same speed against tide and current.

The SUV has been packed. A good bass man is always ready, prepared for what he can foresee. Rods, reels, tackle, all checked the night before. It's the weather you can't control, can't select, can't foresee but can prepare for. The woolen, nylon parka and hat will rebuff the 30 F air temperature, while the rubberized boots will ward off the 50 F water. The half dozen eels are still nestling in their seaweed beds. Bunker and eels, what more can I tempt the bass with?

A quick stop at the marina for some fresh bunker and I'm just a minute from the docks. The 24-foot center console Mako has been gassed up per my phone call early last evening. Getting out of the SUV, I feel the brisk wind has that bite of an early winter. The flags fly to the west; hence the east wind confirms that rough weather is about to invade the coast. The smell of rain is in the air and the wispy, purple clouds confirm the presence of a forth-coming storm. "Where is Harry, my fishing buddy," I exclaim to the wind. Then the cell phone rings and Harry can't make it. He's sick and so is the car's battery. I gotta go anyway. Its that time of year.

I grab all the equipment and carry it like a big bulging beanbag. One trip is better than two. Save time. Rods, reels, bait and all the tackle I can muster with wide-open arms. Two steps down and into the boat, lay the equipment down respectfully, hit the starter button, cast off and head towards the breaking dawn. The wave action in the bay and channel does not foretell those waiting for me off- shore. I put her on autopilot – slow- while I spike the rods and reels in the gunnels. 8/0 Gamasylk hooks have already been strung on 30-pound fluorocarbon line.

As I leave the inlet, I see the arena where I will do battle with my foe, the striped bass. I steer towards the rock pile of an old jetty about one-half mile from the inlet and 150 yards off shore. It was once a magnificent rock pile but the storms have sanded over part of it. It can't be walked on from the beach, only assaulted by boat.

Here the waves are "striper" waves. Two to four feet with a white lashing tongue. The rocks give them an oily look and a low growling sound. One wave crashes over the rocks; the others lash against it and bounce back. A rip is forming. A good sign.

I hear the approaching birds but I do not see any bass. I'm afraid to get too close to the rocks. Some are a few feet below the surface as the jetty is in the state of breaking up. Other rocks are 10 feet above me. This demands a cautious attitude. The Mako rocks and rolls, heaving up a few feet and then slamming down. The noise irritates me. It is an adversarial but necessary condition between waves and rocks. I keep the twin 250s in high idle, just in case.

The wind picks up and I feel the sting of salted ice pellets. I am willing to put up with the rocks, waves, wind and evil looking clouds if the bass show up. The smell of seaweed announces my nearness to the rocks, trans in, power on, back off from the rocks.

The birds, the birds, here they come so are the bass. The bass suddenly are now boiling the water around me. The bunkers are jumping, dashing, flashing around like frightened fire flakes fleeing from the furious flames of a roaring Boy Scout campfire.

The bass roll violently; the birds dive with abandonment. Boiling bass and diving birds are now everywhere. The Mako is drifting towards the rocks being pushed by the thrashing of bass and bunker as I flip my bunker chunk right in the middle of the action, one hand on the rod, one hand on the throttle.

Wham, now I must fight this fish in his arena under his conditions. With deteriorating weather, lurking rocks, driving wind and churning waves, who will win? Will the boat and I survive intact or will the fish and rocks win?

7
Their Stories

7-1
Alfred Anuszewski's Striped Bass 61.0 pounds,
Block Island, RI
Nov. 22, 1984

Introduction to Alfred Anuszewski
and his Block Island Story:

Alfred at 6'4" in a robust triathlon 200+ pound frame is now 51 years old and still lives on Long Island with his wife and two daughters. His "crew" of 10 Block Island surf fishermen does not meet on a schedule but are in contact from time to time. Today Alfred fishes the surf and bay off Long Island, NY but his two young girls have yet to take after Alfred's passion for fishing.

Looking back Alfred feels both Marty McMillan and Steve Compos had the most positive influence on his surf fishing exploits along with the others in his crew.

His story, in part, was published in the magazine called "On The Water" some time ago but Alfred has expanded the events of the day he caught his 60+ pound bass. If you do read "On The Water," you still will appreciate the complete story about the glory days of Block Island.

The story in perspective is greater than its self. It was a time probably not repeatable during our life- time; maybe never repeatable. If never repeated, it is probably the last worthy striped bass story about Block Island. Times have changed since those days in the early 1980s, his crew of 10 has gotten older, and one has died. Alfred was in his 20s with the wind at his back and the world before him. Others of the crew were of a similar bent but tied to parochial requirements of work, work and work. Block Island and the striped bass freed them from the reality and requirements of society. Free at last, free at last. They were unchained for a period of time. Free to roam the rocks of the home of the great bass of Block Island. Freely to trust only in their own individual fishing skills and to challenge the giants who roamed those rocks where the needlefish honeymooned. The Block Island rocks were the home of the striped bass but the needlefish had no reservations only the urge to find a mate.

Alfred's fishing crew of 10 was the essential stars of the striped bass seasons in the early 1980s on Block Island. They fished for unending hours, in daylight and in total darkness as long as the needlefish were there. And they were there by the zillions. It was needlefish mating time regardless the presence of the striped bass. The crew was like gang -busters as they perused the goal of their passion, the striped bass. The crew, a loose group of talented surf jockeys, had their own magical and secret surf fishing techniques. You probably would respect each man in a gang of commandos who had a 45caliber revolvers hanging from their holsters. Likewise each of the "Needlefish Gang of 10" respected the abilities of each other with their own equivalent 45s consisting of rods, reels and needlefish lures. They knew how to use their fishing weapons as well as the gang with 45s. Enjoy his story for the first or more so the second time.

Note: Don Musso, who was essential in providing the needlefish lures for the gang, has turned his plug making business on Long Island, NY over to his son. Without Don's help in those days, Alfred's story would be written but soon forgotten. A fraction of what it could have been. Thanks to Don's needlefish, Alfred's story is memorable and so is his "Gang of 10."

The Land of the 60's

By Alfred Anuszewski

Thanksgiving night November 22, 1984 Southwest Point on Block Island a 61 1/4 1striped bass.

From an old wooden rented rowboat in the back bay of Jones Beach, Long Island back in the mid 1960's, my father and I would fish for flounder in the spring and tommy cod in the winter. We would use a simple drop line to fish, keeping the fishing line between my young fingers waiting for my first tug. Falling in love with fishing instantly, it went right to my heart. This type of fishing with my father was perfection in the simplest form in a young boy's mind. That same year at the age of 8, I saw my first striped bass swim right through a wave while swimming in the surf at Jones Beach one summer day. That fish hypnotized me. I spent the whole day searching for that fish never leaving the water. Never did see it again, never realizing I would spend the rest of my life searching for that striped bass.

Here is my story of my 61-pound striped bass:

From Nauset Beach on Cape Cod to Southwest Point on Block Island in the early 1980's, a small group of surfcasters quietly shared some of the greatest striped bass fishing ever experienced.

I set foot on Block Island for the first time in the late fall of 1983 searching for the giant striped bass that I had been catching from the surf on Cape Cod back in 1981. At that time, no one realized that the historic striped bass blitzes of Pochet Hole and Manomoy Island and the beaching of a 73-pound striped bass in November would mark the closing of the greatest era of striped bass surf fishing on Cape Cod.

I was on Cape Cod in 1981, for that final great year, I was 23 years old and living on Long Island. I was between jobs and had no family responsibilities and had all the time in the world to fish. My fishing partner and I made the decision to leave for Cape Cod in early September of that year. We left Long Island with no return date in mind. Once we arrived we immediately knew something very special was happening; a tremendous number of large fish were being taken. We had arrived right in the middle of the legendary '81 surf run of the striped bass along the sands of Nauset Beach.

That year my fishing partner and lifelong best friend, Marty and I had many great nights at Nauset. All the fish we caught were taken on live eels and the fishing was spectacular at spots like Pochet Hole, Long Bar, and Old Chatham Inlet. I remember that long 12-mile ride over the sand to Old

Chatham Inlet night after night with Marty and we would spend the entire ride strategizing for the night ahead. I miss that ride so much! If I close my eyes, I'm transported back to a brisk early-autumn morning at the Chatham co-op fish market where all the surf fishermen came to sell their fish and talk about the previous night. I remember seeing legendary local Cape Cod surf fishermen with their pickup trucks filled to the brim with huge striped bass. What a night. What a sight. What a Year!

The spectacular fishing on Cape Cod combined with the unique beauty and changing character or Nauset and the back beach, turned me into a life long surf-fishing fanatic. As 1982 came and went the fishing was nothing like the year before. The October blitzes never materialized on Nauset Beach leaving me a Cape Cod surf fishing refugee. I had lost my favorite spot and had nowhere to go. What would be the next Cape Cod?

While surf fishing in our home waters of Montauk Point on Long Island, my surf fishing partners and I would often wonder about a little island visible off in the distance. We knew it was Block Island but that was about all we knew. Little information was shared about the fishing on Block Island and there seemed to be a veil of secrecy surrounding its shores. That was enough to catch our attention, so we decided to pack up and take a trip and fish the island in 1983. We made reservations for the ferry from Rhode Island and we booked rooms at the New Shoreham House in the fall.

When we arrived it didn't take us long to realize that the days of easy fishing on Cape Cod Sands were over; Block Island had cliffs and rocks everywhere. Since not many people lived on the island, we felt like we had stepped back in time to the 1950's. Block Island life seemed simple and pure and I remember seeing the old-style Land Rover trucks driving around the island. The waterfront home building boom had not yet begun, so we had no beach access restrictions at all. We explored the entire island and the more we explored, the more impressed we were. Every fishing spot looked better than the last. There were deep-water bowls and long rocky points, all of which had sea birds sitting in the water. What stood out the most however, was the smell of bait in the air. We could see large sand eels trapped in rock pools behind the outgoing tide and we noticed old rusted pipes coming out from some of the rock boulders, Later, we learned that the pipes were the remnants of the bass-fishing stands of the late 1800's. My imagination went wild with thoughts of the years gone by; "Maybe this was the same Block Island bass stand where Francis W. Miner caught his undocumented 86- pound striped bass in 1887" I said to myself.

When we started fishing we realized that we had stumbled into another world. This world had giant striped bass everywhere. A handful of local Block

Island guys were fishing a strange lure that looked like a pencil. It was called a needlefish. These local fishermen were catching more giant striped bass than we had ever dreamed of; some of them had landed multiple 60-pound striped bass. These locals spoke of the 60-pound stripers as the prize fish, not the 50-pound stripers. On Block Island in the early 1980's 50-pound stripers were common. This was a very different fishing world than the Long Island waters I had come from; I had stumbled upon the land of the 6()'s. The locals never said a word to any reporter or newspaper. Until we came along they had the blistering bass fishing to themselves.

Needlefish plugs in 1983 were like rare diamonds; there was very few around and each one was invaluable. The Needlefish were waiting for a birthplace and they found it on the rocky shores of Block Island. My crew of fishermen had only eight (8) needlefish among us in the classic Boone Needlefish style constructed with screws eyes. Most of the guys fishing Block Island only owned one needlefish, the one tied on the end of their line.

We joined the Block Island locals in a blitz of stripers at Southwest Point at noon one day. All the fish were giants. Every one was over 30 pounds and most of them were in the 40's. Those striped bass tore the screw eyes right out of our needlefish if they didn't straighten or crush the hooks first.

We knew these fish had to be from the same super school we had fished at Nauset in 1981, as the fishing wore on, blitz after blitz, all eight of our needlefish were completely destroyed by the cows. All the fish wanted were the needlefish but you couldn't find a single one on Block Island. One of my friends had an idea. He would find a pay phone and call Don Musso, the plug maker on Long Island and ask him to ship overnight whatever he had in needlefish lures. Color was not important since we would change it ourselves. The next day we waited at the Block Island Post Office like kids on Christmas Eve. Santa Claus eventually came dressed in a postal uniform and carrying a postal bag loaded with 24 wired through needlefish. Don Musso came through for us big time. The fish were everywhere around the island and we caught uncountable numbers of mid-30's to high 40-pound stripers. Ballards Beach, Grove Point, Southwest Point, Cat Rock Cove and Black Rock all gave up fish. A blanket of large sand eels surrounded the island, and the huge school of giant bass stayed right with them. The daytime blitzes at Southwest Point were unbelievable. Forty-pound stripers were thrashing on top, their whole bodies coming out of the water.

I had never seen such enormous bass hitting during daylight with bright sunshine and these fish tore up our new wired-through needlefish and demolished our other plugs. We had an empty coffee can on hand to hold all our straightened and crushed hooks and in between tides we'd examine all the size 4/0 and 5/0 treble hooks in the coffee can. There was a great fishing story connected to each and every crushed or bent hook.

My surf crew realized something very special was going on. This was the kingdom of the great striped bass and Block Island had cast a spell on us. Best of all it was not crowded and all the fishermen on Block Island were gentlemen. In addition to our crew from Long Island there was some locals, a few guys from Rhode Island, Massachusetts and a father-son team. We were fishing in the midst of the true glory years on Block Island, but none of us knew it at the time. It was paradise. We were in striped bass heaven.

November wore on and soon Thanksgiving '83 was upon us. Everyone was leaving Block Island for the holidays and a storm was advancing up the coast but the thought of leaving the island never entered the thoughts of my crew. We knew there was a unique opportunity hidden in that costal storm which should not be missed. Our crew had a great Thanksgiving dinner, which was over by 3:30 P.M, and then we decided to start fishing at Southwest Point.

When we got to the spot the whole rock bar was under white water and the bowl looked black. We had Southwest Point to ourselves. As soon as we started fishing we were into fish. All through the night from 4 P.M to 6 A.M we picked away at the striped bass with Don Musso's wooden needlefish. It was a black night with rain and wind sweeping into the bowl. It felt awesome and mystic at the same time. One crewmember hooked a monster that he battled for a long time, finally landing it deep in the bowl at Southwest Point. In the morning this cow pushed the scale down to 59 pounds. Another crewmember weighted in a fish of 55 pounds and we had many fish between 35 and 59 pounds. It was such a special night with just the four of us at Southwest Point, all alone except for the "Moby" stripers. When morning came the stripers were still hitting the needlefish at the end of each cast so fast that we had trouble getting the line onto the manual pick-up. It was an incredible experience. We left Block Island a few days later and as winter settled in; Block was all we thought about. We were in total awe of the island. We had stumbled upon some of the greatest striped bass fishing ever and we had no idea it was going to get even better. When we returned to Block Island in the late fall of 1984, there was more surf fisherman around but it was not crowded like it would be in the years to come. The island waters were loading with sand eels and mackerel. I had never have seen so much bait; the harbor water was black with it. I knew we were in the midst of a very special natural event, as the largest migrating schools of giant striped bass and massive schools of large sand eels were converging in Block Island waters.

When we started to fish in the late fall of 1984, the weather conditions were downright frigid. The puddles on the beach trails were frozen and we were using thin scuba divining glove and scuba hoods to fish. This arctic weather made the fishing more challenging and in the end, more rewarding. The fish were hitting Don Musso's wooden needlefish in fluorescent glow green during the day and black needles on those dark nights. That year, we fished in a lot of calm water on the south side of Block Island. We discovered that the fish, loved 7-inch Red fins, Bombers and Hellcats. We all became scientist about these lures, loading them in different weights for different spots. We would make holes in the plastic plugs near the balance point and fill them with water.

Toothpicks were used to plug the holes and a dab of glue secured these modifications. Also we discovered the fish were very color sensitive. In our trucks we kept crates filled with spray paints in different shades of green, blue, yellow, and plum. We would paint the plugs right on the beach and then hang them in the truck with the heater on so they could dry. Seven-inch Red fins were spray-painted fluorescent glow green with chrome sides and loaded to a specific weight. We fished them slowly reeling just enough to feel the current. The bone jarring hits from 40-pound stripers on these plugs were incredible in calm water.

We caught many 40-pounders and not one fish weighted less than 30 pounds. We would start fishing at 4:30 P.M and end at 6:00 A.M. We would move all over the island, feeling completely tuned into the island's tides and currents. We talked about the island's tendencies and where the fish would be at what time. One night my partner and I walked down the cliffs of Southeast Light to fish Lighthouse Cove, Sand Bank Cove, Southeast Point and Cat Rock Cove on a falling tide. I believed there were always one or two giants in every one of these bowls. It was a night of a half moon, which outlined every one of these bowls. We battled "Moby" stripers all the way back to Old Harbor Point, totaling nine fish between 35 to 45 pounds, all on loaded 7-inch Red fins and Hellcats. The east side of the island had some of the most classic striper's waters in the world. We walked back to the truck and still had eight (8) hours left to fish. The nights were endless and so was the fishing.

Thanksgiving '84 fell on November 22nd and would be very special to me for the rest of my life. Thanksgiving dinner would be celebrated on Block Island at the High View Restaurant with the crew from Long Island. At my Thanksgiving table was Marty McMillan, Russel Coumo, Dean Diamanpopol, Steve Campo, Jack Vanderkief and son, Tommy Vanderkief. I would also like to mention Sal Sicilano, Jack Linton and Dennis Kuenzer. What a cast of characters, we were young and most of us in our twenties. Our passion to fish was immeasurable. We were in our prime. Talk about luck or talk about how destiny took us to Block Island in one of the greatest era in surf striped bass fishing history. Block Island had many giant striped bass stories and fulfilled many dreams of surf fishermen who came there. As our Thanksgiving dinner went on, our crew spoke of giant striped bass, needlefish, Red Fins and how fluorescent glow green was the greatest color ever created. This table of surf casters from Long Island had many striped bass over 50 pounds that were never reported and one striped bass over 60. These Long Island surfcasters were the true hunters of giant striped bass. They were low key. Their whole surfcasting experiences were kept in secret. These are the men who would share my greatest moment in surfcasting and have a toast to my giant striped bass in the morning in a very quiet way. Never reporting it to the media, always keeping it quiet and hidden in the recess of our memories.

After Thanksgiving dinner Marty and I went to Steve Campo's fishing truck, nicknamed the war wagon, to rub our hand on the famous plastic Elsie the cow head- figure that was glued on his dashboard. This was famous amongst our crew of fishermen for good luck.

We would start fishing at Southwest Point's rock bar. When we go there we found it deserted. The conditions were flat calm and the tide was just starting to go out. As we waded onto the rock bar, I was telling Marty my fishing partner, like I had told him many times before, about the super school of striped bass that I believe existed that could move onto Southwest Point at anytime. A school one mile long with 30, 40, and 50 pound striped bass in the middle of the school with the perimeter reserved for the super cows, the 60 pounders, the 70, and 80 pounders leading the school onto the rock bar. I envisioned these giants with their noses down rubbing on the rocks and the sands, rooting out the crabs and sand eels. On November 22nd 1984, on Southwest Point that super school of striped bass was in front of us. I had my '10-foot Kennedy-Fisher graphite surf rod with a Penn 704 spinning reel loaded with 20 pound test Ande pink mono line: The fishing started slowly. We kept wading farther and farther out on the bar until I started getting little bumps on the black and chrome water loaded 7-inch Red fin. I made five more casts and felt five more bumps. They kept tapping the plug. I switched to fluorescent glow green and chrome Red fin and cast it out, barely reeling and letting the current move it very slowly.

BANG! A hit of explosive strength and the fish took a run down to the backing on my spool on the first run. He stopped and I reeled a little and then he took off again several times more.

This was a fish of a lifetime! Eventually I got him up to the shallow part of the rock bar but it was such a big fish that I couldn't get it over the bar. It ran again and I spent another 15 minutes coaxing it back. With my heart pounding in my chest, I was finally able to beach the fish on the shallows of the rock bar. When I bent to pick it up, its weight told me it was a special fish.

It took me a moment to collect myself and with the giant fish in my hand, I gazed around at the beauty of Southwest Point, whispering aloud, "The Rock, the Rock." This scene was burnt into my memory.

The first cast after the cow, I was instantly into another fish. This turned out to be a 46- pound bass. My partner was landing a fish as well, a 48 pounder. This blitz went on through the entire outgoing tide. Those fish tore apart many of our Red Fins and needlefish plugs, crushing and straightening many of the hooks. Our fishing tackle was no match for these giant striped bass. We lost as many as we caught. They physically and emotionally tore us apart, too. To catch this many massive fish in the rock-strewn waters of Block Island was a great challenge and satisfaction. In my innermost thoughts, I still p our over all the stripers of '83 and '84, I hooked, fought, and lost. I believe some of them would have been world records.

They were soo huge! I have no doubt that these fish were the same school that hit Pochet Hole on Nauset Beach in the blitz of 1981.

When morning came, I weighed my fish on a certified scale. It registered 61 pounds. I had joined the "60" Club! When the scale went down to 61 1/2 pounds the emotion in me was incredible. My heart was singing in happiness. I knew how rare a 61 1/4 pound striped bass was and to catch a 61 pound striped bass on a 7-inch Red Fin made it even more special. These were the best of times, best of friends, and best of fishing. I was only 26 years old and I had already lived a charmed striped bass fishermen's life from the beaches of Cape Cod to shores of Block Island. I knew immediately that I had fulfilled a dream of mine and went to the greatest taxidermist of our time, Wally Brown, to mount my 61-pound striped bass. When we came back on the ferry to the main land from Block Island, that ride from Point Judith, Rhode Island to Wally Brown's house in Falmouth, MA on Cape Cod with my 61 pound striped bass wrapped in a burlap sack in my cooler was the happiest ride I ever made. How ironic it was to go back to Cape Cod with my 61-pound striped bass where my journey had started for this giant fish. The final tally for Thanksgiving night for my partner and I was 23 giant striped bass ranging from 37 pounds to 61 pounds. The next night I walked down to Southwest Point and on my first cast of the night, using a large wooden Don Musso needlefish, I caught a 51 pound striped bass that I released in the bowl at Southwest Point, as I revived the 51 pounder, I felt the strength of its massive tail push off and swim away. There were no words to describe the feeling. I left a piece of my soul on Southwest Point that night, feeling so blessed to catch a 61-pound striped bass and then releasing a 51-pounder the next night. The blitz was the same on that second night. My partner and I had 21 more striped bass from 35-51 pounds. The majority of fish from these two special nights were in the mid- to high 40's. One week later at Southwest Point, a surf fisherman shattered the Rhode Island record for striped bass with a 70-pound giant.   .

Far those two years, our crew from Long Island was part of the great Block Island era of surf fishing. It was a gift to us. Block Island changed a lot of surfcasters that experienced this great fishing that continued through the later 1980's. It was like being in heaven for 7 years and then being forced back to earth, no fishing spot could ever measure up to Block Island, causing some of the greatest surfcasters, who fished Block Island, to lay their surf rods down and leave the surf. They had fished in Nirvana. That is how much influence and power Block Island had on some of the surfcasters. Several years later on a hot and calm day in July 2007, I sat with my wife and two young children on a quiet, deserted Southwest Point. The gentle breeze whispered to me of times gone by. I reflected on how 25 years ago, this sleepy island was responsible for some of the best striped bass surf fishing anyone could ever experience. As the years continue to roll by, I can only hope this great era will not be forgotten. The men who fished here uncovered the spirit of this island and tussled with soul of its major migratory resident, the Striped Bass. Both will be in our hearts and memories forever.

Alfred Anuszewski's 61.0 lb Striped Bass
Nov 22, 1984

7-2
Ray Jobin's Striped Bass 60.8 lb,
Watch Hill, RI
Aug. 19, 1974

Ray Jobin's 60.8-Pound Striped Bass, Watch Hill Reef, RI, Aug. 19, 1974

by Squid Beaumont

Sunday evening, August 18, 1974......... "After watching the local weather reports and checking the tidal charts tomorrow looked like a good day. New moon started yesterday also good a good sign. I planned a date on a warm summer night to meet the bass near Narragansett, Rhode Island so I had to get the gear ready. Best get going, lots to do before I could hit the sack. Tomorrow was another day, and, when it comes to fishing for striped bass, everyday, every tide, every night is different., " said Ray.

Turning the key in my `65 Chevy station wagon, I moved into position and hooked up my trailer and boat. The sun was starting to set, brilliant beautiful swirling oranges and yellows like an early October sunset. It was twilight as I began loading my boat: four (4) custom rods by Murat Tackle, two (2) Penn 5OOM's conventional reels using 50 pound test Ande line and two (2) Penn 704 spinning reels using 30 pound test Ande line; hooks; leaders; extra line; sinkers, all the usual accessories in ample supply. . Fuel tanks were full; batteries were charged; and I had ice. I lugged the bait well over the gunwale and secured it near the transom. Bait was the only missing item right now, and, hopefully, I'll take care of that in the morning. I have to fish for fish before going fishing.

Monday morning, August 19, 1974 ....It's three-thirty am as I leave the house, coffee mug in hand, and head onto Route 1 south for the forty-five minute ride to Barn Island, CT. Bright starry night and the temperature is already at 71 - F. Having fished the last six (6) years in the R. I. Schaefer Salt Water Fishing Contest, representing the Woonsocket Striper Club, this year was no different. I was always hopeful of placing in the tournament with a good fish. One of my famous teammates is Frank Daignault is registered the shore-side division. He and I compare notes even though we are in separate categories; it helps give you a better picture of what's going on, inshore and off shore. He's a great fisherman and a well-known writer about the striped bass.

Arriving at the boat ramp, I notice two (2) boats were already launched and with no one else waiting, I launched and secured the boat. After parking the wagon and trailer, grabbed my gear bag and boarded. My eighteen (18') foot aluminum Star6raft boat along with an 85hp Mercury motor had seen a lot of use but things were in good repair and fairly clean. She was a seaworthy vessel that had motored me safely for several seasons. I started her up and gently maneuvered my way out of the ramp area.

I had planned on fishing along Watch Hill Reef off Rhode Island. A reef structure runs east and west towards Fishers Island, which is claimed by New York although it is just a few miles off the Connecticut shore. Bass like rocks, I like rocks so I fish where they and I like to fish. It's that simple. The tide would be incoming with the flood beginning at 6:30 a.m. and ending at 12:28 p.m. It's 4.45 am as I leave the calm bay waters and head westerly toward Stonington Harbor, just a short run away. Hopefully there will be enough pods of bunker to snag for a day of fishing.

Yessirree, there is bait and plenty of it! It takes me about an hour to snag fifty bunkers (50 menhaden). When the bait-well could hold no more I kicked in the throttle and headed east-southeast. The sun was just coming up as I arrived at my first spot. The weather reports were on target, what a gorgeous day to be out here.

I baited up the bunker like I always do, just in front of the dorsal fin and nudged the boat over to start my first drift with the incoming tide. Idling I dropped my line in and let the bunker swim the way down. After four drifts, of not even a bump, I set off for the next spot. I did this for over an hour checking each of my favorite haunts. Zilch, nothing. Heading toward Weekapesett, I still held out hope the bass might be there. The weather, tide and moon said yes. It was up to me to find the right

Dropping my line and live bait overboard, that first drift pulled a thirty-two (32) pounder onboard. Things were starting to look up. Over the next three drifts, I hooked and landed three (3) more stripers, all in the thirty (30) pound range.

While getting ready for the fifth drift, I saw a friend, Ken Peck, cruising by in his regular boat. I signaled Ken to stop and fish here, holding four (4) fingers up and spreading my hands wide enough to indicate good fish. We fished over the next hour close to each other. The fish were biting and we both caught some nice fish.

On my last drift (you'll see why it was my last), my bait hadn't gone all the way to the bottom, when, WHACK, this fish inhaled my bait and proceeded to take off! Immediately, I pulled back and felt the hook set. When I say this fish took off, I mean TOOK OFF! The whirring noise of my line as it unspooled from the reel was a beautiful sound to hear. The drag set on the reel seemed nonexistent, as the power of this fish was too much for it. I let it play itself out hoping it would soon tire. It seemed like forever before I started working her (I'm thinking it's got to be a female cow) back to the boat. I'm thinking this must be a world class bass because I'm reeling in about 250' (yes, two hundred fifty feet (250) of line, and it's still struggling. Actually many minutes passed with her trying to run out again and again and I determined to stop her. Finally, she's at the boat. Reaching over the side, I can't believe my eyes, it's a HUGE COW! I gaffed her and strain to pull her on the deck. Looking up, I see Ken pulling alongside, big grin on his face. He announces that he just caught around a forty-nine (49) pounder and holds it up. Telling him I also have a pretty good fish, he watches wide-eyed as I weigh my fish on my scale. It reads about sixty-one (61) pounds. I say about, because even at thirty-one (31) years of age, this was one heavy fish to lift and weigh, especially on a boat with my hand-held scale. Ken, the good friend that he is, starts razzing me, that I always catch the big turkeys, and on and on he went. I just reminded him why he stopped here to fish and asked if he was glad. "Oh yeah, you're right," he said with a sheepish smile.

It doesn't get better than this. I packed ice around the fish for the ride in (it didn't fit in my cooler), catch my breath and head for Barn Island. Best thing to do now was to get this fish weighed and registered. Once at the ramp, I loaded up and headed to the Sportsmen Cove Marina (now Lavin's Landing) in Charlestown.

My jaw still drops when the weight comes in at SIXTY POUNDS EIGHT (60.8) OUNCES! HOLY COW! This fish was fifty-three (53") inches long and had a girth of thirty-three (33") inches. Needless to say, this was a banner day!

Over the next few days, as word spread, I received quite a few congratulations from friends and family. There was a nice write-up in the <u>Providence Journal</u>. My Club awarded me the "Top Fish Trophy" and I received a trophy from the R. J. Schaefer Salt Water Fishing Contest. I had earned acceptance into the "Schaefer Circle of Sports Over Fifty-Pound Striper Club", there was no "Over Sixty-Pound Striper Club" at that time. At the end of the season the <u>R. J. Schaefer Newsletter</u> published statistics regarding large stripers caught through their Contest. I learned that in 1974 there were only three (3) fish over sixty (60) pounds; and ninety (90) fish over fifty (50) pounds. Further in 1973, there were four (4) fish over sixty (60) pounds; and ninety-six (96) fish over fifty (50) pounds. The Year 1972 resulted in four (4) fish over sixty (60) pounds; and, fifty-four (54) fish over fifty (50) pounds.

Catching a fish over sixty (60) pounds is not a common occurrence. My fish has a reserved spot over my fireplace. It was taxidermy by Peter Wilson, West Haven, Conn. Peter may not be in business at this writing.

Years have flown by. Since 1968, I have caught sixty (60) bass over fifty (50) pounds in forty-two (42) years worth of fishing so far. In 1973 I came just shy of my first sixty-pounder (60) with a fifty-nine pounds two (59.2) ounces. More recently in 2007, a beautiful cow, again out of Watch Hill Reef, came in at fifty-nine pounds twelve (59.12) ounces, also caught with bunker.

In closing, if you enjoy fishing, you are certainly not alone. I continue to fish, and, as always, realize that every day of fishing is different. Every year of fishing is different. You cannot catch yesterday's fish. There are many variables to successful fishing, i.e., weather; tides; migratory habits of stripers and baitfish; all out of our control. What we can control is how well we steward each of our natural resources. I think we all want our children; grandchildren and future generations to enjoy what we have enjoyed. Take the time to teach a child to fish. My three boys and three grandchildren all fish. I'm very proud to be one of those fishermen who has caught that rarest of striped bass over sixty (60) pounds.

Squid Beaumont, the author of this true story remains a close friend of Rays. His concise report of Ray's fish is accurate and verified by Ray as his true story. Squid interviewed Ray in order to get this story. Ray would like to hear from you if you know his friend Squid.

Ray Jobin 60.8 lb Striped Bass, Watch Hill, RI,
Aug 19, 1974

7-3
Peter Vican's Striped Bass, 76 pounds 14 oz., Block Island, RI
July 20, 2008

Catching A Record Striped Bass

By Donald A. Smith for Peter Vican, angler

Every angler has dreams of catching a record fish. Every time we leave the dock or fish the surf there's a thought that runs through our mind – it would be great to catch a tournament winning fish or break an existing record.

My fishing partner of 10 years, Peter Vican, and I are members of the Rhode Island Saltwater Anglers Association (RISAA). I am one of the 15 founding members of RISAA and Peter was one of the first anglers to join. That's how we connected and became fishing buddies. We share a passion for fishing and can be found on the water every weekend and usually a few nights during the week.

Peter is a three-time winner of the Rhode Island Governors Cup and I have won it once. The cup is awarded annually for the largest catch and release striped bass in Rhode Island waters. Although the majority of our fishing for striped bass is catch and release we do compete in many of the RISAA sponsored tournaments. We also fish in two tournaments at Block Island each year.

We entered the Fourth Annual Block Island Volunteer Fireman's Tournament held on July 18 through July 20, 2008. The event is held to raise funds to buy equipment for the island's Volunteer Fire Department and we have fished in the tournament since its' inception. I won it the first two years while Peter won it the third year. Each year the winners name is engraved on a plaque that hangs in the firehouse.

We arrived at the marina early on Friday evening. I stowed our gear in the cabin of the 24-1/2' Wellcraft Coastal and dumped our eels into the live well while Peter checked out the outboard motor and the electronics. When he started the 225 hp engine he got no amp reading on the gauge. He shut off the outboard and we pulled the engine cover to check the wiring but found no signs of the problem. However the alternator was just not charging.

Peter said, "We have a choice; we can call it a night and have the motor checked out, but we probably won't get anyone to do that until Monday morning; or we can head to the island and just keep the engine running all night because the alternator isn't charging the batteries."

He went on to tell me we'd be able to use our GPS and have our navigation lights and live well pump but we wouldn't be able to use the fish finder, spotlights, or listen to any music or ball games on the radio.

Since we use battery powered headlamps for night fishing not having spotlights wouldn't be a problem. Not having the stereo wasn't an issue either. We figured that fishing blind was better than not fishing at all and decided to go for it.

As we left the marina in Pt. Judith and headed to the island our conversation centered on the effort that was needed for one of us to win the tournament for the fourth time. We pretty much agreed that based on the size of the fish being caught at the Island during the past few weeks at least a 45 lb. fish would be needed to take home the first place honors.

It was around 8 PM when the boat cleared the break wall of the Harbor of Refuge at Point Judith and we headed south towards the island. The weather forecast was for winds at 5-to15 mph out of the southwest.

As we passed through the North Rip at Block Island and headed past New Harbor Peter told me that on his previous trips to the Island, made during the past month while I was away in Bolivia, he had fished our favorite spot, a place we nicknamed the Nest, without getting any fish over 30 pounds.

He said "If one of us is going to win this tournament we'll need more than a 30 pound fish so I'm going to pass up the Nest. Matt has gotten some fish in the high 40's at the Duck's Head and Freddy had a 50 pound fish there earlier this week." Matt is Capt. Matt King of Hula Girl Charters on Block Island and Freddy is Capt. Fred Bowman of Bottom Line Charters out of Point Judith. Both captains are good friends with proven track records for finding big fish. We often trade info about where the fish are. It was Matt King who originally showed us the Nest six years ago.

We motored to one of our tried and true spots, known as the Peanut, and I quickly rigged up eels as Peter set the boat into position for the drift. My first fish was large enough to break my 6/0 circle hook. Peter had a little better luck; he had a fish that appeared to be better than 40 pounds right up to the boat when it rolled in a large swell and spit the hook. Not bad results for a blind drift but not a very encouraging way for two experienced fishermen to start off fishing in a tournament.

Our second drift produced fish in the low 30-pound range for each of us and they were immediately turned loose. With each additional drift we landed fish in the 30 to 35 pound range but nothing close to the 45 pound fish we were looking for.

The drift was perfect for fishing eels and we had plenty of action. There was one other boat in the area fishing about a half-mile away. Other than that we were alone in the 11-mile expanse between Block Island and Montauk Point. The moon rose, partially hidden by low clouds on the horizon and the wind speed finally dropped to the 5 mph that had been forecast.

We fished the Peanut from 9 until 11:00 PM. The fishing was good. There were plenty of stripers, but none that looked like a tournament winner. So far the bluefish weren't bothering us either. We caught less than a half dozen bluefish all night.

Bluefish and dogfish can be a major problem when fishing the Block Island area. Bluefish will destroy an eel in seconds leaving only the head of the eel intact or cutting off the entire rig in a feeding frenzy. Dogfish just grab the eel and chomp on it trying to swallow it. We've often reeled in dogfish right up to the boat and lifted them out of the water before they let go of the eel and swim off.

As the tide slowed we found ourselves being hit by dogfish. They had moved into the area in large numbers. That ended the fishing on this spot for us.

We worked our way back towards the Island trying drifts over a few other spots and ended up at the Finger, another spot named after the shape of the bottom contour on the navigation charts. Drifting the Finger produced no hits on the eels at all. The moon was getting high in the night sky, the wind had died away completely and the temperature was comfortable. It was a perfect night for fishing.

Finally Peter said, "It's time we try the Nest. We'll probably won't get any fish over 30 pounds but at least we'll have some action."

By the time we reached the Nest the current was dying and our drift speed was only about 0.5 mph. Peter lined the boat up for a drift but there was no telling if we'd drift over our spots since there was no wind and the current was going slack.

As Peter lined up the boat I rigged eels on our lines. We fish with live eels almost exclusively. I make all of our tackle and the rigs consist of a 6/0 Gamakatsu Octopus Circle Hook snelled on to a 48" length of Seaguar 50 pound fluorocarbon. A Rosco barrel swivel is tied on the opposite end. During a normal season we will go through 150 rigs, mostly because of bluefish.

When Peter was sure that the drift direction would take us over our waypoint on the GPS he picked up his rod and we dropped our eels. Our drift was painfully slow but we soon hooked up with a double header. The fish we landed ranged in weight from 20 to 25 pounds and Peter noted that this was the kind of catch he'd had on his last few trips to this spot; but at least we had some action.

By 1 am the water was as flat as glass, the drift was just about nonexistent and the bite fell off. Peter had an eel on his rig that was almost dead from being taken by three bass on previous drifts. He put his rod in the rod holder and picked up a bottle of water from the cooler for a drink. All of a sudden the rod bent over and line started screaming off the spool at an alarming rate.

It took quite an effort for Peter to get his rod out of the holder and he held the rod tightly while the fish stripped off line. We fish strictly with light tackle; St. Croix graphite rods rated for 12 to 25 lb. line. Peter prefers a Penn 560 Slammer spinning reel while I use a Calcutta 400 conventional style reel. Both reels were spooled with Tuff Line XP 50 lb. braided line.

By the time the fish stopped his spool was almost empty of line. He started playing the fish but gained little ground because the fish was able to take out line at will. After wrestling with the fish for ten minutes he said that he was finally able to gain some control and turn the fish so it would swim towards the boat. We've often seen Stripers come to the surface during a prolonged fight but this fish stayed down on the bottom. For every ten yards of line that Peter reeled in the fish took back five with what seemed to be little effort. I was glad that we put a fresh spool, loaded with new line, on the reel earlier that night.

I had long since reeled in my line and was standing by to net the fish. I watched as Peter continued to fight the fish. His rod was bent in a "U" shape and I could see the strain showing on Peters face as the fight approached the twenty-minute mark.

At twenty minutes into the fight the fish was no longer making big runs, it was just hugging the bottom and Peter was working hard to reel in line. The line came in slowly and every once in awhile the fish would shake its head and take out a small amount of line.

After putting up what can only be described as a fabulous fight the fish was at the boat; the line was straight down and my watch showed that Peter had been fighting the fish for 25 minutes.

The water under us was around 40 feet deep and Peter now had to bring the fish straight up. I could see Peter straining as he lifted the rod and reeled in line to raise the fish off the bottom. He was sweating from the fight. The fish didn't like the vertical lift either and repeatedly headed down to safety on the bottom.

I stood by with the net while Peter worked to bring the fish to the surface. When the fish finally hit the surface it made every effort to swim away but it was spent and Peter turned it back toward the boat. The fish was clearly visible in our headlamps and we could tell it was big but still had no idea just how big it would turn out to be. The striper made one more small turn away from the boat but the battle was lost and Peter quickly brought it along side where the net was waiting.

I was surprised how easy the fish slid into the net. I rested the handle against the side of the boat, holding it with one hand while I grabbed the rim of the net with the other so I could lift the fish into the boat. I couldn't lift the fish that way and had to use both of my hands on the rim just to keep it from bending under the weight of the fish. As I struggled to lift the fish into the boat Peter put his rod in a holder and grabbed the handle of the net to help lift the fish out of the water. As we swung the fish onto the deck I glanced down at my watch, the entire fight had lasted just over 30 minutes.

As we talked about how much the fish weighed I grabbed the 50-pound digital scale out of the cabin. When I lifted the fish Peter said he couldn't read the scale, it was all lines instead of numbers. I had him do the honors and saw that the scale would get to 55 pounds before the screen went blank and lines appeared. We figured the fish had to go 60-pounds. Neither one of us had any idea at that time how wrong we actually were.

Then Peter said, "That looks like a Governor's Cup fish to me." I quickly shot back at him, "You've got to be kidding. We can't release this fish. We're fishing a tournament and this fish is definitely the winner. You have to weigh it in."

He told me it was a shame to kill such a beautiful fish but agreed to weigh it in when the official weigh-in stations on the island opened in the morning. In the meantime he brought the boat back to our original drift and told me to bait up my line so I could fish. He made no effort to get out of his chair and said his arms were really aching. However, after seeing Peter's fish on the deck it seemed that more fishing wouldn't matter much in this tournament anyway. We covered the fish with a wet beach towel because it was too big to fit in fish wells.

We fished until almost dawn and then headed into New Harbor and tied up at Champlins Marina to wait for Capt. Matt King to pick us up in his truck so we could weigh in the fish. I described the fish to Matt over the phone and had the distinct feeling he didn't believe me because we often go back and forth over the telephone telling fish tales when fishing in a tournament. I told him about the scale going blank at 55 pounds while it's tail was still on deck and told him this fish was something to see. He finally responded to the excitement and sincerity in my voice and after a few seconds of silence he said he'd be right there.

As we unloaded the fish from the boat there were curious onlookers at the marina that came over to see it. They asked how big it was and we said that we didn't know for sure but figured it was between 55 and 60 pounds.

The bass was loaded into Matt's truck and off we went to the Twin Maples bait shop to weigh it in. Back in 1984 Twin Maples was the location where the existing 70-pound state record Striped Bass was weighed in but we didn't know it at the time.

At Twin Maples the fish was unloaded and a new batch of onlookers came over to see it.

Interest was high and excitement was building as the fish was carried into the small bait shop to be weighed. A number of people crowded into the shop to see the weigh in. Peter ended up across the shop away from the scale because the crowd positioned itself in front of him to view the scale. I had my camera and used it as an excuse to get close to the scale so I could take photos. The fish was lifted onto the arm of the scale and John Swienton, the owner, said lets see how good we were at guessing it's weight and immediately slid the marker to the 50 lb. mark on the balance scale. The arm didn't budge so he went to 55 and called out the number. Still nothing, so he went to 60 and called out the number. The arm still hadn't moved.

I was standing next to John while Peter was facing me about eight feet across the floor in the crowded room. He couldn't see the scale readings but had a surprised look on his face as 60 pounds was called out. As John slid the weight to the 65-pound mark I called it out and saw Peter's eyes bulge. When the weight went to 70 I called it out and his jaw dropped. At 75 his face had a totally startled look. The weight was finalized at 76 pounds 14 ounces, a new state record!

Everyone gathered around Peter to congratulate him and shake his hand. Then they wanted to take the fish outside and hang it for photos. People were on their cell phones calling friends and by the time the fish was hung in a tree outside the shop there was quite a group of onlookers with cameras at the scene. People wanted their picture taken next to the fish and had their children's picture taken with it as a frame of reference.

Matt King called Joe Szabo the current Rhode Island record holder, whose 70-pound striper had been in the record book for some 24 years. His reply was "Hey, records were made to be broken." and he extended congratulations to Peter.

After some 40 minutes of picture taking and excitement we found out that even though the scale at Twin Maples was a state certified scale it wasn't certified by the Rhode Island Saltwater Anglers Association. To be recognized by the club for the yearlong striper competition we'd have to weigh it in on a RISAA certified scale. That meant loading the fish back in the boat and heading across the 9-mile stretch of Block Island Sound to the mainland and weighing the fish in at Snug Harbor Marina.

Back into the truck and back to boat we went. It was no picnic loading and unloading the fish and moving it down to the end of the dock at Champlins. The onlookers from earlier in the morning were still around and when they found out it was a new state record they also wanted to take pictures with the fish.

We finally loaded the fish back in the boat and put it into two large plastic garbage bags – one from the head and another from the tail. We then packed four bags of ice into the garbage bags around the fish and covered the whole thing with wet towels.

By the time we reached the Harbor of Refuge on the mainland there was talk on the radio. A voice came over the speaker saying there was some news about someone catching an 80-pound fish. It sure didn't take long for the fish tales to start.

We docked at Snug Harbor Marina and Al Conti, the owner, was there to greet us. He escorted us to the scale for the RISAA weigh in. Because of hanging in the sun for photos and the trip across from Block Island the weight of the fish on the RISAA certified scale was down to 75.4 pounds.

Al was kind enough to take care of filling out the state form and the RISAA club weight slip. He wanted to get some photos of the fish under the Snug Harbor sign at the dock. I had the honor of calling in the RISAA weight to the club. Peter is not the kind of person that likes to bask in the limelight and just wanted to go home and get some sleep.

On Sunday morning Peter picked me up at home so we could return to Block Island for the cookout and awarding of prizes at the firehouse. On the ride to the marina Peter informed me that Don Coyne, a sportscaster for the local TV station, was meeting us at the dock to tape an interview about the fish for ABC news. He also said his phone was ringing off the hook all morning from various newspapers that wanted the story and photos of the fish. He said that he was referring all of them to his secretary, namely me, and gave them my number since the photos were in my camera. He told me that since it was my idea to keep the fish I could deal with the newspapers.

As part of the awards ceremony at the firehouse Joe Szabo was there to shake Peter's hand and congratulate him on breaking his long-standing record. As the three of us swapped fish stories it dawned on me what an experience this was. Not only was I a first hand witness to a piece of sporting history I was also in the company of the history makers. It was an experience of a lifetime.

Peter's fish was officially recognized as the Rhode Island state record at 76 pounds 14 ounces with a length of 54-3/4" and a 34" girth. It turned out to be the second largest bass caught on rod and reel and the largest ever recorded as caught from a boat. Not a bad catch for fishing blind.

Peter Vican's 76.9 lb Striped Bass
July 18, 2008
Block Island, RI

7-4
Mark Sherer's 62.5 lb Striped Bass,|
Block Island, RI
July, 2008

Mark Sherer- 62.5 lb Striped Bass

They say that 10% of the fishermen catch 90% of the fish. There is a group of striper fishermen that fall into this 10% category and we are among the most fanatical and obsessed individuals in the world. We all have goals: our first 40, first 50, maybe even a 60. In reality, we all secretly just know that there is a 79 out there with our name on it, and that is what truly drives us.

I say "we" because my own obsession started when I was a six year-old boy. I would fish with my dad aboard his 18' Lyman and dream of catching a big striper. My dad just liked fishing and was content catching bluefish, mackerel or winter flounder—all plentiful in Narragansett Bay in the 60's. When we fished for these species, I felt like I was wasting my time. Don't get me wrong, it was fun but it left me dreaming of big bass. When I was eight, we trailered my Dad's boat to Weekapaug, Rhode Island. It was October, 1965 and fish were migrating down the coast. I caught my first striper which weighed about ten pounds.

It is 4:00 AM on an August day in 1978 as I launch my 17' Boston Whaler Montauk in Wickford Harbor, Rhode Island. I run to Barrington Beach to meet the *Ocean State* and *Cindy Bet* -- purse seine boats fishing for menhaden. They are just hauling their nets. I pull along side; hand up a scoop net and Ray Jobin gives me two scoops of poggies. He asks me to deliver a bucket of bait to his friend and mentor, Danny Zubeck. I thank him and head back to Wickford, put my boat back on the trailer and drive down to Barn Island in Stonington, Connecticut. I launch and head for Isabella Beach-- on the backside of Fishers Island in New York. I see Danny and his wife drifting, pull alongside and hand over his bait. I know Danny is on fish, but I don't want to crowd him, so I go find my own. I head for Race Rock. The tide is running and the fish are there. I fish until the tide goes slack and head for the barn.

On my way home I stop at Handrickens and sell my fish. In the 70's the price would peak in August because there were not as many fish coming to market as in June and July. (I think I got around $1.50 per pound.)

A fact not widely known by many Rhode Island and Massachusetts fishermen is that the quotas established for those states after the moratorium in the 1980's were based on historical landings. In the years used to establish the new quotas, many of Rhode Island's top commercial fishermen sold their catch in Massachusetts because market prices were higher. I am frequently asked why the Massachusetts annual quota is almost 1.2 million pounds, while Rhode Island's quota is a little over 140,000 pounds. I guess you could say we shot ourselves in the foot.

When we fish with menhaden, most of the time they are fished dead, either chunked or yo-yo'd. Bunker or poggies have probably resulted in the demise of more big stripers than any other one method. For many years, yo-yoing was a closely guarded secret among a few of Rhode Island's top commercial rod and reel anglers. The method was invented by Dick Sevigny. There are few, if any fishermen that have caught more big stripers than this man. In recent years groups have tried to outlaw yo-yoing because it is so effective.

The hardware used to rig the dead menhaden while yo-yoing frequently ends up in the bellies of stripers. For this reason, the On the Water Striper Cup and Martha's Vineyard Striped Bass and Bluefish Derby, have excluded this method of taking fish from their contests. (If you are interested in how it works, go online and you will find all the info you need.)

I get home after selling my fish around 2:00 PM in the afternoon. I need some shuteye so I hit the rack. The alarm goes off; it's now 7:00 PM. I get up, grab a quick bite and head for the ramp at Monahan's in Narragansett, Rhode Island. I meet my old buddy Jack Pimer and we head for the mouth of Narrow River. We fish the Clumps, Annawan Cliffs, Dickens Reef, Whale Rock and then head down to Black Point and Stinky Beach. (The rocky coast line area between Point Judith, Rhode Island and the mouth of Narragansett Bay). The fishing in this area is best on the bottom half of the tide, both incoming and outgoing. We cast eels into the white water around the rocks.

When the fish hits, you feel a thump. At the hit, drop your rod tip but don't go to free spool. When the line comes tight, set the hook. The result of letting the fish "run", will frequently lead to a dropped eel.

We are still slinging eels as the sky starts to glow pink to the east. There is a nice pile of fish in the fish box. This was a typical day in my life at the time.

Work took me to live on Martha's Vineyard and I was introduced to the Martha's Vineyard Striped Bass and Bluefish Derby. Fishing the 1983 Derby is one of my fondest memories. It was the last day of the tournament in October and no big fish had been weighed in. (I think the leader at that point was 42 pounds.)

My friends Steve Morris, Tom Needham, Lou Othote and I left Oak Bluffs around 2:00 PM. We headed to Menemsha where my boat was docked and passed through Menemsha Bite at around 3:30. The wind was blowing 25 – 30 NE. We made it around Devil's Bridge at Gay Head bound for Nomans Land. We arrived on the back- side of Nomans and put Lou on the beach. I had previously scouted the area and found a deep-water beach on the lee side of a point. We were able to nose the bow right up to land to drop Lou off. The plan was for Lou to fish the beach and Tom, Steve and I would fish from the boat. We had VHF radios to stay in contact.

We started picking away at the fish right away. It wasn't hot but the action was steady. We communicated with Lou several times throughout the night and he also was doing ok. Around 1:00AM Lou called on the radio and said, "Get your butt over here. There are big fish on the beach. I've got seven with one close to 50, but I am out of eels and they don't want plugs."

He had found some big fish on the opposite side of the point where we had dropped him. The wind was blowing onshore on that side of the point, so fishing from the boat was going to be a real challenge.

Steve was feeling a little green so he lay down in the bow. I poked around the corner and could see there was a pretty good sea crashing on the beach. I ran the boat while Tom made a cast and immediately hooked a nice fish. I yelled for Steve to get up and grab his rod. I pointed in the dark and told him to make a cast right there. His eel hit the water with a splash and was hit instantly. The hit created an explosion of fire in the water as the eel was struck so close to the surface. Steve set the hook and fought the fish while I ran the boat with one hand and held the back of his slicker to steady him with my other hand. Once the fish was along side, I gaffed it and swung it over the gunnels. I patted Steve on the back and congratulated him on his first fifty.

We decided to call it a night, so we picked up Lou and headed back to Menemsha. As we approached Gay Head, first light was just starting to crack. The tide was now running hard to the east and the wind was howling from the Northeast. We still needed to cross Devil's Bridge-- a rocky reef extending from the beach at Gay Head several miles out into Vineyard Sound. Because the wind was opposing the tide, there was a wall of white water taller than my 19' Lema center console. We crashed through the white water and dropped into a hole which rattled every bone in my body. I looked at Steve and his face was white as a ghost. It had been a long night.

On the ride home in the truck we made a game plan for the weigh-in. The Derby headquarters in Edgartown would close on the last day at 10:00AM. We planned to meet at the diner next to headquarters at 9:00AM for breakfast and then weigh in Steve's big fish at 9:45AM

In the morning all went according to plan, except when we arrived at headquarters. A very excited fisherman was walking out with his big fish which tipped the scales at 45 pounds. He was the new derby leader and was exuberant. Steve, Lou, Tom and I each grabbed a fish out of the back of my truck and the guy's jaw dropped. We had two fish that were larger than his. Steve's weighed in at 49.96 and Lou's at 47.0.

Steve won grand prize which included having his big fish mounted by taxidermist, Wally Brown from Falmouth, Massachusetts; some cash and fishing tackle. More importantly, winning the Derby as a twenty-year old on the Island of Martha's Vineyard gave Steve rock-star like status. He went on to take over his grandfather's tackle shop, Dick's Bait and Tackle in Oak Bluffs. His mount of the big fish still hangs proudly inside the entrance. (Lou disqualified his own fish because Derby rules did not allow beach caught fish from off island.)

In the years that followed, Tom and I often fished together. Finding a fishing partner is not easy. We were compatible, meticulous, dependable and passionate about big stripers. We have stories of many 50's, brushes with disaster and good times. Tom caught two 60's-- one on my boat and the other while fishing with Jimmy Pattersen.

Tom also fished with Wilford Fontain, who held the Rhode Island State record for many years. Jimmy Pattersen actually had four 60's. (Three in consecutive years on the same date, the first on July 14, 1962, the second July 14, 1963 and again on July 14, 1964.) I have been told that Jimmy and or fishermen on his boat caught sixteen 60's during his career.

One memorable trip occurred in November at Block Island in the early 80's. Tom, his son Kevin and I arrived on the backside of the Island in the late afternoon for an evening of slinging eels. There were a lot of big fish and they were in the shallows chasing sand eels. The water was crystal clear. Huge fish were lazily rolling through the sand eels with their mouths open.

The previous trip Tom had a 57 pounder and I had a 58.5 in the same night. We knew they would hit eels after dark, but had not yet discovered the effectiveness of the needlefish plug. We cast eels relentlessly before dark and Kevin caught one 32 -pound fish -- the smallest of the evening. After dark, things got really exciting. We had ten fish for over 400 pounds. Tom had a 61 and I had one over 50.

Staff Carol, the sports photographer for the *Providence Journal* took a beautiful black and white photo of the catch and put it in the paper. The picture was taken on the rocks overlooking the ocean in front of the Top of the Dock Tackle Shop in Narragansett, Rhode Island. We caught a lot of flack for that picture. (This was during the population decline, but before the moratorium.)

On a night in the late 1990's, Tom, John Deterer and I were fishing Old Harbor Point at Block Island. It was just before dark and we were slinging eels in close to shore. There had been a storm a few days earlier and there was a little sea running. The water was milky and cloudy like it gets after a good blow. This condition frequently oxygenates the water and when there is bait present, the big bass move into the shallows and feed voraciously. The fish were here; you could literally smell them.

We had been fishing for a while and as always; I had the bow of my 23' Sea Craft pointed towards the sea. I always focus on the conditions around me and through the years have developed a sixth sense for smelling out dangerous situations. Something made the hair on the back of my neck stand up and I turned to look out to sea. What I saw really got my attention. There was a wave several hundred yards offshore heading our way. This wave was huge. I immediately started my engine and started motoring towards the wave and at the same time warned Tom and John to hold on.

I had been in similar situations in the past and had learned from an old salt years ago how to maneuver a small boat through a big breaking wave. As the wave approached, it began to crest and just before it hit, I gunned the engine to full throttle. This propelled the boat through the wave. White water crashed over the top of my antennas on my t-top. As the boat came out the backside of the wave it dropped many feet and landed with such a jar that it stalled the engine. Fortunately, there was not a second and third wave behind this one rogue, because if there had been, we would have lost everything. As it was, the cockpit was full of water; the boat was listing to one side, we lost one rod/reel, a gaff and our eel bucket with all of our bait. We were all completely soaked and severely shaken but no one was hurt. We were lucky.

It was July 2008 and I am home having dinner with my kids and Roe. The phone rings. It is Carl Webster, a friend and employee at the Point Judith Fisherman's Company. He had just received notice from RI Department of Environmental Management that the commercial striper season was to end the following day. I told everyone at the table that I was going to sleep right after dinner. I set the alarm for midnight.

I arrived at Point Judith Marina at 1:00AM. The weather was good; no wind, clear skies and I knew the tide would be perfect. As I passed through the West Gap in the Harbor of Refuge, I plugged in the waypoint SW of Block Island which I intended to fish. I switched on the autopilot and leaned back to enjoy the beautiful starlit night. When I arrived at the spot, it was 2:30AM and there was another boat there which I did not recognize.

I set up to make a drift and as I approached the structure where the fish should be I got hit. I landed a fish in the thirties and went up for another drift. On the second drift, I got hit again. I could tell it was a nice fish because it made a long run but then came up pretty easy. When the fish came up along side, I lip gaffed the fish and attempted to lift it over the rail with one hand. I got the fish's head up to the gunnels and it slid back into the water. This was definitely a two-hander.

Once the fish slid onto the deck, I remember thinking, "Nice fish, and definitely over 50." I slid it in the fish box and went up for another drift. I fished for the next hour and a half without another hit and then around

4:00AM, I caught another fish. It was keeper, so I took it up to throw in the fish box. When I opened the box the big fish looked even bigger than before. No ground shrinkage here. In the back of my mind, I'm thinking, "How big?"

It took me a few more drifts to get my last two fish to fill my commercial five fish limit and by then the sky was starting to brighten. It was going to be a picture perfect sunrise. By this time my curiosity was getting the best of me, so I broke out the 60- pound Boga grip and grabbed the big fish out of the box. It buried the needle which stops at about 62- pounds. Wow! I was stunned. I immediately called my fishing partner, Tom and give him the news. He was very happy for me and asked me to call him back as soon as I weighed it on Al Conti's official scale.

I plugged in the West Gap, set the autopilot and headed for Snug Harbor Marina. At the dock we put my fish on the scale and the digital readout registered at 62.5 pounds. A lifelong dream had been realized. After weighing the fish I went over to Point Judith Fisherman's Company to sell my other four fish.

Then I called my friend, Don Deberidino, who worked at the Department of Environmental Management Fisheries Office in Jerusalem to ask him if he would take some pictures for me. We took our time and set up some really nice photos. Tom Meade, outdoor writer for the *Providence Journal* featured one shot on the front page of the sports section along with a nice article. At the time I was entered in the On the Water Striper Cup, fishing for Team Dick's. The fish won me the "Striper of the Year" award and was the first 60 ever caught in the Cup.

After the photo shoot I took the fish back to Snug Harbor. Joe Mollica helped me wrap the fish in cotton sheets, place it on a sheet of plywood and wet it before freezing it for the taxidermist. (This protects and preserves the fish.) Joe and Lowry at NE Taxidermy did a skin mount for me. It is by far the best striper mount I have ever seen. It looks like it could swim off the wall.

In the days that followed, I heard from many people-- old friends and acquaintances that I had not heard from in years called to congratulate me. All of my current social friends, fishing buddies and some people I didn't even know contacted me. My fiancée, Rosemarie came home from work the following night saying she couldn't believe the number of people who were aware of the big fish! People even came to her office to comment about my catch. There was also a lot of chatter on the Internet. Fishing news travels fast!

The week before I caught my 62.5, a 70 -pound fish was caught at Orient Point, New York. The week after, a 68 was speared by a diver at Watch Hill, Rhode Island and eight days after my catch, the Rhode Island state record was broken with a 76 pound 14 ounce monster. All of these fish were 55" in length. All caught in about a three-week period within a thirty- mile radius. I have wondered if these fish were all from the same year class.

I think I fished harder last year in 2009 than I had since I was a kid. I sold my 26' Regulator and downsized to a 21' Contender. I rigged it myself with all of the latest electronics. Garmin 4210 chart plotter with a vision card, that gives me detailed bathometrics, bottom contour and structure, Furuno 1724 Radar, Furuno FCV-585 fish finder, Ray Marine autopilot, and Icom VHF. All of these components are interfaced using NMEA   0183 and have helped to increase my productivity by being able to find the fish and stay on them.

With the smaller boat my fuel consumption went way down and I could trailer to where the fish were. What a year! Every time I left the dock I knew there was a sixty or bigger out there with my name on it. That didn't happen but we did manage to catch 21 fish over forty pounds during the season. The biggest was 47 pounds and was caught by my good friend, Captain Dick Smith.

There is a concerted effort by recreational striper fishermen and Stripers Forever to stop the commercial harvest of stripers. I am a charter captain as well as a commercial rod- and-reel fisherman. I have many clients who are fly fishermen and I enjoy nothing more than to see their excitement when I put them on big fish. In my opinion many of the attitudes and opinions of the recreational fisherman are based on emotion and lack of understanding of the big picture. Biological data tells us that the biomass is healthy. Just because you caught all the stripers you wanted at a particular place at a certain time of the year doesn't mean that will happen every year.

Stripers have tails, they swim and they swim to where the conditions are optimal for their survival. There are more stripers outside the EEZ than most fisherman can imagine. These fish are healthy and they are protected and they are there because that is where the bait is. In my opinion based on my experience and knowledge of the safeguards that are in place, we will not face another collapse in the fishery as we did in the 80's.

Tony, the author of this book, asked me to answer a few questions and also describe my tackle:

1. Is the RI quota still five fish?

The RI annual commercial quota for rod and reel is around 146,000 pounds. The June season opens June 6, 2010 and will probably last about three-four weeks. It will close when 75% of the quota is reached. The season will re-open on September 13 and remain open until 100% of the quota is filled. The daily limit is five fish and you can fish Sunday through Thursday. (No fishing on Friday or Saturday.)

2. How much do you get per pound?

During the 2009 season, the average price I received was $3.00 per pound.

3. Describe your method for drifting eels.

I use an 8 ½' or 9' graphite custom rod with a Garcia Ambassador 7000 or Shimano Calcutta 700B.

Line: I use 25 or 30- pound clear blue Stren during the day and 65- pound Power Pro at night. (I do not get as many fish on the power pro during the day, so I assume they can see the line.)

I use an egg sinker on the main line with an 80-pound Spro barrel swivel connecting the main line to a fluorocarbon leader. I use a stopper above the egg sinker to stop the sinker from sliding up the line. (The depth of water, amount of tide and wind will determine the weight of the egg sinker.)

I prefer Gamakatsu 6/0 Octopus Circle hooks.

I fish on structure or contour lines. Fish concentrate and migrate on a daily basis along these contour lines. Traveling along these lines and over structure will allow you to locate fish. Good electronics and knowing how to use them will help you stay on the fish when you do find them.

Mark Sherer's 62.5 lb Striped Bass
July, 2008
Block Island, RI

7-5
Ted Nimiroski's 60 lb Striped Bass,
Narragansett, RI
Aug. 13, 1958

This is my story of how I learned about striped bass fishing. It's a tale of my family, heroes and friendships, rescues along the way and being allowed to fish with some of the greatest striped bass anglers, both men and women, in the State of Rhode Island.

Bio of the Bass and Me

June 1952

I was 15 years old when my mother said, "Let's go for a ride to Norton Reservoir, I want you to meet someone." We pulled into the reservoir entrance where the Wading River empties and immediately saw a game warden and a man fly fishing for large mouth bass. In that era you could not keep large mouth bass until the first of July. Bill Chase, the game warden, said to me, "See that man out there with a fish on?" Mr. Chase was watching as the angler was releasing a fish without taking it out of the water." He said, "That is the way to release a bass as it won't hurt the fish." After a half hour or so he drove off. The man in the water wearing hip boots was the person my mother wanted me to meet. His name was Ernest Richmond. He hollered to my mother, "Did that SOB leave?" My mother said, "Yes, he did." Ernie came to shore holding a stringer of large mouths from three to five pounds apiece. Ernie was not a law breaker by nature, he simply wanted to release the fish in front of the bait shop where he worked, so he could show customers that there were bass there by making a few cast either with fly rod or casting outfit. That was the first day I met Ernie and he immediately became my hero.

Sept 1952

The Portuguese community held a festival in Norton, Massachusetts every fall and Ernie was from that town. He graduated high school with Joe Fernandez whose market was the main sponsor of the festival. I'll always remember the festival because it included a four foot long piece of beef roasting on an iron stick. Of course, since Ernie was a classmate of Joe's, those guys got the tenderest cuts. There was wine, whiskey, plenty of beer and fireworks at the end of the nightly event, including a few memorable fistfights due in part to the wine, whiskey and beer.

My mother took me to the event and during the fireworks display, while everyone was looking up, Ernie would pass me the beer bottle and I would chug as much down as I could. He then became my superhero. Of course, in those days, as long as you had money it was okay to buy as much booze as you want.

March 1954

Just prior to my enlistment in the United States Air Force on March 23, my mother took me to meet Ernie for some words of encouragement and some pointers on how to get along in the service. He had given me his ring with his initials on it as a good luck charm. My father, being a great provider, was also a heavy drinker and was quite abusive when drunk. My mother had told me that as soon as I went in the service she planned to leave my father. I told her to go for it and not worry about me; I would be all right. I tried to emulate Ernie by requesting gunnery school but modernization had deleted the use of men for that function. It had become an electronic responsibility and I was sent to learn how to repair electronic fire control systems, which became my lifelong livelihood.

Nov 1957

I received a letter from my mother saying she and Ernie had gotten married on the first day of hunting season. Go figure. I think he conned my mother into being his bird dog. He shot two pheasants on their honeymoon. I was stationed on Chitosi AFB, Hokkaido, Japan at that time. In October the Air Force reassigned the 4th Fighter Wing back to Seymour Johnson AFB for those who had more than six months left on their enlistments and for me, who happened to be one of the unlucky few left on their enlistment, had to stay another five months to await orders for separation. It was the longest five months of my life. It was the longest five months of my life because I had no pay for booze, nothing to do except wait, wait and wait some more. I decided to hock the ring Ernie gave me, so we could buy some Japanese beer and Saki wine. I knew if Ernie ever found out, he would have disowned me. I never admitted that I hocked it. I just told him I lost it, though I'm sure he had his suspicions.

Feb 1958

I got home around the end of February 1958. It was an exceptionally cold winter that year. Both my Mother and Ernie were working at the Foxboro State Hospital, Ernie as a painter, my mother toiling in the kitchen. On weekends we decided to do a little ice fishing for pickerel and perch and anything else that would bite. That kept up until late spring. Then, we went trout fishing and a little bit of pond fishing for pickerel. I also found out that my mother and Ernie bought a summer cottage at Breakwater Village, in Narragansett, Rhode Island. It was a little homestead-covered 20'x 24' building with a toilet but no shower. It had a kitchen and just enough room to sleep to get out of the rain.

May 1958

Ernie and my mother decided to take me striper fishing off the railway trestle in Warren, Rhode Island. We were using sand worms and as luck would have it, I caught the first fish. I held it up and asked Ernie, "What should I do with it?" He told me grab it by the gills and tail then shove it up my butt. They both laughed like hell...my first striper...I was hooked.

July 1958

We traveled to the cottage for some serious tries at big fish from the surf. Ernie was up early the next morning and went to the nearby lighthouse off the point to try a little surf fishing. During his try, while moving from place to place, he stepped on a bag of striper lures. It was a bag with Atom Swimmers and Poppers...about 10 of them. He picked up the bag and on the walk back to our cottage, he asked several people if they knew of anyone who lost this bag of plugs. Around noon, a lady appeared at our door and said that her son, Gary Bryson, had lost them. Ernie handed over the bag. Later that afternoon Gary, who was about 14 years old, came over to thank Ernie and a lifelong friendship was started. A couple of weeks later, Gary's mother, Jan Kosacz Bryson, painted a beautiful picture of a sailing schooner and gave it to my mother and Ernie as a thank you for Ernie's honesty. It remained in our cottage until someone broke into our place and stole it. Gary's mother and husband Bill were the nicest people you would ever meet and immediately gained Ernie's and my respect. Bill and Jan were so happy that their son could go fishing with someone who had an adult mind, not realizing that Gary really was the one who had the adult mind and that Ernie and I were a couple of beer drinking, smoking, hell-raisers. I have given credit to Gary, as of this day; he has not taken up any of Ernie and my bad habits. Gary and his family are considered part of my family, even though we are not related by blood. Gary is godfather to my daughter Deborah as I am to his son Gary. Now my daughter is godmother to Gary's granddaughter, Anna.

Gary's grandfather, Mr. Kosacz, owned a mahogany speed boat with a 10 HP motor on it and it was suggested that Gary and I go cast some eels to try to catch a few larger stripers. We trailered the boat to the ramp in Galilee and went around the Point Judith light to a cove located in back of the Bonvue

Inn. We made a few casts and both caught our first two large stripers. These fish weighed in around 25 lbs each and we were both really addicted to striper fishing now. As fate and life had it, my fishing was over that year as I had gotten a job with the Air Force as a civilian at The General Electric Plant in Utica, New York.

Aug 1959

I would say that was my luckiest year of striper fishing. One afternoon I was sitting at a local bar, the Bonvue Inn, having a couple of beers and looking out the window. I noticed some fish rolling on the surface chasing bait. I watched them for about an hour and thought, "I'm going fishing." I headed to Gary's cottage and found another friend, Ron Wojcik. Since Ernie and my mother were back to work, Gary and I hooked Gary's trailer and his new 14ft fiberglass Howard boat to his station wagon and headed for the ramp at Galilee, launched the boat and headed for the area where I had seen the fish. By then they were gone, so we decided on rowing our usual route starting where the fish were seen and heading north to Scarborough. Eels were cast off the back of the boat and rowing gave a lift motion to the eels. Coupled with the quietness of our movement this method was deadly for catching fish. We rowed about a half-mile, slightly past the Sheep Pen, turned around and rowed back. On the first leg of the trip nothing happened, and we were about halfway through our second pass, when I felt a familiar bump. I dropped back and set the hook, only to have a giant fish strip off around 30 yards of line and head for a rock that was just under the surface. Pop! The line and the damn fish broke off but I did see her tail as she waved goodbye. She was big. It was getting dark and the sea was flat. There was no wind and we had music on the radio, a bottle of Mother Goldstein wine, and Gary rowing. In my mind's eye, I had it made. Our arrangements were the guy rowing would continue until someone caught a fish, then that person would row. Gary kept rowing and I had another bump but the fish never picked the eel back up. Now Gary was getting a little irritated that I kept losing and breaking fish off while he rowed. It was pretty dark now and Gary was still rowing. His reel finally started to sing. As Gary rowed, he flipped the reels clicker on while laying the rod off the back of the boat. As luck would have it he landed a 25 lb striper and had to keep rowing, which made it okay with me, since I was feeling no pain, drunk on wine. Another half hour went by and I had another bump. I dropped back and set the hook; only to have the fish head out to sea peeling off around 75 yards of my 40lb test braided nylon Ashaway line. I thought, "Oh no, not another of these big guys that I can't stop," as my thumbs were still sore from fighting the one that straightened my 7/0 hook the week before.

On that trip I had caught 5 bass over 35lbs and had one fish on for 15 minutes before straightening out my 7/0 O'Shaughnessy hook. This giant finally did stop, turn and made another couple of short runs before she came up on her side. Gary put the gaff to her and lifted her over the side into the boat. It was my turn to row, so I put on another eel and set my rod down and went about 50 yards when my Penn 200 started to sing again. I set the hook on that one, fought it and landed another nice fish and at the time we knew these fish were monsters but not sure how big, so we fired the motor up and headed in. We got back to Breakwater Village where a local guy had a bait shop named Bucky's. We put the biggest one on the scale and it weighed a whopping 61.8 lbs! The other fish weighed 52.7 and the other 25 something. We then found out that Bucky's was not an official scale for the Knickerbockers Beer contest that was going on. We would have to wait until morning when Ed Fishes tackle shop opened. Ed got there around 6 AM, opened the door and we put the fish on his scale and they weighed 60.0 lbs and 51.0 lbs! Wow, was I happy! Ed had a connection with a Providence Journal photographer/writer Staff Carroll and he came and took photos and wrote an article about these fish. I felt like I was on top of the world. I was the luckiest fisherman alive using a beat up old Horrocks Ibbertson rod, Penn 200 reel and braided nylon 40# test Ashaway line, which would now qualify me for their Nifty/Fifty Striper Club. After a friend of mine mounted my bass, I brought it to the Horrocks Ibbertson main office and it was displayed in their front window until I left Utica, NY.

July 1961

On the 8th of July I married my beautiful wife Charlotte. She was the best thing that ever happened to me and, of course, trying to be like Ernie on his honeymoon went hunting. I told Charlotte the first week we would go to Maine and the second week we would go to the cottage at Breakwater Village and maybe do some fishing. At the time we had a 14ft Aerocraft boat that was popular with Cape Cod bass fishermen. Since we could launch from the surf, I took my wife out and decided to explore the Narrow River in Narragansett. It's well known to have many large stripers near the mouth and I figured that some big fish might be upstream in deep pools of water and maybe we could sight fish them. We had no luck that day so I decided to turn around and show my wife the beautiful beaches along the Narragansett shoreline. We headed out of the river. During our time in the river the seas picked up and there was a good roll at the mouth. I told Charlotte to hold on and we pushed the aluminum boat thru the breakers. She was sitting in the front seat and was not prepared or holding tight enough when the boat slammed a wave. She hurt her back to the point that she cried. From that point there was nothing I could do but take it real easy for the ride back to Point Judith. That area had gotten real snotty around the light and thru the gap off the east wall breakwater. That event certainly put a damper on our honeymoon but it didn't stop me from fishing all night the rest of the week. My wife was quite upset with me for leaving her alone all night and when I caught a 35 lb bass, she told me what I could do with it. She didn't stay mad for long as I did get her pregnant with our first child. I guess we really did have time for a honeymoon.

28 Sept 1961

I had worked with my wife's cousin, Ray Novak, and he introduced me to another striped bass fisherman named Arthur Donovan and we immediately bonded. Art had a 15ft plywood boat and we tried and caught many schooling bass in the Merrimac River. I convinced Art to try night fishing and we set out around 8 pm and had caught maybe 30+ fish, trolling small Atom Swimmers. It was around 10 pm with an outgoing tide, we trolled outside the mouth where a sandbar was located. We got in too close and I yelled out to Artie, "Watch out," and he gunned it, which pitched and rolled us over into the river. When we went over, while in the water, I could see the battery hanging right side up with the cables still attached. I pushed myself from under the boat and spread-eagle on the capsized bottom of the boat while Art was hanging onto the bow eye with his fingers. Fortunately, a 42ft charter boat named the Knickerbocker, saw our lights disappear and they started searching for us. Capt Red Hilton owned the boat and they looked for what seemed an eternity to me. I found out later that it was a half hour or a little more and then fog started to roll in. I'm still not sure if I was scared or not but I think I did a little praying and had thoughts, "Me and my stupid mouth." If I had kept it shut the wave would have broken harmlessly in the boat. Then again, you never know for sure what would have happened. The charter boat decided that we must have gone in. Fortunately through heaving wave action, they caught a glimpse of our bow light that was still lit and came over and pulled us out of the water. Someone on shore had called the Coast Guard and we were transferred to their boat to search for our boat in the fog. We finally found it and got it upright and brought it to the boat ramp that we used in Newburyport. Then found the nearest bar that was still open. I had shed my boots and hunting jacket while trying to swim to the charter boat that saved us. All I recall is the bartender saying, "It was pretty cold for swimming, boys." I didn't care what he said while I was shivering, frozen to the core. The next day there was an article in the Lawrence Eagle Tribune Newspaper about 2 inexperienced fishermen rescued from the Merrimac River. That was certainly a blow to our pride but I must admit it was true and maybe there was a reason. I did have a few times when I saved others and it did convince me that there is a God.

June 1962

While we still had our aluminum boat, I decided to buy a 16ft fiberglass Lone Star boat and tried to do a little more fishing in water that I knew best around Point Judith. There was plenty of water we wanted to fish along the Narragansett shoreline and until then we were confined to rowing along the east wall and the area from the lighthouse to Scarborough Beach. One foggy night we decided to fish close to home. We generally launched our boat from the surf. We would go out from the gap and followed the break wall, while we rowed towards the lighthouse, listening to the foghorn for guidance. We were in the corner of the wall and rowing to the light when we heard a splash and felt a line come over our heads. It was a surfcaster trying to catch a fish in the fog. Ernie grabbed the line and jerked it a couple of times and we rowed pretty fast to make it appear like it was a fish. Ernie started pulling the line by hand until we heard the guy scream, "I have the world record on, I have the world record on," to one of his buddies. It was all we could do from laughing and we kept doing it for about a half hour. We had a hundred yards or so of monofilament in the boat with the eel. Ernie then put the eel in the middle of the wadded up line and threw it over the side and the guy hollered, "I lost him, I lost him." The next morning Ernie went surf casting in the same area and found all the line along with the knife the guy used to cut the line off. Sometime afterward, I was not too proud of doing that little prank but I admit it was funny at the time. Later that summer with the bigger boat, we got to meet more people on the water who happened to be some of the best striper fishermen in our area.

One of the best was a fellow named Jim Mitchell, who had ten fish over 50 lbs and two over 60 to his credit. I first met Jim on the water and got to know him and his fiberglass Herters boat. You could see through his boat when he put his lights on to unhook a fish or put another eel on. We knew Jim for at least two years before actually meeting him at the boat ramp with a beach buggy named the 'Eel Slinger'. Until then we knew each other by our voices. He also happened to have his friend Al (Red) Tedeschi with him that day. We eventually became good friends and started hunting together in Maine and Pennsylvania when I moved there.

Jim was one of the hardest fishermen and hunters that I knew. One night while we were rowing well outside the surf line, we spotted Jim's boat inside the surf where there was a good roll on and swells were maybe 6ft high in front of and to the right of him. We said, "How thc hcll did he get in there," but we continued rowing. Later on during the night Jim said the bass were really in there tonight and he had 15 fish from 25-40 lbs. But he left because he had little freeboard and didn't want to completely swamp his boat. We couldn't figure out how he got in there since there would be surf breaking in front of him, to the right, to the left and it looked real dangerous. I'm still not sure how long it took Gary to figure it out but we knew we had to get into that zone. The secret was timing. We would wait for a wave to break on the left side of the pocket, run into the pocket, and drop the anchor and start casting towards shore. After a while we figured it out. We caught many big bass in there but never would do it if Jim was fishing in the area. Another time when Jim had his uncle with him and I had the Lone Star boat, I saw him sitting low in the water and asked if he needed a hand. When I pulled next to him he must have had 20 big fish in the boat including one of his 60's. He grinned and said, "All these are mine and my uncle caught a fish that weighed around 35 lbs." I put most of his catch in my boat except the 60- pounder and met him the next morning. He said that he caught a couple more until he ran out of eels, then tried a rubber one with no luck and decided to come back in. Another night, fishing with Red Tedeschi near the reef inside Black Point, Red had a fish on for quite a while and it finally broke off. The next day the brothers from the Christian Brothers seminary were taking their morning walk in the same area Red had been fishing and they found a 63 lb bass in the seaweed off Stinky Beach where they were fishing. Red got a look at the fish and it had his line and hook still in its mouth. How do you tell the spiritual people that I want my fish? Red just said, "Have a great meal on me."

Another night while we were rowing we heard a boat running wide open, off shore. It would stop and then run again wide open. This continued all night while we were there. The next day when I saw Jim, he gave me a clue to what was going on. You could see the bass in the light of the phosphorous and when the angler spotted fish they would cast an eel, let it lie on the bottom until the bass picked it up, catch the fish and do it all over again. That worked when there was phosphorous in the water on dark nights. We tried it with them and it's a wonder that we never ran into each other. When questioned about this technique by other fisherman, we told them it's a new Polish game we were playing. I don't think anyone ever found out about Jim's secret of catching bass when the water was lit up. It was fun but also scary, since you had to stand up high on your seat so you could see the school of bass.

During that time, we began to meet new fishermen. Denny Dillon was a great All-State Rhode Island basketball player who was going to URI (University of Rhode Island). He fished with Ernie and me. As I remember, I think he caught his first fish over 40 lbs (around 42), when we gaffed it and put it in the boat. Ernie clubbed the fish over the head with a weighted club he called the "Persuader." When Denny earned his captain's license and got a new boat, he named the boat "Persuader." I'm not sure if that club had an influence on him naming the boat or not but I would like to think so.

Another great fisherman I took out and helped catch his first bass over 40 was named Lou Storti. We were fishing in the Sheep Pen when Lou got a hit and he said, "It's a small one." I got the gaff ready, put on my head lamp and gaffed a 40+ lb green fish and pulled it over the side of my boat and watched it come to life and beat the hell out of my boat. We both got up on the seats to get out of the way of that guy as that fish nearly destroyed my boat.

Sometimes we would weigh fish in at Joe Tattories Bait shop in Narragansett. Joe was a great fly rod fisherman who fished with Joe Brooks, outdoor writer for Outdoor Life Magazine. They were the beginners of the fly fishing era for striped bass that exists today.

The only fish that we figured were close to or over 50 lbs there. I had met Jim Patterson and another of his friends from Massachusetts. Jim was another great fisherman of that time and you had to respect him as he lived in New Jersey and traveled every weekend like I did. He fished the same area as I and we kept out of each other's way. He had great fishing friends like Slim Borsay, and his wife Joy, who also caught many bass over 50 lbs. You just had to admire these people, as they were working classes, but fished to make a few extra bucks like the rest of us did. I continued to fish every weekend that I could and did not stop until my job took me to Cape Canaveral, Florida.

Aug 1965

I earned a job promotion and moved to Florida, towing my Lone Star boat with me. I was the lead quality control person on a space program named Lunar Orbiter, which took pictures of the Lunar landscape for the Apollo Mission. As a result of being the lead quality guy, my wife, at age 23, was invited to attend the launch with the VIP's, which sent a Limo to pick her up. She was thrilled to pieces over that. That launch and the spacecraft had taken the first pictures of Earth from deep space with the lunar surface in the foreground. Those pictures made the front page of every newspaper and magazine in the world. I didn't care for the saltwater fishing in Florida at the time but did take my friend out and caught some fairly large king mackerel up to 45 lbs. Most of my fishing was freshwater largemouth bass fishing since the St Johns River was in my back yard. My mother and Ernie came down that Christmas and I took him out saltwater fishing, catching sea trout on every cast and netting large blue claw crabs and large shrimp, all nice ones in those days. I also took Ernie fishing on the St John's and he was in his glory, fly rod fishing large mouths up to 8 lbs. He also caught one of the biggest pickerel I ever saw. Had to be at least 39 inches or better. Never measured it, just released it. We also caught some big alligator gar and bowfin that we threw back.

One night while running wide open on Lake Pointsett, which is basically cow pasture flooded over, I heard a "snap" and Ernie said, "Don't look now but you just went through a barbed wire fence." Sure enough the next day there was a hole in the fence. Wow, was I lucky? When I looked my boat over there was a scratch about three inches below the windshield on the hull, a little higher and that wire would have taken my windshield off...along with my head. I never ran wide open again in that lake except at times where it was real shallow, especially at the mouths of the three lakes we used to fish.

I enjoyed my stay and made friends, one of which asked me to move to King of Prussia, Pennsylvania, where he was setting up a new space program named Manned Orbiting Lab which was supposed to be manned by three military people. With the Government, when you were in a commodity like Space Systems and if you were any good, supervisors would seek you out, and of course I wanted to get back closer to my fishing area and I asked my new boss, "When can I start."

1967

I'm not sure where Ernie and I were, but we did miss one of my family's biggest and proudest events. My godfather, Edward Strzepek's, son, Steven caught a 56 lb 6 oz striper while rowing in the same area as I had caught my fish. I do know that both Ernie and I had a lot of influence on Steve and his brother Richard liking striped bass fishing and the meaning of "take a kid fishing" proved itself to us again and again.

May 1968

I started working in King of Prussia and it took about three months to get my top secret, special access clearance. I was also trying to figure out how to make it easier for Charlotte to pick me up on the way to Point Judith since I worked east of where I lived and getting to the Point would be on the way. While living in Pennsylvania, I experienced some of the best sea trout and flounder fishing in the Delaware Bay and of course early Rockfish (Striped Bass) in the Chesapeake Bay near northeast Maryland. I made friends at the local Polish Club in Coatesville and Phoenixville and went fishing with my friends quite a bit. When I bought my house in Glenmoore, a telephone worker named, Joe Zaleski came to install the phone lines and saw my 60 lb fish hanging on the wall said to my wife, "I have to meet your husband.

He will fit right in with us." And, so it came to be, one of my favorite areas outside of Point Judith.

I had a yellow lab retriever named Buff and I lived in the heart of the Amish country and the best pheasant hunting east of the Dakotas. The Amish people were very generous about letting a man with his dog use their land, and when I shot a bird I would give it to them all cleaned and continue hunting until either Buff or I tired out. I will admit that it was me that tired out first.

Ernie and my mother came to Pennsylvania often as the fishing season was over and Ernie was a very great wing shooter. One day while we were hunting on a farm that I had permission to hunt, Buff flushed a cock bird and I pulled up on it and shot it at close range...very stupid of me to do... and Buff went to retrieve it. Ernie said, "That's the first time I ever saw a dog make a retrieve three times on the same bird." The wings were separated from the body.

Gary also came to Pennsylvania. It was very hard for him to get time off since he was a teacher. He did come and we got our limit but sadly I shot most of them. It wasn't that Gary was a bad shooter, just reflective of a habit that I had developed by hunting alone. I was quick on the trigger. It wasn't all about hunting in Pennsylvania, as during the spring of each year we would go Blackback (winter flounder) fishing. I would take orders from the people that worked at GE and go fishing with Ernie and Gary and fill up a 151 quart Igloo cooler, bring them home and have my wife fillet them and sell them for $1.50/lb. Some weekends I would have at least 75 lbs of fillets and I would pay my wife $ 3.00 per hr. We both made money and were happy.

Aug 1970

During the VJ day weekend in RI, the Hi Neighbor Narragansett Beer Company sponsored the Pt Judith Bass and Bluefish Tournament, which I was entered. It was the first time that I had entered it, since living in PA made it real hard for me to get away all the time. Ernie and I fished all night without much success, maybe a 25 lb fish or so. When daylight came I saw Jim Mitchell and he said there were some pogies (bunker) off Narragansett. He told me to get some and use them for bait. I did have a live well on board in the event the guys from the fish trap would be unloading their catch, but being a holiday, they were not working, so off to Narragansett we went. I did have snagging hooks and we managed to get about 3 of them before some idiot charged thru them and scattered the school. We went back to Scarborough where we had fished all night. I put on live bait and had a chase in about 10 min. The fish hit the bait then picked it up and dropped it about 5 times before I felt comfortable to set the hook. The fish made a couple of short runs and I thought that I had lost her since she was swimming towards my boat. Another long run and a couple of short runs and she came up and Ernie put the gaff in her, lifted her over the side and said this is a pretty big fish, let's go weigh her in. Got back to the dock about 10 am put her on the scale and she weighed 55.2 lbs. There were a lot of big fish around and never thought that the weight would hold up to win the contest. I had just quit smoking and had a bad cough and was chewing Hall's Menthol Lyptus cough drops and almost passed out from the cough, Ernie kept saying (Ted, you look like your turning blue). It turns out that I had Bronchial asthma that would have turned into emphazema had my doctor not put me on antibiotics once for 30 days and double strength for another 30 days. My wife had to work and could not join me but she was real pleased when I received the $500.00 check for first prize and the extra money from fishing.

That would mean that I could buy a new boat that I had been looking that was in the Delaware Bay area. The hull was a Ray Hunt designed Seabird that was used for Marine Patrol in the Delaware and Maryland area; a super hull, which got me thru some very bad seas.

July 1971

My son Brian was born and where was I, at the Polish club celebrating with my buddies instead of being with my wife at the hospital. Dr Korbinitz called me with the good news and off to the hospital I went with a bottle of scotch that I had promised the doctor. My wife accused me of not bringing her flowers and that might have been true, as I was riding so high that I barely remember anything. Things were looking up. A new baby son and a new boat coming the next year, things were really looking up.

I had asked my wife to have the baby induced so that I would not miss the bass tournament and she did. Can't say enough of how blessed I was to have her for a wife.

About a month later we decided to have our son's christening at St. Mary by The Sea, located in Pt. Judith and I decided it would be the christening to end all christenings. I invited all my fishing friends and we had one big drinking party. We ordered 12 cases of beer, gallons of whisky, gin, vodka and any other alcohol that was made. After hours of drinking and the party being almost over, we were standing near my car in front of our place when a swan, which was flying, decided to release its digested meal splattering us and my car pretty good as someone yelled, "Duck," while we looked up. It was not a nice feeling but we all laughed like hell while covered with swan poop. It was a great event with people ending up in places that they should not have been, including me, along with hangovers to end all hangovers.

Aug 1972

In August when the tournament came, I had to fish alone, as Ernie was off doing something and Gary's wife Helen, was in the hospital getting ready to deliver their second child. It was around 9 pm when I cleared the East Wall and noticed a sailboat where it should not have been. It was blowing around 25 knots and I circled around to ask them if they needed help. They were screaming that they were hung up on the bottom of the reef and were breaking up," Please help us." I wasted no time and yelled, "Throw me a line and I will try to get you out of there." When I got the line and secured it around my rear cleat and started to pull them, the rope broke as a big wave caught their boat and it surged enough to get the boat off the bottom.

I quickly circled them and told them to throw the anchor into my boat and I will try towing you in the Lone Star. I had a gas compartment and I just jammed the flukes of the anchor into it, took a quick wrap around my other cleat and got them free. I got them inside the Harbor of Refuge and said you will be all right now and they hollered back," No, we are taking on water," so I towed them to the Coast Guard station in Galilee and tied them to the dock. A nearby dragger called them on the VHF and told them that there was a boat in trouble tied to their dock and sinking. That got them down there in a hurry. I asked if they needed more help and they said, "Yes, their car was parked at Jamestown Dutch Harbor," and they asked if I would be kind enough to take one of them with me to get it. I did and they told me the story of what went wrong. They were planning a trip to Block Island for the weekend and they went under power when they got close to the Pt Judith Light. The seas were real rough and an unsecured line washed off the bow of the boat, got caught in the prop and they were left to the mercy of the sea. Any way I told them it ruined my fishing and wished them luck on the repairs to the boat and they went on their way.

And I decided to stop at Gary's to see if the new baby arrived. When I arrived I saw Helen's mother and Gary having a drink and they offered me one as baby Eric Bryson was just born. Gary is not a person who drinks and I though what the hell, my fishing is ruined lets jump in my camper and go check on the guys that we knew were rowing behind the Bonvue Inn. We did, and a couple of our friends had a couple of small bass, maybe 30 lbs, nothing impressive. The next two days the wind blew a steady 35kts and fishing was done for that tournament for me. Little did I know that the people in the sailboat wrote a letter to the tournament committee explaining how I saved their lives and the board awarded me the Sportsmanship Award. That invited my wife and me to the banquet for a baked stuffed 2 lb lobster, which we were very proud of. Thinking about it now, I would rather do something like that rescue, than winning back- to -back tournaments and catching more and larger striped bass. Maybe it's a payback from when we flipped over in the Merrimack River that September night. The rest of the year was quite successful as far as catching and selling bass. I know that I caught another 51 lb fish casting eels outside the Sheep Pen and we got to fish more around Dickerson's Reef in Narragansett and also a few places around Jamestown. On my last fishing trip of the year, I was with Gary and we were fishing off Beavertail Light heading back towards Narragansett and I noticed water squirting thru the floor. I looked at Gary and said, "That's it for this boat, its served us well." Next year we will be fishing with the Seabird, which had also been used for marine patrols on the Delaware Bay. I went to a marina that I knew in East Greenwich, RI and ordered a new 21ft runabout- outboard but had to wait until spring for delivery.

Mar 1973

Received word that my new boat was ready and I had already ordered and picked up a trailer from an OMC dealer in Coatesville, PA. Charlotte, my 2 children and I were ready to go to Hialiah, Fl to pick it up. We arrived in Florida to a wicked cold snap. We dropped off the trailer at the Seabird factory and headed south to where it got a little warm at Knights Key. We pulled in a camp ground for a couple of days, didn't do much there as I was anxiously waiting to pick up my boat and head north to see an old friend that I use to fish with. His name was Bill Ramey, he like me, did not like the Florida climate because he was from Colorado and didn't like the 'Gooey Bog' as he called it. Here he and I caught a great number of large mouth bass and saltwater fish. Disney World had just opened and my wife decided that we should take our children and Bill's youngest daughter to see the exhibits there. I'm glad we did and that was one of the best days away from fishing that I had ever had. We also had an 8 mm camera and took 6 rolls of film, as memory. It would be at least 25 years before we would have a chance to do it again. We dropped off Bill's daughter and I decided to stop at a fish store I knew on Merritt Island. We decided to pull into a campground at Titusville to cook up the crabs and shrimp I bought. After boiling and cleaning them, I had around 2 lbs of shellfish ready to eat. My 9 month old son decided to clear the table and everything went on to the camper floor which also had quite a bit of sand since it was where the campground was located. Needless to say my wife had to make something else. I'm not sure what we ate but it wasn't what I had been craving for since I moved out of Florida. I never made that mistake again.

Arrived back in PA and needed to buy an engine for the Seabird and there wasn't much available back in 1973. I decided on a 135 hp Evinrude from the dealer where I bought my trailer. The only problem with the Seabird was that there was a cutout on the transom, and you could only mount a standard size shaft engine there.

Ernie had gotten promoted to 'boss' painter and one of the requisites was that he had to have rigging expertise and thorough knowledge of knots. I called my mother and Ernie. I invited them to help test drive and break in the new engine and also try for some early striper fishing in Maryland. They came to PA late Friday night and we headed for northeast MD early Sat morning. Ernie secured the bow line while I climbed in the boat put in the drain plug, ignition key, jumped in my truck and backed down the ramp pretty fast to slide the boat off the trailer. When I looked back all I could see was my boat headed out in the Chesapeake Bay about 50 yards away. I yelled at Ernie, "Glad I wasn't 50 ft up on a scaffold with the knot that you tied." From that day on I always put the bowline on myself. The problem wasn't over. I had to figure how to get my boat back since no one was around on the water or cottages where I could make a phone call. I started to look underneath some cottages and found one that had a small surfboard type-floating device so I borrowed it. Found a big stick to use as a paddle and went out to retrieve my boat, while listening to Ernie laugh like hell saying, " I wish I had a camera to take pictures of this." At that point I was so mad I could have kicked his butt but got over it when I got the engine started and let the burn in sequence begin.

We started down the bay where I knew some bass might be. I recognized a friend from the Polish Club, Ronnie Monko. I headed toward him but he didn't recognize my new boat and was acting very nervous until I got closer to him and he hollered, " Ted you SOB, you just caused me to throw over 2, 30 lb bass." He had been using a gill net and it wasn't legal at that time to keep fish over a certain length and when he saw my boat, which type was used for marine patrol, he thought he was going to get arrested for sure. Ernie, who also had met Ronnie, had another laughing fit. Ernie had one great sense of humor especially when it as at the expense of someone else.

We did get some fishing in and caught enough for a meal that night. He told my mother how our day went and she also showed no sympathy and laughed also. I can't say my feelings were hurt but I did get valuable lessons about bigger boats.

The first time I had my family on the Seabird was on the Delaware Bay fishing out of the Mispillion River just south of Milford, DE. The state had just built a boat-launching ramp and I put my boat in and headed into the bay for some weakfish. We were around 25 miles south of the river near Lewes, DE and I noticed some large thunderheads headed my way, I fired the boat up and started to head back to the river and it started to blow. My wife went below in the cabin and had Brian on her lap. We got into a 5ft chop. When we would hit a wave, I put my head below the windshield, I could see my son laughing like heck. He thought it was real funny. My daughter was riding up front sitting alongside of me and when we would hit a wave, it would come over getting us soaked. I couldn't crank it up to go over them and just rode it out for at least a couple of hours to get back in. I had heard later that the winds reached 75 mph and there were 20 something boats capsized on the bay that day. I must say that day gave me complete confidence in the Seabird.

A couple of days later my neighbor, Eileen Mooney came over to my house and asked if I would go to the Wilmington Hospital and cheer up her husband Dan, not saying what was wrong with him. The next day I found the room Dan was in and found him standing at the window overlooking a cemetery. He turned greeted me and said," Pretty soon I will be down there," and proceeded to tell me that he had a blood clot on the brain and there wasn't a way to shut off the flow of blood.

A few months later he told me that he had been contacted by John Hopkins University and they would like to try a new procedure of calibrating a BB to the size of the artery that was feeding the blood to the brain. They had tried it once before and the patient passed away and hence it would be a risky operation. I told Dan don't worry as you are a good man very devoted to the Catholic religion and God will take care of you. The next time I saw Dan he told me that the operation was a success. It was a very painful experience since they kept him awake on the operating table watching an overhead video of the BB moving and the tremendous pain that felt like someone putting an axe in his head as it was put in place. The second bb was just as bad when put in place to stop the flow of blood.

He also told me of an experience that he had with the charismatic movement of the Catholic religion where he was called up on stage among others. The priest began praying and he said that he passed out and could view his body with a vision of Christ coming out of his chest. All I could tell him was that was a sign of God protecting you. I know Dan is still alive today in 2010, although my daughter talked to his wife just before Christmas and Eileen said Dan had some sort of problem but she did not elaborate.

I know that during the late 70's they came to Pt Judith and I took him fishing on the Seabird in CT and we caught a lot of 30-40 lb fish. That made them very happy. I must add that I had now met another loving family who were neighbors, which made me a better person today for which I am also eternally grateful and blessed knowing them.

We were fishing off of Watch Hill, RI drifting on an outgoing tide in a 4 ft chop when my 135 hp Evinrude engine quit. It seemed in the early days of mfg they did not install a baffle to prevent water being sucked up into the carburetors, hence dead in the water and drifting out to sea, when a large sailboat with a drop dead, gorgeous, naked lady at the helm went passing by with a lot of my fishing buddies motoring along side and following like baby ducklings with their mother. A real bad day for the razzing me, sad to admit, I got after wasn't very nice.

Aug 1974

I took a transfer back to New England and worked at the Avco, Wilmington, MA and moved to Londonderry, NH. It was a lot better than traveling from PA every weekend as it was only 2.5 hrs and I fished every chance I got. I also lost respect for the fish and was more concerned with the money end of it.

One foggy day Ernie and I snagged about 8 pogies, tried fishing all around the Narragansett shoreline, got nothing and decided to try at the light house. We put 8 baits over and caught 8 fish including 1 Ernie caught that went over 50 lbs. We ran out of baits and went straight to the co-op, where we sold the fish. After we sold them Ernie said," GD it Ted, you didn't even stop and take pictures, what the hell's the matter with you." I shrugged it off but thinking about it later, he was right, I should have known better.

Seeing I had the bigger boat and motor, I became more adventuresome and started to fish the waters off of Cuttyhunk, MA. We would get up at 4 am, get on the boat and run way up in Narragansett Bay, get menhaden at sunrise and fish all day. I bumped into Denny Dillon and he was fishing with a Dick Lima, who designed the center console 26ft Bonita. He said, "Why don't you follow us to Cuttyhunk." We knew the captains of the menhaden boats and when they made their sets we would pull in close to them, hand them our nets and they would fill them with as much baits as they could hold and we would put them in our live wells. Head for our fishing spots, catch our fish and head home to sell them at the co-op before it closed at 4 pm.

One day we went out there and caught 24 Bass over 40 lbs even one that weighed 25 lbs and sold them without taking a picture. That convinced me Ernie was right about taking pictures.

We pretty much did this until early September and one-day, we saw Ernie lose one of the biggest stripers we ever saw. He had the fish on for about 15 min and it surfaced and was laying about 15ft from the boat. The fish looked to be close to 6 ft with a tremendous girth and for some reason the hook just came out of its mouth. All I could say, "Ernie, nice fish but she will be bigger next year," I can't write what Ernie's reply was but it wasn't nice. I will add that he did everything right, didn't try to horse it, just bad luck and you can't imagine how disappointed Gary and I was.

The Pt Judith Bass and Bluefish Tournament started with real crappy weather and I don't remember fishing much at all but do remember a fellow fisherman named John Martini winning the Bass Division with a 53.5 lb fish. John fished out of a small Boston Whaler off of Cuttyhunk. I'm not sure but I think he won 2nd place with another 50 something lb. I am not sure how many 50+ pound fish he has but from what I hear it is in the 50+ range. I can verify that he is one great hard fisherman but I have to add, he was never lucky enough to break the 60. I wouldn't bet that he wouldn't break the 60 mark.

Aug 1975

My friend's wife, Betty Tedeschi, Red's wife, won the Woman's Division. She caught a 32.5 lb fish going back to 3 July 1959. She was delivering her first child and Red was out fishing with Jim Mitchell. Red had caught a 52.5 lb bass that night. There was a light on the Cranston Fire Dept. He had no place to store the fish so he took it to the upstairs bathtub, filled it with ice, until he could bring it to the Italian Club for a delicious meal. The 60 lb fish that I caught ended up as table fare at an Italian restaurant in Utica, NY. It was a place where a bunch of GE guys and I used to go for lunch. All I can remember is the owner's son, Vinny. I wish I had that recipe for baking stripers. I still can taste that fish 50 years later,

June 1980

My son Brian and I were fluke fishing inside the East wall and there was a big sea on with waves breaking over the wall. I did notice a man with his 2 children walking along the wall and thought I better keep an eye on them since they would wait for a wave to break and then proceed to move further out along the wall running for about 10 ft at a time. I pulled fairly close to them and hollered," You better get back, it's pretty dangerous." Not knowing they were foreigners and not understanding what I was saying, they ignored me. This kept on for another 15 min and one great big swell crashed over the wall putting them in the water. I raced over to them and the guy was holding his son about 6 years old and he was crying. I grabbed him and put him in my boat and the guy grabbed on to my bow rail. I backed out since I was in between some breakwater rocks. I slowly moved toward the beach that was about 100 yards away until the guy touched bottom and I passed his son to him. All he could do was show a gesture of gratitude and off they went. I don't know how his daughter made it back to shore but she was there when I brought her father and brother in. Once again maybe it was a payback from the Merrimack River or a destiny of my son being in the Rescue Department of the 2nd largest fire departments in the state of Rhode Island.

Another situation was when I had my friends from PA fishing with me. They were Tony Tryanski, Ron Gorsky and Bob Hartman, guys that worked for General Electric whom I became friends with. It was blowing pretty hard out of the northeast and the only calm fishable water was along the area south of Jerusalem. We trolled that way and threw some eels off the Charlestown breach way without any success. I said to the guys, if we go in now, we can make it to a bar before it closes and I cranked the boat up. I got inside the Harbor of Refuge and was moving at a good clip when I spotted what looked like a man sitting on something in the water. I pulled hard over and missed what was a drunken guy who stole a pram and was trying to get to Georges Rest where they had a rock band when he got swamped by a big wave from a dragger that was heading out to sea for its fishing trip. We heard people yelling on shore," Help, Help," so I got closer to him and Tony pulled him over and tied the pram off. In the meantime I got on the radio and called the Coast Guard who were already on their way. I pulled over to the dock of the CG station and one of the crewmen knew this jerk, who started to give us some shit about saving him. Tony retained his anger and composure luckily for the idiot, as Tony could be one mean Pollock, if he had to be. The next day the wind lay down and we caught a lot of nice bass in the 40 lb range.

Sept 1980

I was the Supervisor of Quality Assurance at the General Electric plant that manufactured turbine generators for the 688 Class Attack Submarines being completed at the Groton Ct, Electric Boat Shipyard. Naval Sea Systems Command preformed an audit at my facility, saw my operation liked it and gave me an offer to go to work at EB since they had no one there with that expertise working for the government. It was close to Pt. Judith and I immediately said yes. My wife on the other hand had a great job working as an executive secretary for the Manager of International sales for a Company named, Balzers. The main headquarters was in the country of Liechtenstein. She was deadly opposed to us moving for various reasons, mainly she feared my son becoming a commercial fisherman, which is a dangerous and hard occupation. Of course, I won out and I started on the last week of September.

We bought a partially completed home and for the first couple of weeks, I lived at our cottage at Pt. Judith while I worked on my new home to get living conditions set for me so I could be closer to work. With the help of my father, who was a First Class Engineer and also was a master plumber, he hooked up the water so I could shower and also the bathroom for a toilet.

Once completed I moved my camper to my driveway so I could sleep in it and then started to finish each room and move my bed and sleep in the rooms in the house. In March with the help of my mother, Ernie, my wife and I completed the house and had an offer from someone to buy my house in NH. In April I sold the NH place and my family was with me once again rather than just weekends, which had brought tears to my eyes every Sunday when they had to leave.

I didn't do much fishing other than for fluke during the year as finishing off a new home required a tremendous amount of time. Things I just couldn't put off.

Aug 1980

The Pt. Judith tournament ran and I'm not sure who won the seniors but my son Brian won the Jr. Division with a 10 lb bass also my godchild, Gary Bryson and his brother Eric also won prizes for various species. It made all of us proud as heck. During the awards ceremony a fantastic surf fisherman, who won the surf division, was given a new Kunan surf rod that he proudly gave my son. I'm not sure of how many 50+ lb fish Gene Champlin has caught but I would bet it is more than one. Gene Champlin is one classy person and I hadn't seen him for quite a while. When I heard that he was working in maintenance at Breakwater Village, I found him and told him who I was and if he remembered giving that rod to my son. He said yes and then asked how many fish did he caught from the surf. I told him that Brian is a great boat fisherman and never does surf fishing as he had barely enough time for the boat. Anyway he thanked me for looking him up and said good fishing to me. Another great surf fisherman is Andy Lamar, who caught many big bass, not sure how big, but he is another class guy.

1982

There was a moratorium put on of catching and having striped bass in your possession and our fishing became mostly for summer flounder or fluke, as they are sometime called. We did very well most days and would catch up to 2 to 3 hundred pounds. A lot of my friends switched over to Blue Fin Tuna fishing but I think I made just as much money inshore as they did chasing those fish around. Anyway at that time you pretty much had to have a great loran and a good fish finder and a boat big enough to get you back in when the weather got crappy.

That was not my game at the time and I stayed away from it with the exception of when it was real nice and the seas were flat. I do remember one day we tried it with hand lines and had no clue what we were doing. When the Styrofoam float went under and line started peeling out like crazy, Gary set the hook and the 300lb test line just broke. Like I said, we had no clue what we were doing, although we did help our friend Lou Storti and Walter Martish untangle a line that a 300 lb fish wrapped itself around there anchor line a few times.

That was the end of our tuna days until I bought the Terminator.

1988

On May 8th I put my papers in for an early retirement from the government, as the last few months being a supervisor in a plant that required 5 people but only having 3 including myself. When I trained one, they would reassign him to another facility and I thought the hell with this after they pulled it on me twice. They never said goodbye; kiss my ass, nothing and never heard a word until the end of the year when I received a letter saying it was approved and I would get retroactive pay back to May 8th. It was time for a long waited celebration.

I had wanted a JC Boat for years and every time I thought that I had the financial funds, the price was raised to $25,000.00. Finally when my father passed away I sold his house and found one on sale for $75,000. It had been listed for $ 92,   000.00 and I thought it was a good deal so; my family went to a marina in Boston, MA for a test ride. It was real crappy with a steady 25+wind out of the northeast. I pinned the throttle and the boat went thru the 5 ft chop and never pounded, I was sold. I put a down payment on it and had the option of running it back to RI myself or having it shipped. I told my friend Barry Cherms about it and he said, " Nice boat but you will be sorry you bought it, as you would have liked fishing out of the Seabird much better." In a way he was right but I did fulfill a dream about owning a JC, as they were one of the best head sea boats made. The boat showed up and we put it on blocks and covered it for the winter.

We began thinking of a name for her and my son said how about the Terminator. I questioned him why that? He replied," Because you and your friends terminated all the bass." What could I say, the moratorium was still on. We couldn't wait until spring to launch it.

1989

Launched the Terminator and went cod fishing on the east grounds of Block Island and it was real crappy. The boat went thru the chop and never pounded but not having an enclosure or a tower, I got soaked. We caught around 30 small cod up to 10 lbs and headed in. Got back to my slip and had no clue how to back it in as she was a single screw, deep keeled vessel. Now I had to think about the expense about running the boat and a tower. I called my friend Red Tedechi and he had a fireman working for him named, Ernie Delmonico, who was an expert welder and could make fighting chairs along with tower. The name of his company was Flash Welding. I called him and made arrangements to bring my boat up to Appanoug, RI and have it hauled to Ernie's shop, which was located in Cranston, RI. It seemed like forever before Flash (Ernie's nickname) got thru with putting the tower and roof cover on and I still did not have an enclosure. One of Flash's friends was one of the best isinglass installer in New England but he had health issues and I decided to run the boat back to my slip and have someone do it for me.

The person that I selected did a lousy job and I decided to try doing it with my eventual co- captain Fred Bowman, who is another great striped bass fisherman. I'm not sure how many 50's he caught but a lot of people on his charters got them. Any way we decided that we would make the enclosure out of lexan on both sides of the boat, with a window that opened in the middle that was separated by two smaller windows. I found out that Fred was not only a great fisherman but also a great marine carpenter and I am not sure what I would have done without him. I met Fred at my dock. He was a part time commercial lobsterman and owned a 26ft General Marine Hull that was manufactured in the state of Maine. After talking with him we decided to try to get our captains license since it would be the only way I could afford to operate my boat. After a couple of months of school, we went to the Coast Guard Headquarters in Boston for the exam. I went first and Fred a couple of weeks later and we both passed on the first try, which was unusual at that time. The license we trained for would allow us up to unlimited tonnage provided that you had sea time on the lower level. That was all right with me because I had no desire to work larger boats or ferries.

Once I had my license I started a Chapter S corporation that was named 'Quality Sport Fishing' and stared advertising in magazines like the 'Fisherman' and in other local places like bars and restaurants where I was known. We made up brochures with recent pictures like Fred standing with a 500 lb Blue-fin Tuna that he caught on stand up gear and some pictures of big stripers etc. The first year we had 25 trips, which include cod, bass and blue fishing and also some tuna trips. I did make some money but spent it just as fast as I made it.

The next year was better with more charters but Fred decided to go it on his own. I admit that there was a little tension between us, not sure why but it was a good move for both of us at the time. I think that was then I learned that the desire for fishing was over, when it became a business. Barry Cherms was right about having more fun with the small boat.

The next couple of years got progressively better to the point that I had built up my business to 100+ charters a year and quit the trips around the end of Sept. I would move the boat to Cape Cod and do commercial fishing for giant Blue fin tuna with my friends Jim Mitchell, Red Tedeschi and another co-Captain named Bruce Duboir. I also found out after a couple of seasons that it was a rich and young man's game and you couldn't go there running money scared. We did catch quite a few medium size Blue fin tuna and I did make enough money to cover the expenses.

April 1993

My best friend had passed away from prostate cancer and during the viewing a gentleman that I had never met, addressed the audience and said, "Ladies and gentleman, the reason that I am here today is because of that gentleman Mr. Ernest Richmond, who was our tail gunner on the B-17 aircraft named Mag the Hag. I was the pilot of that airplane and the number of tail end attacks that he stopped and also the number of enemy aircraft that he was credited for shooting down, leads me to believe that he was the best gunner in our wing if not the whole US 8th Air Force. Cmdr. Jim Robinson, lived in Mass on Cape Cod made that special trip to attend Ernie's viewing. He also said, "That if you didn't like Ernie, you would not even like anyone, including yourself," which made us feel real proud of our Ernie.

I had never met a man who was so well read, a collector of Native American artifacts, which were donated to Middleboro MA. He could also write poetry and he was one of the best all around fisherman and deer hunter that I knew. I could not have had a better teacher of fishing hunting and life in general, which had made me a better person for which I will always be eternally grateful. His love for his grandchildren, which were not blood connected, was and is the best of grandfather's love could ever be and they also had a great teacher of life and love. It is without question of how much respect and love we all had for Ernie.

I decided to have my son take the captains course, which ran me a few hundred bucks only to have him decide at the last minute that he didn't want to sit for the exam. I asked him how come and he said Dad," You will make me do all the trips." I'm not sure about that being true but I do know that he is a better offshore fisherman than I was and that has been proven many times. When I was fishing off the Cape on another friend's boat, he took the Terminator with another of my friends and caught a 400+ lb Blue Marlin, a couple of 150 lb yellow fins and blue fins and also fought a giant for quite a while because he didn't know my 130 Class gear was at home and not with me, as he thought. He was using 50 lb class stand up gear.

1997

Red and our wives took a trip to Alaska with our campers for 2 months as I had another close friend and co-captain named, Lynn Safford running my boat for me. I had met him while working at EB and he also was a great offshore fisherman. One time while he was running my boat for me during a shark tournament, he won both the largest of the tournament with a 457 lb Thresher and also the largest Mako weighing over 250 lbs. He was also a great marine mechanic as he helped me out of a lot of jams. I had also put the Terminator up for sale because I was getting sick of the proposed changes. Lynn took the potential buyer on a test run while Brian and I were at the NASCAR race in Charlotte NC. The boat sold and I'm not sure if I was happy sad or both. I wasn't too happy about the price since all I got was 50 cents on the dollar from what I had invested.

We went to our winter home around West Palm Beach, Fl and started looking for small boats again. I found a 23ft Sea Craft, no engine but with a small 20 hp Johnson outboard for $ 5,000.00. I put a brand new 225 hp Suzuki engine on it, called Brian to come get it as he had a 4+4 pick up and mine was with me. He arrived here with a friend of his Brandon Cleary and decided they wanted to go to Key West. They took my camper and went fishing, caught a few nice fish, came back, we went to the marina, picked up the boat with the trailer on it and headed home, not without problems. The ball on the hitch worked itself loose somewhere in Maryland and they had a hard time finding another ball. They finally managed to find one and made it back to RI without further trouble.

When I got home in March, I had talked to a marina owner in Watch Hill, RI about a slip in the area. I knew the area very well and fished it often limiting out with my charters just about every trip and it would save me an hour run from my usual slip. Before I sold the Terminator I had talked to him and he didn't see a problem with the smaller boat.

We brought the boat there in early June and Brian and I went fishing to a rip that I knew. I caught 2 bass around 28 lbs, turned to Brian and said, you own it - boat, motor, trailer, fishing rods, lures, everything; the hell with it I just don't enjoy it any more. I'm still not sure why, just one of those things.

Brian continued to use the slip in Avondale for a couple more years, getting his share of sellable bass and fluke. Not sure when Brian got his captain's license but it was after my friend Lynn Safford bought a 32ft Brendan and my son started to mate for him. They also had many successful charters since I had given Lynn the names of the people that chartered my boat and they are still booking trips with them today. There are so many people that I fished with that I know have caught 50+ lb stripers and they are Ernie Richmond, Gary Bryson, my cousin Steve Strzepek, Lou Storti, Bill Waring and Denny Dillon.

The people that I know that have caught 50+lb stripers but did not fish with me personally are: Bob Barneschi, Barry Cherms, Ted Stempian, Danny Zubic, Ray Rao, Tim Coleman, Slim and Joy Borsay, Fred Bowman,

Junior Benton , Ray Jimmis, Fred Galleger, Dick Chatowsky, Ed Vallett and John Martini. The following guys have caught numerous 50 and 60+ lb stripers are a family friends Joe Wojcik, Tom Needham, Jim Patterson, Bill Gavitt, Mark Sherra, Charlie Dodge, Joe Szabo, Tom Detmar, Dick Sevigney, Ray Jobin and Barry Cherms.

Most of these guys have caught multiple 50 + pound stripers. I'm not sure if they know how many of them and thought it would not be important to keep track of the numbers and with that I agree with the exception of some day, you might want to or have to tell your story, as I have to Tony Checko, author of 60+ pound club who has given me the opportunity to make sure these great striped bass fishermen and legends, will be remembered.

17 September 2007

Another sad day in my life as my mother, Charlotte Strzepek Richmond passed away from a rare blood disorder. Words cannot express how great a lady she was or how blessed I was for having her as my mother and I know that I could write another biography of the wonderful things that she had done for other less fortunate people that she both worked with and in her later years, others. To describe her, she was a very loving and compassionate person who was always there for her parents, brother, sister her son, grandchildren, great-grandchildren, cousins including those that lived in Poland, which she visited 6 times. Likewise for people who lived in our community in Florida, as she was a member of the Kool Kats, a group of seniors, which entertained elderly people in hospitals and nursing homes.

11 May 2008

Another devastating day, my wife, Charlotte Bartula Nimiroski, also passed away from cancer and I thought husbands are suppose to die first and thought how will I continue on without her. She and my mother were the reason that my son and daughter became the wonderful caring adults, both of them putting up with me during all my stupid endeavors. I must also credit my daughter, Deborah for making some changes in my household that made my wife's loss less painful although I don't think that you will ever get over the pain that you have when you lose a love one.

Dec 2009

I had decided to leave for my annual stay in Florida early planning to stop at Seymore Johnson AFB home of the 4th Fighter Wing to which I was part. I had made contact with a liaison specialist, who handled the museum at the base and continued to the 8th AF Museum in Georgia. It was the first time that I had not spent Christmas with my family since getting married. When I stopped at Seymore Johnson, the specialist had a health issue and was not available for me to get on base so I continued to the 8th AF museum. When I signed in and went to the first exhibit, I lost it, and couldn't continue as the first exhibit showed the suffering of the Nazi victims and also the hardships that our Airmen went thru, made me cry. *Who said that grown men can't and don't deserve to cry.*

Ted Nimiroski's 60.0 lb Striped Bass
Aug. 13, 1958
Narragansett, RI

Ted Nimiroski with other stripers
1958
Narragansett, RI

7-6
Joe Szabo's 70.5 lb Striped Bass, Block Island, RI
Nov. 1998

Joe Zebo's, 70.5 lbs. Striped Bass, Block Island, Nov, 1984

For years I fished Long Island Sound, NY from Scott Cove to Montauk Point with my Dad (Joe) and uncle (Gabriel). Flounders and striped bass were our usual targets. Depending on the weather we fished most nights casting plugs and even tried trolling some of the time. I caught my first 50 lb bass when I was 11 years old in a flat bottom boat in Long Island Sound. Later my Dad and uncle built a lobster boat that brought us to a new level of activities-commercial fishing. This 17 foot wood skiff was hand -built by them from plans they had purchased. They knew it was dependable.

The week I caught the big bass the weather was bad the whole week with a strong wind from the northeast and a big swell from the southwest. My Dad, a friend and I had been fishing for striped bass for about a week and caught absolutely nothing. We went out at all hours trying to catch one without any success. It was around Thanksgiving that my Dad, a friend and myself went out fishing just before nightfall. My Dad kept detail records of the weather, tide, moon, bait for every fish caught so we felt pretty confident we knew what to expect. We knew the full moon phase was not good for night fishing for bass and the backside of it could be much better. I asked, "Dad why we are fishing the full moon." So he turned it around and answered me," Joe, when are you going to take me to where you take your friends? You know, where there are fish?" I asked him, "Why did you want to fish during the full moon?" Dad replied, " It might not be the best time for bass but I can see better during the full moon." I had no comment. My friend got a little disgusted with the poor fishing and the tit -for -tat between my Dad and me so he headed home.

We had purchased some big live eels from Twin Maples Tackle Shop (on the island) and went off to try and catch the big one or just any one. The wind was blowing hard that night out of the northeast, which made it easier to cast if the wind came up from behind me. We fished all over Block Island from the north end of the Island, Graces Cove, Black Rock and finally Southwest Point where the wind was at my back.

After fishing for some time my Dad wanted to move onto another location when I informed him that this was the best spot on the Island where I take my friends so we stayed and kept fishing. Soon Dad decided to go back to the truck to get something to drink. I had my 11 foot surf rod with 30 pound test line spooled on a Penn 704 spinning reel. With the wind blowing hard out of the northeast I made an unusually long cast and when the eel hit the water and I immediately had a bump. Then nothing. It felt like I had lost the bait. I began reeling in slowly. It seemed forever. About 50 feet from the shoreline I finally realized the fish was swimming in with the bait. There was a big swell coming out of the southwest pushing the fish towards me. I set the hook and held him in front of me just beyond the breakers. I stood my ground and would not let him run out. I trusted the line, leader, hook and the knot. The fish swam left, and then right, then just stayed beyond the front breakers. It's common to find big bass just beyond the breakers especially on a dark night. They can be in 2 to 3 feet of water at this time. I fought the fish for about 10 minutes mostly in front of me and finally landed it with the help of the incoming swells. At that time I thought I caught my first 60 lb fish. I began yelling with excitement and my Dad came running to see what was going on. He thought I had injured myself or got swamped by the breakers. When Dad saw the size of the fish he said it was 70+ pounds.

Twelve hours had passed since I had caught the fish when a couple of friends of mine suggested we get the fish weighed, it could be a record striped bass We all started guessing on how large it actually was and decided to take it to Twin Maples to weigh it on an official scale, then to the local Post Office with its scale. Sure enough it took the Rhode Island State record of 70.5 lbs. largest stripe bass caught from the beach. If I weighed it soon after it was beached, it might have gone 73-74 pounds. I decided to have the fish skin mounted to remind me of this great night of fishing with my Dad. To this day the fish is mounted on the wall at Rebecca's Seafood Restaurant on Block Island.

Joe's State record lasted for 23 years until surpassed by Peter Vican's 75.4-pound striped bass caught (by boat) on July 18, 2008, Block Island, RI.

Joe other note-worth records like catching over 30 big bass in a single night and hundreds of 30 and 40 pounders over the years still take second place to his 70.5 striped bass that put him in the, "The Striped Bass 60+ Pound Club."

7-7
Bill Gavitt's 63.8 lb Striped Bass, Block Island, RI
1970

Bill Gavitt's 60+ Pound Striped Bass plus other memorable fish

Being asked to recall a few really big stripers? No problem, right? Well, if you removed the memories of the events leading to attaining such success, you'd be right!

It started innocently enough; a kid growing up on the Rhode Island coast with a love of the outdoors and fishing. At first, it was just schoolies at the peak of fall migration, when "everybody" chased bass. Unlike most, I wasn't satisfied with dawn and dusk raids. I listened to enough stories, to know there were better chances at times when some people we're home!

It took part of a lifetime, a U.S.N. timeout, and some help from some new friends, who knew when and where to catch much bigger fish. Two years after my Navy obligation ended, I took my first 50, two or 3 am., at Charlestown breach way, last half of the outgoing tide, in October.

Now the obsession was firmly rooted in, and so began the journey. Along the way, lifelong friendships were formed. Henry La Foutain, who had fished with Jerry Slyvester, a very well known striper expert; the Barris brothers, Steve and Gloria Oscella, Mat Squillante, and also Charlie Dodge.

Charlie was a Block Island native, living and working in my neighborhood, when I met him. Soon, we were traveling to the island, staying at his parent's house, and figuring out the best spots on Block Island. Charlie's knowledge of access spots to the shore, sped our learning curve, and soon we were racking up unbelievable catches! When we started at the islands, it was just like the mainland surfcasters fished, dusk and dawn. I don't recall seeing another caster in the middle of the night! It's hard to hide success such as we were enjoying, but at first it was almost like a private fishery.

The big fish really started to come now, thirty's and forty's were common. Fast forward a couple of years, now the island is a lot more popular, the word was getting out, but we were still pretty much undisturbed. One night, Charlie, myself, and a fellow named Ron worked until midnight without a fish. It was one of those damp, breezy nights that really make you miserable. Charlie was fighting fatigue and a cold, and decided to save him self for a better night. Ron and I dropped him off at home, went to Ron's, where he lived on a boat in Old Harbor, and had coffee and toast. After probably twenty minutes, we went back out, and for whatever reason, went back to Black Rock, exactly the same spot we had left! Ron went left, and I went right, and I hooked -up the first cast! Then I hooked another really good fish, and after a struggle, I got it out of the surf. After unhooking it, I estimated it at the middle 50 lb. range. After more good fish, and a 22 lb. bluefish, the bite slowed, but I was still seeing Ron's light going on, so I moved down. A couple of casts later, bang, a good fish on. When I beached that one, I told Ron, "this one's in the high forties, and I've got a fifty back up at the beach! When it was over, just before daybreak, it became obvious I was wrong; these fish were really big! As it turned out, the first one was 63.8 lbs., and the second one was 55lb. Poor Charlie!

There was one 50+ pound bass that sticks in my mind. It was late in the season and I decided this would be the last night fishing. As I recall we didn't do much because of the high seas and dirty waters. After daylight and not wanting to quite, I drove around the island looking at the condition of the ocean. I discovered a clean area of water below the Mohegan Bluffs at Southeast Light. It was not very big but on the lee side of a point with white water breaking across it. It was quite a hike down to the Bluff, before the stairway, but I couldn't resist urge. I was casting a line green needlefish plug by Stan Gibbs. There was fish there. It was probably about 9:30 am, not when you would expect to catch big fish especially this close to shore. I remember I was only able to get strikes on that needlefish and the fish were big and used the wave and current action to their advantage. Time after time they would hit and run to the nearby rocks about a good cast from me but off to my right and left. Once they were there they would rub the plug off their jaws and all you would get back was the plug with straighten hooks. It seemed a game they were playing with me. I tried every plug in my surf bag but ended back using the small Stan Gibbs line green needlefish. I robbed the hooks off every other plug in the bag to repair that needlefish. I landed some impressive fish before a fish rolled on the plug right in front of me but did not strike. I quickly shot out a short cast towards the same spot. As the lime green Stan Gibbs needlefish got near the spot, the bass launched its self completely out of the water and engulfed the plug in mid-air. Because this was so close to me I managed to turn it before it got to the rock pile. It was probably the best battle of a 50+ pound bass I ever had.

Another 50+ bass came at the Southwest Point on a Danny Boy swimmer. It was windy and very rough and difficult to fish any surface swimmer. Those plugs cast well on a calm day but not in that wind. Timing became critical. You needed to land the plug just over the breaking wave and get it swimming in the pull of the next wave. The fish were wild making spectacular surface hits but quite often, as it is common with big surface swimmers, they would pull off. We landed a few fish that were in the 50lb. range.

My best boat caught fish was 59.8lbs and was caught at Watch Hill. We were fishing live sculp and I got a call from my friend Bruce Vass. He said they were doing pretty good and I should join him. I did with my fishing partner that day, R. J. Boudreau, and we stopped at one of my coordinates just inside of Bruce's position. We started catching fish immediately drifting over the same spot time and time again. On one of the drifts I had a fish grab the scup and when I set the hook it made a lazy circle all around the boat but deep down in the water column. When I got it up to the boat, it hovered under it. Finally when I saw the swivel and leader I grabbed it but the fish was still under the boat. I set the rod against the railing and pulled hard dragging the fish out. As I reached over to grab the jaw of the bass, the boat rolled with my weight shift. It bumped the bass. The fish exploded and dove straight down. I let go of the leader and I dove for my rod. The leader was wrapped around the guides by now so I pointed the rod in the water right at the fish as I untangled the line. I yelled at R.J. " I need help. This is a real big fish." Eventually I brought the fish back to the boat. R.J. got his hands on its jaw and the bass was in the boat in one graceful swoop. The scale stopped at 59.8 pounds just shot of the 60- pound club mark.

I entered into competition fishing after reading an ad about a new tournament trail. The ASA was well run and managed by Jack and Diana Holmes with partner Bob Flocken of the South King Fish Association tournament trail. I met many new friends up and down the east coast and the competition honed my skills. Fishing tournaments are an unforgiving business. I seemed to have a knack for "not quite good enough". In the hunt for "Angler of the Year" status, second and third place had a grip on me. Eventually I made it to the top in a year that saw a 49lb. average weight per tournament. That was the last ASA tournament in Virginia. In a tournament in Delaware Bay we needed a good fish to win. In the past we had not enjoyed much success here, so I changed my approach. Chunking bunker is the game down there so I dramatically changed the way I had fished in the past. We decided to leave the more popular well-known fishing spots and try to find new ones ourselves. We found a spot that produced fish that kept getting bigger and bigger. We were almost out of time because we had a long run back to the weigh-in station. Just at the last minute a fish picked up one of my baits and made a long run to the left, then surfaced and ran with the tide. Knowing it was a good fish I was very careful and took quite awhile to get it back to the boat. When it came into sight I knew it was a good one and told R.J., "Forget the net and we're gonna grab this one by the jaw." I was afraid with the tide something might go wrong and we would break our net as we have done many times before. I led the fish in close and R.J. reached down the liter and grabbed the jaw and hauled the fish over the rail. We had the one we needed, another 50ish and outside our home waters. We packed up as quickly as possible, hauled up the anchor and raced to the scales on the opposite side of Delaware Bay with the winning fish.

I had several night catching 40 and 50 pound bass over the next few years and finally I had a couple of fish just over 60. Unbelievably, we we're catching so many fish, I didn't regrettably didn't get any pictures, or really do much more than ship the fish to market. Charlie Dodge, and myself, filled the back of his jeep to overflowing on one tide at Southwest Point. Probably there were thirty or thirty-five fish over 20 lbs.

Through all of this, one thing is obvious to me. Contrary to popular believe, surfcasters are more opt to catch these really big fish. I know several boat fishermen, who could fill my truck with 50's, they've caught, and most only have one legitimate" 60."

I believe part of this has to do with the fact that really big fish are becoming more vulnerable in turbulent water. This rough water is close to shore where bringing in a boat would be suicide. It's where ALL my biggest fish have come from, sometimes twenty feet from where I was standing.

I myself, switched to boat fishing around 1986. The physical part of surf fishing wasn't as easy anymore. Since then, I've managed two 50's up to 59.8, but not one over 60.

There are times when I think about a November surf trip to my old spots, but I never seem to make it!

7-8
Richard Colagiovanni's Striped Bass,
66.0 lb
Watch Hill, RI
June 30, 1997,

64.0 lb
Watch Hill, RI
Oct 5, 1964

The Elusive Sixty Pounders..............

My fascination with striped bass has filled over forty of my sixty years. Before I delve in and share my fortunate captures of 60-pounders, I would love to share with my readers, anglers of intent, pursuers of striped bass, some background on our fabled fish, and some background of me as it relates to fishing.

Called with respect: striped bass, striper, rockfish bass or just plain fish, they are colorful, spirited, majestic, worshipped, eaten and sold stripers. Fish pursued by commercial interests ranging from sport fishing publishers to trap fishermen, by recreational anglers ranging from executives to vagrants lucky enough to possess a fishing rod and a few plugs.

Striper: A fish totally adapted by eons of evolutions and natural selection to effectively swim in surf, estuaries, coastal ponds, bays, sounds and oceans.

My eventful introduction to stripers was on a summer holiday. The year was 1960. The Green Inn, a summer holiday hotel located along the Atlantic coast, Narragansett Rhode, Island. The hotel of vintage Victorian Era construction loomed above the surf-kissed shoreline only a few yards away. In the suite's morning room that faced the eastern sky and the waters, I admired my newly acquired Penn Squidder fishing reel with thirty-six pound-test Ashaway squidding line. I had practiced casting and could perform short casts with fair accuracy and with the occasional backlashes. I was told to use my thumb to slow down the revolving spool. A nondescript six and a half foot solid fiberglass rod with an enormous wooden butt held the reel. This was my surf stick. Studying a recent issue of Salt Water Sportsman magazine, I replicated the fishing knots illustrated. A large rainbow colored Atom swimmer was attached directly to the line.

As I glanced out the window to the sea, the surf churned a frothy white, contained by slate green slicks between the turbulence. Water sloshed over Volkswagen car sized rocks.

Gazing out at the waters I noticed a few birds, terns. A few moments later a squadron of gulls joined in. The slick waters sandwiched between the white combers were dimpled with scores of silvery flashes baitfish. Small flashes, big flashes, small splashes, big splashes caught my eyes. Small bait fleeing in panic and large fish rolling amongst the combers.

Fishermen began to materialize on the rocky shore. Lures arched out into the melee. Rods bent. Reel drags screamed in protest. Bulbous, silvery fish about three feet in length, with darkened backs etched with horizontally stacked stripes were hoisted from the waters. Stripers!

On my third cast a hefty whitish form ate the dancing Atom Swimmer plug. My meager fifty-foot casts were adequate as the bass were tight to the shore in the wash, "penning up" terrified baitfish. Luck was on my side with a magnificent striper finally tired at my feet. A nearby fisherman used a steel gaff to secure my prize.

I studied the varied iridescent hues of the fish. What caught my eye on that eventful day was the specialized glamour look of this mystical fish. I was almost twelve years old.

As the decades rolled by I was becoming proficient in a variety of stripers fishing techniques. Live bait. Dead bait. Use of plugs, metal, umbrella rigs, tube's worm, jigging, light casting tackle and the fly rod. Graced with contacts with the some of the best striped bass anglers, I was brain washed with effective bass catching techniques and methods. Further on with a select group of others, I refined and created some of my hot striper fishing techniques. With opportunity to fish over 100 days per year, countless thirty, forty and numerous fifty pounders tallied up.

Narragansett Bay, south coastal Rhode Island, Block Island, Fishers Island and the "Vineyard", being the locus of the catches. Water conditions varied from near gale force to glass calm conditions. Some nights were so calm one could easily hear giant stripers suck down a surface swimming Danny or Gag's surface v-ing needlefish. Days of glass calm and sunny skies were successful trips too. The best fishing may have been in stormy days.

I teamed up with Joe Macari throughout the intermediate years, 1975 to 1985. Night trips to Block Island were our usual site for striped bass fishing and adventures. We would cast eels, needlefish, Redfins and Danny swimmers from the boat into four to seven foot deep waters that surrounded the rock strewed shore line. These rocky points with submerged reefs were the hot spots for stripers.

Some nights the 20-mile return trip from the Island to the Rhode Island mainland was challenged by dangerous waves driven by strong and gusty northwest winds. Joe's 17-foot Montauk Boston Whaler delivered a whale of a ride. In a storm when we left the backside of the Island, the full force of the 4-8 foot seas was felt on the small boat. Continuous sheets of water engulfed the little vessel on many a homeward trip as its passengers hovered beneath the windshield watching our catch sloshed around the self- bailing hull. In the dark with little moonlight the wind whipped the top of the waves to white foam. The seas appeared more white than dark at these times.

We thought about pulling into the Old or New Harbor on the Island and wait for calmer winds. The thought of sleeping in a small open boat in the late Fall did not appeal to us. Hand bailing to assist self-bailing was preferred to than sleeping in an open boat during a storm. Joe would concentrate on the throttling of the engine in order to keep the boat nearly level while I did the bailing.

Thanksgiving eve 1979 was a very successful trip for Joe and me. That day the wind howled so hard and the sea pounded so loudly that we had to shout at max dbs to communicate. The brutal conditions produced seven bass: 4- 50s and 3- 40s+. It was a good trip in a bad storm.

Several years later while night fishing at Block Island, Joe and I had a very close call with a rouge wave. We were fishing the Southeast Lighthouse corner of the Island when a 10- foot wave lifter Joe's 20-foot Wellcraft up at a 45-degree angle. The water poured over the bow, gunnels and over us. Joe had placed the bow of the boat facing the sea and the motor idling; standard procedures when eeling or plugging close to the shore. I saw the moving wall of water approaching us and yelled, "Joe, get on the power, now." This allowed him to immediately throttle up and blast through the towering wave. We lived to fish another day. Other fishermen have lost their lives at Block Island fishing by boat close to shore. Only the meek should fish with sand under their feet.

Then to my gratitude, in the span of several years, the waters granted two, yes two, 60+ striped bass; a 64- pounder on October 5, 1994 and a 66-pounder on June 30, 1997.

The October 1964 pounder was a fantastic thrill for me. When the scales at a Watch Hill Tackle store registered at 64- pounds plus a bit on this certified scale, I was delighted. So delighted, I did not sleep for a day and a half!

The day of the 64-pounder was a whirlwind of activity. Weather conditions were of a cold front blasting thru a warmer October air mass. The breeze was a stout nor'wester at 15 knots with occasional higher gusts. I recall vividly the details of the day. It started off with a two-hour delay, as my fishing partner could not locate the truck keys! My fishing partner of seven seasons was Ray Masciarelli Sr. We probably fished over 600 trips together during those years.

Finally on the waters we fished the last half of the incoming tide on the Watch Hill reefs. I can still see the ominous skies, dark clouds racing by, the tide waves billowing up, rebelling against the wind. I can replay the 80-to-100 yards initial run of the fish with the tide. I can still feel the chaffing of the 30-pound test Berkley Big Game mono line on the lip of the reef. I immediately backed off the drag on my Garcia Ambassador 7000 reel-making adjustment to my drag. The line probably lost over half its original strength during the bottom rub. The waters were all riled up as the Watch Hill reefs are know when a booming tide is against the wind. May I add, it's not for the week of heart to fish under those rough water conditions. The fish was finally wrestled near the boat where it did one final dive. The gaff struck home and the prize was aboard. Three way rigs with dead fresh menhaden was the gear used while drifting with the tide. This fish won the 1994 L.G.F.A. Annual Fishing contest in the Striped Bass Division. Fish was 54 inches in length and 30 inches in girth.

The 66 pounder day of capture was on the last day of our fishing week. That month of June, Ray and I caught many, many stripers of various sizes. Several days before the capture of the 66, I caught two- 50 pound plus bass on two successive drifts (a few years back Ray Sr. caught two 59- pounders on the same structure minutes apart!). As Ray Sr. operated his 20- foot Sea Craft the "Janice M" (named after his lovely daughter-who holds the I.G.F.A woman's world record striped bass of 57 plus pounds on 80- pound line from the same body of monster fish). We searched the spine of the Watch Hill reef complex for a concentration of the big fish that we had been catching all week. We finally located the monster fish group and began to routinely catch 40- pounders on just about every drift. I was using a three-ounce bank sinker on the rig. Eagle Claw bronze 7/0 hooks were employed in both monster bass captures.

Then, my whole dead three-way rigged menhaden was sucked down in the forty-foot depths. I set the hook into a solid fish that, after realizing it was hooked, it started to make a beeline towards Fishers Island, New York. The green tinted thirty-pound Berkley Big Game monofilament line melted half way off the reel. I remarked to Ray, "This fish is a good one!" After repeated shorter runs and dives, the fish was boat side. Ray gaffed the monster and we both dragged the trophy striper over the gunnel. The Seacraft bow fish locker was too small for this monster. I wrapped the fish in my Gruden tops and bottom rain gear. Later that day, a certified scale indicated 66 pounds. The fish won the L.G.F.A. 1997 Annual Fishing Contest in the Striped Bass Division. This trophy measured 56 inches long with a 31-inch girth. Two days later, I guided Joe Macari on his 20- foot Wellcraft center-console, "Salt Shaker" to the reef. He scored with a 57- pounder!

I have IGFA certificates declaring my 64 and 66 pound bass as the Annual Fishing Constant winners in the 1994 and 1997 Striped Bass Division.

For several seasons in the 1980s I operated a 27 –foot charter boat called Big Red out of Newport, R.I. We fished for tuna and bluefish for tourists from New York City. Our aim was to get them tired catching fish and motor back early to the docks.

To say the least I was delighted to be honored by the striped bass gods to catch a second sixty plus pounder! I did sleep that night about three or four hours, an improvement over the no sleep night of the sixty-four.

In retrospect on occasions, I reflect upon the journeys of my trophy striped bass that took them up and down the Atlantic coast; from birth at their nursery in the Chesapeake Bay, to the annual coastal migration to the New England waters. I think about the age of the fish spanning over many of the twenty-five years. The 25 years of coastal commuting this fish has endured driven by length of days, availability of food, and water temperature. I contemplate the 25 years of storms, predation and pollution the bass endured before a hook attached to a thread of line on a reel attached to flexible pole of fiberglass, that gave me these wonderful fishing experiences. Skilled fishermen that shared some other fishing techniques with me are; Jack Gouda, George Simes, Bill Mancini, Tommy Bartolomeo, Dick Sevigny, and John Martini. John may be a different record holder having caught over 65 bass weighing more than 50- pounds. Catching a 60-pound bass must be a rare event, ask John.

With great respect, I honor this fish of a lifetime and the men who have shared their experience and knowledge with me.

Richard Colagiovanni's 66.0 lb Striped Bass
June 30, 1997
Watch Hill, RI

7-9
George Cheshire's Striped Bass 64 lbs 8 oz.,
Virginia Beach, VA
Dec.14, 2007

George Cheshire- 64 lb Striped Bass

I am fortunate to live in Virginia Beach on a cove of the Lynnhaven River at the mouth of the Chesapeake Bay, and I am able to enjoy some of the east coast's best inshore fishing. Striped bass, locally known as rockfish, have always been my favorite and over the last 45 years and I have fished for them from Maine to North Carolina. I've fished long cold nights and crisp fall days. My tackle box is crammed with plugs, and jigs, but I often use cut and life baits and even sea worms. My long held dream was to catch a 50- pounder, but the biggest ever landed on my boat was a 25- pound fish and it was a guest that caught it. We have a resident population of stripers in the bay but the big girls are ocean run fish. The same ones that spend the summers up north around New England show up in the Chesapeake and off the ocean beaches in the late Fall. So, in December 2008, when there were reports of big, ocean run stripers being caught near the eastern shore, I had to give them a try.

The 14th of December was a relatively warm- maybe 50 degrees - sunny and calm day, and I loaded up my old 22' Grady White with its 200 hp Yamaha motor and left my dock around nine in the morning. First stop was Bubba's marina and bait shop to gas up and buy a few eels that I slipped into a bucket of saltwater. It was about 45 minute ride on the glassy looking water across the bay to the deep channel near the high span of the Chesapeake Bay Bridge-Tunnel. It was mid tide, and the current was flowing slowly into the bay.

I set up on the ocean side of the bridge in about 45' of water according to my depth finder, figuring that I would drift through the bridge and up the channel towards Kiptopeke and Cape Charles. Somewhere along the way, I hoped to catch a bass. Any bass would do but I didn't really expect anything more than a nice schoolie for dinner. There were a few boats in the area a bit north of me but nothing close by so I enjoyed having a piece of the ocean to myself. By the way, I often fish alone, and I enjoy the solitude.

I put out two rigs. The first bait was hung fairly deep on a pretty good bass rod. I could feel the eel moving around and I thought that any chance I had of catching a trophy bass would be on the deep rig. With the other rod, I was anticipating catching a few schoolies, so I put my smallest eel a few feet under a float and watched it drift out about 50 feet from the boat. That rig consisted of a medium action Ugly Stick spinning rod, a Penn reel spooled with 12-pound test line, a short leader, and a circle hook. It will handle a

10-pound striper but probably not a monster. I certainly didn't expect to catch a big fish on the top rig.

As I drifted lazily, hunger set in so I dug out my brunch – sardines and crackers. I drained the oil from the sardines into the calm bay waters and imagined that the oil would be a tiny slick that would attract some big cow bass. "Fat chance," I said to myself.

I had checked my watch on arrival and it was about 10:15. I finished my sardines and sat back to wait. It was a beautiful day but the current wasn't moving much, so I began to think about moving closer to the bridge. But then I noticed movement around my float. Suddenly the float disappeared. I was excited at hooking up so soon, and I hoped my first striper of the season would be big enough to keep for dinner.

When I picked up the rod, line was already steaming off the reel without much resistance, because I had neglected to check the drag. It was set a little light for a striper – any striper. I held the rod up high trying to put some pressure on the fish but the drag was just too loose, so I began to brake the spool with my thumb – not too much but enough to increase the drag. That worked, and I could feel the strength of the fish. It seemed to be bigger than a schoolie, so I thought that maybe it would be a good fish of about 36 inches. I looked around for the big net and realized that it was in the cuddy cabin. So I carefully made my way forward, keeping a tight line as I grabbed the net and laid it over the seat back. Thank goodness I didn't lose the fish in that maneuver.

We tugged back and forth a little while, and I began to appreciate the strength of this bass. I revised my estimate of its size. Maybe I would get a fish more than 25- pounds - if it didn't break off the light line. I don't know how long we struggled, but it didn't seem very long before I had the fish coming to the boat. When it came into view, I realized that it probably was at least a 25- pounder, and I got more excited.

The fish came to the boat rather docilely and lay on its side. Fighting that light rig had worn it out. It was bigger than I thought. I wasn't sure how big, but I was wondering how I was going to get it into the net and handle the rod at the same time, while not breaking the fish off from the light line. Sometimes there are disadvantages to fishing alone!

The fish was laying still, gills flaring as I retrieved the net. I went over in my mind how I was going to get the fish in the net without dropping the rod or breaking off the fish. If I put the net in front of the fish with my right hand and held the rod in my left, perhaps I could direct her into the net. Then I could drop the rod and grab the net with two hands. Of course, big fish have the habit of coming to life when confronted with nets and causing commotions often leading to their escape. I know this from countless humbling experiences.

I took a deep breath, lowered the net into the water in front of a pretty good size cow bass and gently tugged her forward with the rod held high in my left hand. Amazingly, she went in without a struggle. Wow! I dropped the rod and grabbed the handle of the wide striper net with both hands. Bracing myself against the gunwale I attempted to lift her but the net handle began to bend. Wow again! Quickly, I grabbed the rim of the net in my left hand, moved my right hand to the other side of the net, and tried again. This time I could lift her and I gave a heave and pulled her over the side into the boat. Oh, my aching back. Mind you, I was 67 years old at the time, and my back was a problem.

Looking at the fish laying still on the deck, I was shocked at the size of it. It was huge – much bigger than any striper that I had ever seen. Holy cow! I had to get going and take her back to the dock and the scales. I pulled in the other line, started the engine and headed back to Bubba's. I checked my watch. It was just 11:00.

On the way back across the bay, my mind was racing. I'd caught a trophy striper, and I was sure she was a 50- pounder.

After tying up the boat at Bubba's I tried to lift the fish, but I could barely lift its head, much less lift it out of the boat and onto the dock. So getting out of the boat I went into the dock office, where I saw Dimitri, the owner of Bubba's. I've known him for many years, and when I told him that I needed help with lifting a fish, he grinned. He came down to the boat with me, looked at the fish, and said, "Let me get a rope." Running the line through the fish's mouth and gill plate, the two of us were able to lift the fish onto the dock and drag it to the scale. One of Dimitri's employees, a strong youngster, lifted it onto the scale- it read 64 ½ pounds! Dimitri was beside himself and more excited than me. He quickly went in for a camera and even called to see what the current state record was. (The state record had been broken a week before with an even bigger fish, but a month later a 73- pounder took the record.) One fellow told me that if the fish had another week or two to gorge on the menhaden in the bay it probably would have gained another 5 or 6 pounds. Maybe so, but I didn't care about that.

After a lot of congratulates from other fishermen on the dock, I took the fish home, which is just a short distance up the river. My wife was out so I set up to take some pictures myself. The problem was that the fish was too heavy for me to lift and I wanted to hang it up on a piling for better pictures. I jerry rigged a way to get it up, but it was with great difficulty that I finally got it hanging on a piling. My poor back was screaming! My wife arrived, and after some "oohing" and "aahing', she took the pictures.

After that the fish came down and the butchering began. There were so many steaks and fillets that we couldn't possibly have eaten it all, so I spent the afternoon delivering fish to friends and neighbors and telling my story over and over.

Months later, I received my Virginia citation for my trophy bass, and it made me reflect on the experience. First of all, although I had always wanted to catch a trophy striper, when I finally did, it was anticlimactic. Maybe because the catching of it turned out to be unexpected, relatively quick and easy, and it just wasn't a big deal as I thought it would be. Consequently I didn't have the mount made, the mount that I always said I would have if I ever caught a 50- pounder. Maybe it was the very sobering experience, when I found two really large roe sacs in the fish's belly and realizing how many baby stripers are produced by these big cow bass. It was a very unusual season, because so many big bass were caught last year in the waters off Virginia, and it bothers me to know that we killed so many of the big brooders. (Later a fishing editor of a local newspaper claimed nearly 2000 rockfish over 40-pounds were caught that year.)

Anyway, I've decided to never kill another big bass. I'll certainly fish for them and I'll continue to take smaller fish for food but I'll never take another trophy fish. I don't need to because I already caught my fish of a lifetime.

George Cheshire
Virginia Beach

George T. Cheshier 64.5 lb Striped Bass
Nov.14, 2007
Virginia Beach, VA

7-10
Sherwood Lincoln's 63.0 lb Striped Bass, Fisher Island, NY
1980

Bio of Sherwood Lincoln

Sitting at the table with this giant of a man you feel it would be wise to make friends with him. Surly he must be 6'4" plus and not too far from 275. As he speaks with his booming voice you detect a gentleness and patience and firmness gathered from the years of commercial fishing for the striped bass. He knows his business and is now willing to talk about his adventures but much of which he request be held for a book he working on like " Confessions of a Commercial Striped Bass Fisherman" or something similar.

For 10 years he patrolled the water from Cape Cod to Fishers Island. The first few years were "in training "with friends who had "no training from me attitudes." Secrets are secrets and fishing secrets have to be discovered alone. He said he didn't catch enough bass for his own and his wife's supper in the early years but learned bits and pieces from others as he crafted his skills. Fishing for a living can be a scary life. Storms, waves, winds can peril the occupants of a small 20-24 foot bass boat. If you don't fish in the storms, with gale winds and man-size waves, you will not catch fish. Some of his friends have lost their lives fishing under these conditions.

Sherwood will tell you must accept discouragement from a poor days fishing but not the guff from your competitors. Stand up and state your case less you will be overrun by unfriendly forces. A 6'4" frame standing tall in a boat coming to inquires why you cut his line is showing you why you better stand up and state your case else............

Although Sherwood has mellowed over the years his entanglements with other fishermen in similar circumstances is not unknown. He is well respected by those who will stand for their own rights and express them. They all knew where Sherwood stood. He says Jason Colby;(his story is in Book I, "The Striped Bass 60+ Pound Club"), is a good and respected friend. My bio of Jason said you don't want to mess with him and Sherwood stands right along side him. Maybe a little taller, only in height.

Sherwood Lincoln's 60 lb striper story..............

When Tony called and asked if I had ever caught a 60 lb striped bass my first response was, who are you? And how did you get my unlisted & unpublished number. Turned out that Tony had been contacting fishermen up & down the coast that have caught 60 lb stripers for his second book on large striped bass. He got my number from Captain Jason Colby who runs a charter boat called the Little Sister which charters out of Quincy Harbor (Mass). Jason is noted for his consistent limits of jumbo winter flounder, cod and striped bass.

Jason and I met during a freezer filling flounder trip in Quincy. We became instant friends because we were both "pin hookers" back in the good old days. Pin Hooker is slang for someone who is a commercial rod & reel fisherman. Commercial meaning we sold our catch which were caught by using "sport fishing" methods. I pin hooked from about 1974 to 1984 mostly for stripers, but occasionally for flounder, scup, black fish, weakfish and blues.

In earlier years Jason fished out of Montauk NY and I fished out of Southeastern CT. I believe this is the best area to fish from a boat for stripers north of New Jersey, yes, even better than the Elizabeth Islands or Cape Cod.

I lived in Old Saybrook Ct at the mouth of the Connecticut River and trailered my boat to fish the waters from the eastern end of Long Island Sound out to Montauk Point, east to Block Island and back to Watch Hill. These prime waters include many reefs and well-known places such as N. Rip, Southwest reef at Block Island, Great Eastern at Montauk, the Watch Hill reefs off Rhode Island, the Sluiceway and the Gut. The best striper fishing, when the jumbos arrive every spring, is mid May until Thanksgiving. I believe more 50 & 60 lb stripers have come from this triangle than anywhere else along the coast.

What does it take to become a "professional" fisherman? First you have to love to fishing to the point of obsession. You must also have a wife who understands the nature of this lifestyle and realizes that there are times when it requires investing 12 hour trips 7 days a week, weather was not important. A positive never fail attitude is a necessity. When I first made the transition from sport to pro I thought I had what it takes to make a living.

That was 35 years ago. My first year in this business didn't produce enough for a good fish fry!

Fortunately my wife had a job that could sustain the household until I became more proficient.

Each year catches improved as I got better at it. After several years I came to realize I didn't know it all and never would. It's just too complicated too many spots and too many techniques.

Remember back in the 70's & 80's before the striper stocks crashed, there were almost no regulations. Striper stocks dwindled. By the early 80's the only fish left were large. My average striper weighed 36 pounds, a nice size fish by any angler's standards. Fifty pound plus fish were not uncommon and while sixty pounders were never common, a lucky angler maybe could catch one or a half of one in a lifetime on the water. – You'll see later what I mean.

Tony's request was to write the story about catching my sixty-pound striper with some tips and a short story about my striped bass fishing.

Most of my striper fishing was done from a boat. In the fall when the weather turned bad we would cast for stripers from the beach on Cape Cod. Fishing from the beach was almost as good as from a boat but less dangerous. At any rate I never became much of a surf fisherman. It was too much work, too cold, and too unpredictable and sand got into everything!

One evening in late October or early November my friend and excellent fisherman Frankie B invited me to do some surf fishing with him at the Cape, before weather was going to turn bad. I jumped at the chance. Frank's truck had a cap and was set up like a dune buggy with large tires, a cooler mounted on the front and rod racks all over. It had sleeping arrangements in the back, which allowed us to stay on the beach all week if we wanted.

Well we loaded up the truck and headed for the Cape. Now remember stripers were worth a lot of money so about everything pertaining to catching them was top secret. I was new at this surf fishing game and did not know the Cape very well.

It was pitch black when we arrived and I think Frank took advantage of my ignorance. I'm sure he drove around in circles because we passed the same house three times! When we finally drove out onto the sand he drove to & fro for another half hour. I was beginning to think that the spot was so secret he didn't even know where it was! When he finally stopped there were no buggies in sight. I was instructed to keep all lights limited. We put our waders on and baited up, then walked 40 or 50 feet to the water. Frank was using a live eel and I was using a loaded black and chrome red fin plug. "Loaded" means water is added to the plug to make it more neutrally buoyant and cast better. The surf was perfect. The sea breeze was heavy with the smell of feeding stripers.

I was very excited!

We began casting and retrieving, but my plug just didn't feel right. I complained to Frank but he was busy landing a fish so I continued casting. Frank landed his fish and dragged it up to the cooler. When he returned I took a long cast and grabbed him and almost forced him to take my rod asking him to see what was wrong. He handed me his rod and started to reel mine. Three or four turns on the handle and he was into a big striper, a fish that turned out to be a 50 plus pounder. That proved to be one of my best nights ever surf fishing. We caught 13 bass over 38 pounds. Frank caught three 50's with his first 50 caught on my rod, which weighed around 55 pounds. This was one of the few times I caught more fish than Frank and my total was seven. My biggest weighed in at forty-nine and change. Oh – by the way, I forgot to mention why my plug felt funny on the retrieve. The reason was the "loaded plug" and the fact we were fishing inside the outer bar, in only three or four feet of water. The plug didn't feel right because I was reeling too fast so it was dragging on the bottom! Lesson learned, I slowed down the retrieve and the bass started biting. Well there's Tony's true story and the moral of this story and a good tip on how to catch large bass – never cast and let your buddy retrieve the lure – and always know where you are casting.

Before I tell you about how I caught half of a sixty-one pounder let me say this again catching a 60 plus striped bass is and will always be a rare event. I personally know several fishermen who have done it. These fish were not caught by accident, all of these guys are really good fishermen and know what they are doing. Bear in mind, most of the fishermen on the coast have never caught a forty much less a sixty.

The "Seaweed Sixty" is a story about catching a half of a sixty-one pound striper!

Around 1980 a friend Perry P asked if I would take him striper fishing some time. I had mixed emotions as this was my livelihood and bass were worth a dollar fifty to two dollars a pound.

I knew Perry a short time but could tell he had integrity and could be trusted. The first time we went fishing together was on the south side of Fisher's Island at what was then a "secret spot" called the Airport (*not a secret anymore!*). The spot is located close to the end of the S/E runway and is known for large stripers. Large fish were holding there based my recent trips. I had several back-to-back good days catching large fish including a few fifties.

We were live lining mackerel. Live lining is the most exciting way to catch striped bass. It's quite simple. Hook a live bait throw it out and drift over the bass. You haven't lived until you have seen the sight of four or five 40 to 50 pound stripers chasing a one and a half pound mackerel on the surface. If this doesn't get your adrenalin flowing then maybe you should take up bungee jumping for excitement! But I digress.

Sometimes, in fact often, the bait is harder to catch than the stripers. This day was no exception. We had to motor down the beach as much as 5 miles to catch some very uncooperative mackerel. The 45 gallon bait well with 800

GPH bait pump keeps at most 8 to 12 large mackerel alive for a short time. Once we caught enough we would race back and proceed to live line them. Perry was having a tough time. He kept losing baits because a mackerel is so strong it will pull the drag off a reel when it is being chased. For a beginner it's hard to tell when the bass has the bait, but he picked it up fast and caught a few large stripers. On our second trip back from making bait Perry hooked a large striper. This fish made one run and went to bottom in about 25 feet of water. The fish sulked and Perry could not move it. We spent some time trying to get the fish off the bottom. Remember we were in the middle of a blitz of very large stripers so Perry recommended we break the fish off and get back to catching. I decided to take his rod and see what I could do. A fish in the box is worth *–well you know!* I drove the boat with one hand and worked the rod with the other. The fish could be felt but would not budge as the boat was worked around one way then another. It was about ten minutes before I started to gain some line. The strain on the rod was unbelievable. The fifty-pound line was close to breaking but up she came very slowly, until a huge ball of seaweed, kelp and a large almost dead bass rose to the surface. I handed the rod to Perry, gaffed the bass and hauled the whole mess, seaweed and all in the boat. Hence the seaweed 61. Although this was a very good day, fourteen bass 35 to 61 pounds, it could have been better were Perry more experienced and the mackerel easier to catch. This could have been two or three times better. Figure I should get credit for catching a least half of that 61- pounder.

P.S. Perry bought a boat, became a very good fisherman and we are still friends after all these years.

The story about my 63.4- pounder is not much of a story. The fish was caught in the same place. The only difference was yo-yoing with dead bait. The fish makes one good long run, then a short run and like most big bass a little splashing and on heavy equipment she is history! That's the story of how I caught one and a half 60-pound stripers.

A few words about conservation, I believe fish, all fish, are a valuable renewable resource. When plentiful enough can be harvested and made available to those who do not have access to the water. The state and federal agencies have done a deplorable job of conserving our public resources and today we are in tough shape. Catch what you can and release what you can't eat. Teach your children conservation.

Best Blitzes!
Sherwood

Sherwood Lincoln's 63.0 lb Striped Bass
Fishers Island, NY

7-11
Albert R. McReynold's Striped Bass, 78.5
pounds,
Atlantic City, NJ
Sept 21, 1982
World Record

Most of this story appeared in Book I, "The Striped Bass 60+ Pound Club" but how do you eliminate a world record striped bass story until there is another one to take its place. I have added information which should inhance the story and have the reader contemplate what you would do if you hooked a world record striped bass. Good luck or maybe it isn't good luck. It all depends on you and your wits. Read and learn from Al's experience. Some one will probably do it and have the same extradunary conditions imposed on him or her. Get ready to learn how to handle the event of your fishing life or maybe your entire life.

There have been a few stories written by sports writers concerning Al McReynolds world record striped bass of 78 pounds 8 ounces. It was 53 inches long with a 34-½ inch girth. There have been many opinions expressed over the Internet and at the local tackle shops about this catch. The night he caught the bass, he gave the reporters so much information concerning the difficulties with the storm, jetty and of course the bass, that he recommended, if anyone caught a world record fish, they should keep the details to themselves. Once the news media heard about the catch through reporters or other interested parties, several versions of the same story emerged.

It has been said that Al fought the bass for 1½ hours, others estimated it was a 3 to 4 hour battle, still others claim no bass can fight for more than fifteen to thirty minutes. If Hollywood is any indicator of the medias' need for gossip, true or skewed, it can be expected the same was needed from a "star-like" fisherman as Al. Today one may find it difficult to locate where Al hangs out. By being obscure in the general public arena, he can avoid more and more questions about the same story.

To one's knowledge it was September 21, 1982, about 7:30 PM and 2 1/2 hours after low tide when he started fishing with his pal Pat Erdman from the Vermont jetty off Atlantic City, New Jersey.

It was a dark and gloomy night ..... not quite. The marine forecast for Atlantic City wasn't too bad; temperature of 65 F with a low of 55 F. Fog present in the early morning and later in the evening. Some rain in the morning and the visibility 2 miles or less. Wind 10 to 20 knots from the north and northeast with waves at 3 to 5 feet. It doesn't sound like it could have been a terrible day or night, surely not a Nor'easter by any interpretation since the barometer at 29.96 inches changed very little during the day.

If the actual weather was different at the Vermont jetty than the forecast, then a 40 to 50 knot gale could have been called a Nor'easter. The Rebel black top, silver body, 5-1/2 inch plug was tied directly to the mono line and could have been thrown from the south side of the east-west facing jetty, in fact, a metal Hopkins might have landed in Delaware Bay. The skeptics can be assured that the lightweight Rebel plug could have been cast southwards from the jetty in a Nor'easter. High tide was at 11:04 PM and low tide was at 5:04 PM at the Steel Pier. The moon, if visible in the storm, would have been nearly half full.

Jetty or groin rocks are slippery and dangerous anytime of the year whether in daylight or nighttime. I imagine he knew this rock pile very well and he had on his white boots and rain paints. There may have been a bit of twilight at 7:30 PM since the sunset at 7:00 PM, while the moon may have given some reflected light until it set at 9:36 PM. The neon lights from the casino and boardwalk would have given him some additional visibility as they danced on the turbulent waters.

Al at thirty-six years old had been fishing most of his life. His spinning reel was a Model 710 Penn loaded with 20-pound test mono line. He was at a good fighters' age with a 9-½ foot rod with the Penn "old work horse reel." With reliable equipment ready to do battle with an equal adversary, the striped bass, the savvy old bass knew his arena as well as Al knew his, maybe even better.

Al and Pat could see the bass thrashing their tails and rolling their bellies along the breakers. Mullet were terrified scampering along the beach even leaping on the rocks along the Vermont Street jetty

The wind of the Nor'easter was at a gale force by now, singing through his rod and reel. The waves lashed up and over the hanging rocks threatening to dislodge anyone who thought they were stronger than a ton of water on 100 tons of rocks. This was Al's arena, wild, rough and dangerous.

Pat Erdman was his fishing pal during this battle. He had already caught several bass before Al hooked his trophy. Directing the fight like the second man in the corner at a boxing match, shouting, "move here," "shine the light there," "don't force him," etc. Near the end of the battle both were soaking wet. Sliding around the moss laden jetty rocks can be expected during a Nor'easter. Pat's assistance would have been critical in such a situation to save man from the briny sea and take the world record striped bass from the briny sea. Al first fish was a 15-½ pound weakfish but the next cast was the fish of a lifetime.

When hooked the bass ran with the current towards the open ocean, and then sped towards the beach, finally right at the jetty. Several times during this 1 ½ to 4-hour battle, the fish just stopped. The author has also had bass that just won't move, probably like Al's did. You stand there, holding on, waiting for the next move. You can't move it. It feels like a dead weight but also like a rational being thinking what his next move might be. Experienced striped bass anglers say the bass dig themselves in the sand, broadside facing the angler. Sooner or later it will move, as a deer that stares at you and takes a rigid posture. The deer doesn't know what to do but eventually it will move on just like a bass. The 9 ½ foot rod and 20-pound test mono line held its own. The fish wandered to the beach, then towards the rocks, then down deep, then towards the surface while all the time they couldn't see it. It's dark with only reflected light from the distant casinos doing a disruptive jitterbug on Davie Jones's watery dance floor. Finally she shows herself. It's the biggest bass they ever saw. Back and forth they went, Al and the fish. Finally due to the moss-laden rocks, Al found himself sliding down into the water; neck deep joining his adversary in his arena. Pat tried to moderate the situation, directing Al towards a positive outcome but both Al and the bass are in the water. Pat's assistance was necessary in order to save both man and fish.

With both Al and the fish visible from the distant flickering lights of the Boardwalk, Pat shouted, "It's a really big one. Oh, my god, Albert, don't lose him." Pat grabs Al's clothing as Al got one hand through the fish's gills and out his mouth has he struggled up the rocks, soaking wet from top to bottom. "He got bigger and bigger as I looked at him." Al said. When they got to the shore Pat and Al danced around knowing they had a world record striped bass.

It was late at night by then, hence all the tackle shops were closed and they had to wait until morning to have it weighed. They wrapped the bass in a wet blanket in order to minimize the loss of weight. With the big bass hanging over the hood of the Jeep they had to wait for the certified scale that would confirm the world record catch. At Thomas (Cocky) Campbell's Marine, Bait and Tackle Shop in Northfield, New Jersey, they couldn't believe what they saw so the owner call everyone he thought should be interested. It weighed 78 pounds, 8 ounces surpassing Bob Rochetta's 76- pounder caught off Montauk Point in N.Y. in 1981. Campbell put the bass in his freezer and put a $100,000 insurance policy on it. Abu-Garcia gave him $25,000 for being the weigh master and watchdog. Nelson Bryant, outdoor writer for the New York Times heard about the fish and told Al about the $250,000 prizes money he should get.

At 78 pounds 8 ounces it surpassed all line classes, male, female, and junior records. A true world record. With documents signed, scale certified, witnesses included, it was official.

Here was Al handing over his rod, reel, line and fish for further confirmation that the regulations had been met. Soaking wet from the night on the jetty, he had to get to the Beach Patrol and to work. He admits his reading and writing skills were not up to par hence the snakes came out of the grass, or waters in this case. Al was glorified by the sporting goods world, equipment manufacturers and by strangers he never knew including Government officials. We all have our 15 minutes of fame and Al got a lot more time to bath in it. How did he handle it? You got to ask him yourself. From my personal contacts with the people he brushed against, not very well. He may be still looking for a good, trustful friend. His fishing friend, Pat Erdman, I think is referred to only as a "friend", not by name, in the Salt Water Magazine story. If you need to read the whole truth and nothing but the truth get a copy from the library or from SWS, Sept. and Oct. (2 part story) from 2004 as Al presented his story to them. The version above is the best I could surmise from the New York Times and Philadelphia Inquirer newspapers, the Internet and a limited portion (by law) from his story in the SWS Magazine.

World record fish demand exciting stories and it can be found in the past issues of the SWS. Although Al might have said he would cut his line if it ever happened to him again, I don't know anyone who would contemplate doing it. Would you?

Al and his family, wife and three kids, were born in Atlantic City. He was a commercial fisherman since the age of fourteen moving to where the business was; New Jersey, Massachusetts and Nova Scotia.

He received his $250,000 check from D.L.Blair of Abu-Garcia Company at the Explorers Club in Manhattan, New York City, N.Y. After several weeks of checking and rechecking, the IGFA, Abu-Garcia Administrating Office and D.L.Blair declared Al the winner of the *Striped Bass* prize. Al and his wife, Karen, were picked up at their Atlantic City home by an Abu-Garcia official, driven to N.Y.C. for dinner at Joe's Pier 52 restaurant and spent the night at the Hilton Hotel, N.Y.C. Breakfast in bed, of course.

Web sites comments give interesting views about this event.

1. I thought it was pretty cool hearing it from the horse's mouth. I thought he fought that fish 1-½ hours. In the story he writes that it was over 4 hours.

2. It's a shame that he caught as much crap as he did for catching it. He even goes as far as saying if he could have another chance he would cut the line.

3. Skeptic in me wonders how true the story really is. Only Al knows for sure but I enjoyed it nonetheless.

4. His friend helping him was Pat Erdman. The plug was a black over silver Rebel and the battle was for one hour and forty minutes (from Bob D'Amico's story).

5. Even an hour and forty minutes is too long to fight a bass on a jetty in a Nor'easter.

6. I know that there are many fishermen out there right now who wish they were holding that rod bowing to that cow.

7. Easily the strangest account of that catch; I've read all the others.

8. Did he really say he would have cut the line if he could have foreseen all the problems that this fish caused?

Other Notable 60+ lb Striped Bass

Barry Cherms 60+ lb Striped Bass
and others

James Patterson,
66.25 lb Striped Bass,
Pt. Judith, RI
6/10/1964

Jim Mitchell
63.0 lb Striped Bass,
Pt Judith, RI , 1960

Kevin Needham, Tommy Needham, Mark Sherer
61.5 lb Striper
Nov 19, 1983
Narragansett, RI

ALL-TIME BIGGEST SURF-CAUGHT STRIPER
Weighing in at 65-lbs., 10 ozs., was this record striper recently taken by Neil Cordeiro of Provincetown, Mass., fishing the nearby Race Point surf from the shore.

THIRD LARGEST EVER TAKEN
Third largest ever taken, this 66½ lb. striper was landed by Donald Nee of Charlestown, Mass. at Cuttyhunk, Mass., one of the real "hot spots" for striper fishing.

"I have used Ashaway for 15 years without disappointment" and there could hardly be anything disappointing in this 65 lb. bass caught at Point Judith, R. I. by James Paterson, Jr. of Westwood, New Jersey.

Peter Sparuk of Hyde Park, Mass., made connections with this 64-pounder at Cuttyhunk, Mass. while fishing with Captain Bob Smith.

James Mitchell of West Warwick, R. I. fishes "with confidence when using Ashaway Spinning lines" and here's Jim with his 63 lb. bass caught at Point Judith, R. I. on 20 lb test monofilament.

Bernard O'Demers of Holden, Mass., with his 60 lb. 8 oz. striper taken at Cuttyhunk, Mass., says he's used Ashaway almost exclusively for 15 years and it can't be beat for strength and durability.

Thaddeus Folcik of New Bedford, Mass., caught this 60½ lb. striper at Nashawena Island, Mass. on 45 lb. test Ashaway Squidding — "and would use no other on big fish."

Peter Millara of Quaker Hill, Conn. commented after taking this 60½-lb. striper at Race Point, Fishers Island, N. Y., "Good to know when a large fish makes its first long run, the line can take it."

60+lb. Striped Bass
from the 1950s

Ron Wojcik   Ernie Richmond
61.0 lbs.   3 other bass
8/58 - Pt. Judith, RI

Steve Smith 64.0 lb Striped Bass
Naragansett, RI
Nov. 1982

Tommy Needham, 61.5 lb Striped Bass,
Narragansett, RI Nov 19, 1983

2/1/2010

Willie Hilton and 61.0 Striped Bass
caught off Pasque Island with an eelskin
June 30, 1958.   L= 50 1/2" G= 30 "

8
Tips from the "Story Tellers"

Alfred Anuszewski

1. Fish from dusk to dawn.

2. When you retrieve your lure or eel, do not rush to get it in. Slow down your retrieve to a crawl and stopping the retrieve numerous times as you bring the lure or eel back to you. Making this lure or eel look like the weak one or injured one of this school of bait. That's the lure or eel the giant striped bass will strike.

3. Search for baitfish with your eyes and your nose.

4. Fish in nasty weather like rain, strong winds and frozen late November nights.

5. Keep you fishing tackle in perfect shape, also change with the times as fishing tackle gets better and better, year after year increasing your chances of catching that real large striped bass.

6. Learn to listen when fishermen you respect talk about catching giant striped bass. Let all these fishermen you respect do all the talking. You do all the listening.

7. Help other striped bass fishermen succeed. I believe it will come back to you ten fold.

Ted Nimiroski

1. Get to know the areas that have known to produce large bass and learn it well, all tides.

2. When fishing from a boat, try using the reverse function on your motor so that you may present the bait right in front of the fish, eventually they will take it either from annoyance or hunger.

3. Live bait, eels, squid menhaden/ bunker, small skip jacks, bluefish, skup/porgies or fresh bait. Enough can't be said enough about using the freshest bait possible.

4. Great fish locators. I had found using the latest technology Fish Finders available has its rewards many times over.

5. Patience, if you can follow the above tips will get you fish.

Richard Colagiovanni

1. The past years I have used with great success a Frabril Company's large hoop Conservation Series net for the final capture. The mesh is such that it provides equal pressure when supporting the fish therefore minimizing the fish's protective slime and reduces any internal organ damage.

   In the years 1970 to 1974, my 1967 4 wd Ford Bronco saw action on the beaches of Cape Cod National Seashore. I targeted the bayside of Great Island near Wellfleet Harbor/Village from time-to-time. I sniffed around the island in a vain attempt to locate pirate prate booty, alleged to be buried there. Then on days when the water was flat, I targeted stripers from my 10' aluminum John boat powered by a 1950s 3 horsepower Evinrude outboard motor. Granted a small boat but I was a lightweight then. After anchoring up a bit offshore, along a slight drop-off, I would sling eels and cast Bob Pond's Atom swimming plugs. The fish would swim -by about every hour or so and I would fish those critical minutes hard. I would sound the depths with an 8 -ounce bank sinker attached to a tarred hand line. Dawn and was my prime fishing time. My catch was sold on the Cape. I also fished from the beach on the Oceanside from Race Point

Lighthouse down to Cape Cod Light via 4 wd. When selling out in P-town, I would often reward myself with a beverage at the "Old Colony" tavern, in celebration. The beach was still a bit like the Wild West 40 years ago, limited restrictions, not over crowded.

2. With the advent of ethanol fuels, definitely use a gas treatment in your outboard or inboard such as Star Tron Enzyme Treatment. This product is worth its weight in gold in preventing the gasoline from breaking down and causing headaches. A dead engine at the ramp or on the water can rapidly ruin a pleasant day of striper pursuits.

3. Try to fish for stripers during a steady or falling barometric pressure. Most often, the falling air pressure prior to a cold front will encourage the bass to eat.

4. Always check your line/leader and hook/knots after each fish caught.

5. Try to use the freshest baits (i.e. menhaden, hickory shad, scup, etc.) and keep them cold and iced before and during use.

6. Try to fish times that coincide with the absent/minimum boat traffic while fishing from shore or boat.

Sherwood Lincoln

1. Sharp hooks always out fish dull ones. Fewer drops.

2. Use braided line.

3. Use only the freshest bait.

4. Smooth drag will also stop you from dropping fish.

5. Buy an Eldridge Tide Book and study.

From Other Notable 60+ Club Members

1. Fishing the surf, rod, reel, line and the rest must be balanced. The rod cannot be tip heavy hence load your arms and wrists. A 9-foot modern rod with a 12- ounce-spinning reel will give you close to the ideal balanced package.

2. Do not fish at the edge of the surf. Many strikes occur right at that edge and by moving back about 10 feet on the sand you will fish the edge.

3. A very high percentage of the big fish are lost right at the surf line. Move the rod from near vertical to near horizontal as the fish nears the beach. The fish will probably roll at the surf line and a vertical held surf rod might pull the hook out of its jaws as it goes upside down.

4. Use a reel that works well with braided line; you will never change to a different material.

5. Check the sharpness of the hooks after working sandy and gravel beaches and after landing a few fish.

6. Point you rod always in the direction of your presentation even follow the current with it.

7. Go early and stay late. Document the tide, wind, baro pressure, water temp and season. The bass knows or feels these variables, you need to know them.

8. At low tide the bass locate near the deepest water. At high tide they may be anywhere. Go to the beach at low tide and find these holes.

9. Go fish where they are catching fish, fish with what they are catching fish, fish when they are catching fish. Good luck

9

A Southern Shift?

Only fine wine stores carry Don Peron Champagne, only the very stocked liquor stores carry 40-year old Black Label Scotch and only in high-end jewelry stores will you find Rolex watches, likewise for Rolls Royce at exclusive auto dealers. Find a 60+ pound striped bass at Race Point, MA, Montauk Point, NY and Sandy Hook, NJ may be a "yester- year" event since now the big cows are more common off Virginia Beach, VA and vicinity. There were over 10 striped bass of 60 pounds or more caught in Jan.'07- to Jan. '08 in Virginia waters. This rare event became a common catch. Will it be "one for the ages"?

These are probably the same bass that left the Chesapeake Bay vicinity in the spring of '07 and went north to follow the menhaden, mullet and other baitfish. During the summer they got their fill along the Massachusetts, Rhode Island, Connecticut, Long Island, New Jersey, Delaware and Maryland coastline and arrived in the Virginia Beach/Chesapeake Bay area. History has documented it and put a time and place for the miracle; the time and place where so many 60+ pound bass were caught over one year. An event even Cape Cod, Montauk Point, Sandy Hook etc can't claim, can't even recall a reasonable challenge in past years of this number of big bass. Most likely the bass sneaked around Race Point, slid down Nauset Beach, hid around the rocks of Cuttyhunk Island and Block Island, blitzed Montauk Point, skirted Sandy Hook, did a wide bend around Barnegat Light's sandbar and kept the same distance offshore until the warmer waters off Virginia Beach. The 40-degree water temperatures up north were not as attractive as the blend of "Virginia's southern waters."

In 2008 according to the Virginia Saltwater Fishing Tournament, over 1400 anglers registered trophy striped bass over the year- long program. These anglers weighed in 123 bass bigger than 50 pounds and 10 cows passed the 60- pound mark- the heaviest at 67 pounds. Is this a Southern Shift or a big tsunami or both?

These 10 big bass were all caught while fishing from boats. Hanging an eel from a floating bobber ambushed most of these cows. Yes, a freshwater-type floating bobber. I don't think the color made much difference. How much simpler can you get? No multi- depth parachute rigs pulled by a 3-5 knot trolling boat, no Montauk Point 2 to 4 pound trolling spoons, no chum buckets stuffed with oily trash fish, just a 50 cent bobber hanging from a carbon fiber boat rod instead of an old unimproved bamboo cane pole. Yes, the high- tech literature wasn't read by the bass probably because they didn't have a permanent mailing address. During their annual migrations along the eastern coastal states, they may have established "Rock Boxes" in lieu of a P.O. Boxes. Do you know the location of a "Rock Box?" If not check with Virginia Beach and vicinity or scan the locations of various groins and jetties highlighted in another chapter of the book or in my first book.

In the late 1950s, early 1960s along Cape Cod, MA many big bass called this home. Although 60-pound bass are never common, a few were registered. Keep in mind that there weren't 2 to 3 million striped bass anglers seeking their haunts along the east coast. It was Frank Woolner, Henry Lyman, Wilford Fontain, Jason Colby and Al Ristori who plodded the sands or navigated from the stern of a bass boat loading up on 40 to 50 pound bass. Many were shipped to the local fish dealers, especially in Provincetown, MA. Those were the days of big bass, later to be repeated in the early-mid 1980s, and then the moratorium was imposed on fishing for striped bass. The recovery completed by 1995 may have led to today's miracle at Virginia Beach/Chesapeake Bay. No longer may we be able to regard Race Point, Montauk Point, Sandy Hook, etc. as the mecca of the striped bass activities. The South has risen again and the bass seem to….. like Thomas Greeley " Go West young man" is replaced by " Go South Striped Bass Anglers."

The Chesapeake Bay- Bridge Tunnel looks like a big rock pile to the rockfish. No use calling the striper rockfish up north, although there are plenty of groins and jetties for the rockfish to pick a snack at his favorite rock. There are approximately 520 of these northern rock piles. The Bay- Bridge Tunnel is the only rock pile for snacks around Virginia Beach. Grits are not served here but all the varieties of crabs, clams, worms and a great number of smaller bait and game fish. The bass will eat everything, less the rocks.

Mathematically this is a much better opportunity for success by the striped bass/ rockfish angler since this is the only available rock pile.

Although many of these southern big bass were caught in the ocean, Chesapeake Bay area is their home base, even though many may never have crossed the official line between the Bay and the Atlantic Ocean. The fish from the north probably migrated past the Wachapreague, Smith Island Flats, Fisherman's Island and finally crossed the Bay and the tidal rips at Cape Henry, then onwards to Virginia Beach. A little further south you may find these bass off the EEZ deeper waters of Corolla, North Carolina.

Many observant and devoted fishermen say bass will spend the winter at or near the local groins as well as jetties and not migrate with the rest of the clan. Where the surf waters may hover around the high 30F degree temperatures in the northern winter waters, the deeper warmer waters pass 3 miles out off the same beach may keep the bass in the local waters. A short swim to the rock pile for breakfast, lunch and dinner is a reasonable expenditure of energy. No use in chasing winter flounder, hake, whiting etc in deeper waters while the seashore rock pile offer tasty morsels in- residence.

In some east coast states striped bass fishing is open all year except in the local rivers, bays, coves, etc. These rivers, bays, coves etc are scattered along the coast for an added food supply for the local bass. The non- ocean waters are usually protected from fishing till after spawning during springtime.

Years ago New York City wanted to fill in some of the Westside of the Hudson River in order to construct high- rise apartments. The law required many government agencies get involve in ascertaining the impact on the environment. Marine scientists discovered the shipping docks and storage structures along the river were the winter home for a massive amount of striped bass. Filling this area might destroy the population. We know that changes in water temperature over a short period of time will kill the resident fish. The unexpected winter shutdown, several times, of an east coast nuclear power station has killed thousands of fish. They only counted the game fish. Fish seem to adapt their body to gradual temperature changes over a period of time. We don't know the impact of removing their residence especially in the winter from the accommodating water temperatures and salinity at the south end of the Hudson River to some uninhabitable waters. Therefore the building was postponed until piles were sunk into the river bottom and the housing development was hung over the water. Both fish and people seem satisfied.

Is it time to close the book on those cool October evenings with a full Fall moon rising at Race Point? The rolling sand dunes look lonely enough like some moon scrape in other worlds. No rocks here for the bass to trap bait, no sand bars to challenge the waves to moderate its fury. Just the flat, sandy, pebbled stage, like time gone by, looking for action from its actors. The same for Montauk Point, south side, north side, rocks, rocks and more rocks. The eerie rotation of the lighthouse at night may give you the feeling someone is watching you. He's higher than wide but when the moon is nye; he's a good friend but not so with the surrounding rocks. Better to angle your cast to avoid the barnacle-laden rocks that will cut your braided line in a flash and your mono in a flash and a half. Will the southern migrated bass result in elbowroom between the surf jockeys at the "Point?" No more tangle lines, short tempers and "whose fish." No more "fish on", no more " my favorite rock is occupied", no more no mores. Maybe but...

It's a long walk from the parking lot at the doubled decked World War II concrete armament building to the "rip" at Sandy Hook. Loaded down with full gear is only for the young or strong; half gear for the 60+ anglers. It's like shuffling through a field of stubble hay at some mid-west mega farm. Each step included the dragging of sand and other loose material with you. You earn your way to the "rip", there is no taxi to take you there, you take yourself and you take only what you need. Successfully dragging a cow bass back will be your " strong man's citation," well planned and well earned. Now if you are not in training for the trek to the "rip", there are several parking lots prior to the "rip" which have a shorter walk to the beach. There is even a "Fisherman's Beach" with parking for the summer time anglers while the other parking lots are reserved for the summer bathing crowds. All the parking lots open up for anglers after Labor Day.

Fish that haven't moved from MA, R.I., CT and the Island to the Hudson River must round Sandy Hook. Some bass may choose the local rivers in the Raritan Bay region and move in with the juvenile 2-4 year old bass while the rest head south towards Barnegat Light. Here the large sweeping sandbars steer the bass many hundreds of yards off the beach and around the lighthouse. October surf jockeys wait for those times when the bunkers get caught inside the big sand bar. Then it's on to Atlantic City, the present address of the World Record Striped Bass at 78 pounds 8 ounces. Pass Delaware, Maryland towards Virginia Beach/Chesapeake Bay. Those bass still moving south chasing menhaden will be found along the Outer Banks, North Carolina, Oregon Inlet to the Cape Hatteras Lighthouse.

We have plotted the old migration paths of the bass, discussed their options along the way and hinted that the big cows may have forsaken their old favorite haunts. Numbers are numbers and they do tell a tale about past times but trend lines indicate that big bass are southern gentlemen and southern ladies. Time and numbers will write the final chapter of this "Southern Shift."

If any questions still are unanswered you may want to talk to those who made this shift possible. The results of the Virginia Saltwater Fishing Tournament 2007- Striped Bass:

<u>Lbs.</u>	<u>Name</u>
67 lbs 6 oz.	Donald Riesgraf
65 lb. 3 oz.	Roger S.Tisdale
64 lbs. 8 oz.	George T.Cheshire
64 lbs. 2 oz.	Robert Blackwell
63 lbs. 4 oz.	Nick Smith
63 lbs 0 oz.	Bill Claar
62 lbs. 1 oz.	Wayne Rickman
61 lbs. 6 oz.	Jay I. Bechtel
61 lbs. 4 oz.	Matthew Fine
60 lbs. 2 oz.	David Wilson

In the story section of the book and you find stories written by some of the members mentioned above about their 60+ pound striped bass.

10

Bass Vision Revisited
What tools do they have?
What tools do you have?

Water acts as a filter to the eyes of all fish. Objects are visible after the light protons strike the water and then move through the water table refracting and reflecting in the water to indicate colors- violet, blue, green, yellow, red or a combination of all colors-white. Objects in blue waters will tend to look bluish, green waters to look greenish, clear water to look near true color. Water is a filter which effects vision for man and fish.

It is important to select colors that are most sensitive to the retinas of the fish. Having a blue colored lure in blue tinted waters or green colored lure in green tinted waters may be a poor choice unless the fish has its maximum sensitivity in this color region. Each species of fish has maximum color sensitivity to certain colors in the water environment no matter what the color of the water. This gives them an advantage to locate prey. You do not want the color of water (filter) to attenuate the color where the retina is most sensitive.

There is an adage in nature that says that you do not want to be an obvious target for those that prey on your species. Many animals that are preyed upon have a natural camouflage built into their outer layer. The camouflage nearly match their environment, hence makes detection difficult for their prey.

Deviate too far from your gene-generated colors that provide a natural protection, you become more visible, more in- danger and more of a target.

There are not many animals or fish that have a natural color of white. The reason is obvious. White stands out in bright and poor light conditions.

There may be no place to hide. Even very low light areas cannot give total protection.

Although most fish species have retinas that have maximum sensitivity to certain colors, white color is more easily detected in any level of light. White color emits nearly 100% of the light photons that strike its surface. If you do not know the maximum color sensitivity of the fish you seek or the waters are stained and dark, white colors lures may be a better choice than any other color.

Large Mouth Bass

I know of no scientific study that tested the vision of striped bass in their natural habitat. What has been done is the testing of fresh water large mouth bass has been done but most all fish have similar light sensitive retinas. The color spectrum goes from about 200 nm (dark purple) to over 800 nm (dark red). In between you have the blues, greens, yellows, white, orange and reds. Large mouth bass have two types of cone cells to see red and green (720nm and 460nm). Carps with four cone cells can see red, green blue and ultra violet. The human eye can detect colors from approximately 400 nm to 700 nm, with maximum sensitivity at 420 nm for blue, 530 nm for green and 568 nm for red. Fish fall into this overall range also but with different maximum sensitivity for blue, green and red. You want to fish with colors they can easily see.

Each species of fish and animals have different abilities to distinguish the detail in shapes. This can be called visual acuities or sharpness. It is the ability to distinguish differences between two different points in space or on a surface. The greater the visual acuity or sharpness, the less chance a bass will be fooled by a poorly presented live bait or lure.

For instance, a dog has about 2.8x times less visual acuity than man, a blue marlin about 3.7x times less, tuna 3.7x times less, large mouth bass 10x less, flounder 11x less, and a carp 17x less. Now you know why it is easier to fool a carp than a blue marlin.

When it comes to distinguishing color and relative sensitivity to color, it depends on the number of cones their retinas contain. Yellow is generally the color which most fish have some sensitivity. This is around 500nm. Blue and purple as well as reds are less sensitive to most fish except the striped marlin where it has its most sensitivity to green about 450nm and much less to orange and red at 600nm.

The best information on large mouth bass indicates that orange/red is the most sensitive to their eyes (630 nm, red-orange and a second peak at 530nm, yellow-green). Studies have shown that color sensitivity decreases considerably as water depth increases. At 6 ft. in stained water, the large mouth bass can barely distinguish the yellow/ orange colors (this is their most sensitive color range). Purple, blue, green all look the same.

The lighter and brighter the lures, more of the photons (light energy) are reflected to the eyes of the fish. White color will reflect 100% of the photons and black zero. Successful night fishing is highly dependent on some form of light. The quality and nature of the water can also absorb reflected photons before the fish's eyes receive the image.

Aside from color and sharpness identification, distinguishing motion is also an important ability of fish. Predators need to see motion in order to identify a potential prey. The ability of a fish to see motion is related to their flicker frequency (CCF). For humans we have a CCF of around 50 to 60 cycles per second. That is the frequency your TV picture or computer monitor needs in order to appear as a steady state picture. As things move across the screen you can distinguish a motion because you have a continual picture in your mind and not a snap shot of one frame at a time. CCF rates vary with the temperature. For man with a steady 98.6 degrees Fahrenheit body temperature, this is not very important, but for a cold-blooded fish its water environment is very important.

As fish move to colder waters in the fall and winter, their ability to detect the motion decreases. This affects both the prey as well as the predator.

Some fish like tuna, lamid sharks and swordfish have the ability to keep their bodies warmer than the surrounding waters. This permits them to seek prey at greater and colder depths.

Keep in mind the relationships between fish's color sensitivity, sharpness, and water temperature and water depth. With this knowledge you will improve your luck.

If watercolor appears blue (peak sensitivity at 470 nm) there will be extremely low illumination at a depth of 400 meters (about 1200 feet). If watercolor is green (peak sensitivity at 525 nm) due to organic matter, the illumination is gone at 150 meters (about 300 feet).

Note that each species of fish must adapt to their environment in order to feed successfully. There are 25,000 different species of fish. They may all be fish but each species has its special gifts in order to survive. We humans, also have our special visual gifts, which are mostly all the same because we are one species, Homosapiens.

Striped Bass

The striped bass has in its eyes (retinas), rods, single cones and twin cones.

The cones are used for daylight vision and the rods for nighttime. The size of the cones grow in length with age but rods do not.

The work that has been done specifically with the striped bass vision has been done in the laboratory using actual striped bass retinas. This has indicated the <u>rods</u> of the striped bass have a maximum sensitivity at about 528nm (green), <u>single cones</u> at 542nm green/yellow) and <u>twin cones</u> at 605nm (orange). Rods overall range is from 500 nm to 650 nm; cones from 500 nm to over 700nm.

This means the striped bass vision at night is most sensitive to light green using its rods and in the daytime it is most sensitive to green/ yellow/ orange using their single and twin cones. See Figure 18.

The human retina has the max green sensitivity at 535 nm, very similar to the striped bass rod sensitivity at 528nm. What the human eye sees as a green lure in very poor light, relatively will the striped bass may see shapes, not true colors at 528 nm.

Although the human eye has a good sensitivity in the purple/blue region at 450 nm, the striped bass does not need superior sensitivity in this region, which is associated with great ocean depths. This is not their region for chasing prey.

Being a costal fish, they would be more inclined to be feeding successfully in water depths, which corresponds to what their retinas easily see- green, yellow, orange/red . These colors can be seen in moderate ocean depths of the costal region where some light is present.

We can conclude that the striped bass vision with their rods (night vision) cannot distinguish true colors but shapes of black to white and with their single and twin cones (daylight vision) best for yellow/orange/ red color. Be aware they do see colors from violets to reds, across the visual spectrum, as does the human eye but not with the same sensitivity. They don't turn off their daylight sensitivity cones when the sun goes down but add their rods for night vision. Any color sufficiently highlighted against an adverse background can more easily be detected i.e.; black against white or visa versa.

What you see of green and red on the bait and tackle shelves is approximately what the striped bass sees but the bass is in an environment where colors will be attenuated by depth, water quality and the direct light from the sun or reflected light from the moon.

These colors present the most sensitive colors for striped bass under lighted conditions. At a depth of 30 ft. or more, light would be attenuated severely; all lures may just look dark. The fish may substitute smell, sound and motion for lack of color in search of food.

In ocean waters with clear sky at noon, light penetration remains only at

45% at about a depth of 1 meter, 15 % at 10 meters and 1% at 100 meters. Violets and reds are heavily attenuated at 1 meter where red and oranges are absent at about 10 meters. **It seems to indicate that a lure fished at the surface to about 3 ft. (1 meter) would give the fish a better chance (everything being equal) to see the lure more often than those lures fished at 30 feet or about 10 meters.**

A green/yellow/orange light colored lure may be the best combination of colors at any time, day, night or any season. This puts a hole in the rule of thumb-black for night and white for day fishing. White reflects 100% of the light photons hence it will have a better chance to be seen at greater water depths regardless of other colors which may be more sensitive to the fish's retina. At night the contrast of shapes between water, lure and sky plays an important part in identifying prey.

Some scientists say that having eyes with cones and rods is not a conclusive indication that fish see color. It is merely an indication that they have the organic instruments to see colors. A field test of the striped bass in its environment is the only sure way to conclude the bass see colors. Who wants to make up the test? An analogy is; if you see a man with arms and legs, it is not a proven fact that he can lift a glass or take a step. You must verify the hypothesis by a test. A visual test in this case should be conclusive.

Fish eyes never stop growing. Their eyes become bigger and the retina packing density increases which means their vision becomes more acute but the density of cones cell is much less than the human eyes. Fish also have the natural ability to repair eye injuries.

Most fish look somewhat green in color because this is their camouflage in saltwater or freshwater. If you look much different than the "greenish" tinge you are a mutation therefore easily detected and easier caught. The color white is an odd color that stands out against most all colors in the ocean. Although fish's eyes may not have the peak sensitivity to white, which is the combination of the three primary colors- blue, green and red, the motion of white in a surrounding medium of green-blue seawater is easily detected. Fish do attack white colored lures but not because that is their most sensitive color of their retinas but it is a contrasting color against the background and has motion of a prey. We know striped bass retinas are peaked at light green, yellow and light red. Crabs, bunker, eels, sand eels, and by catch fish have some if not all of these colors built into them. A wise old bass may pass up a white colored lure but something like one or more of the colors above, which fits their memory and sensitive retinas, may get their attention.

One of the most popular striped bass foods is a clam; it comes in gray, light gray, dark gray with a touch of color. Smell may be a better selling point to a bass rather than color in this case.

Smell is another tool for the fish to use in-lieu of color. Sharks apparently can smell prey miles away. Most fish have similar abilities hence the oceans would be left with decaying remains of dead sea-life. Little goes to waste. Chum bags have been use for ages to attract everything in the ocean. More smell equals more fish of all kind and a fresh clam is the "piece de resistance" for even a fully rounded bass, preferable opened and chucked, of course.

Some lures, failing to leave an oil smell behind it, have turned to making noise. Metallic balls rolling around a hollow echo tube can send sounds over long distances as the Navy has learned. The fish have their own unique sonar systems hence another tool to find and catch prey. With some brain material, much experience, sensitive to color, speed, smell and noise, you have a fish not too different from our God given tools. We humans use our tools on the surface while the fish prefer the subsurface. Our intelligence hopefully keeps us out of sight, speed, smell and noise of our prey.

Striped Bass Vision

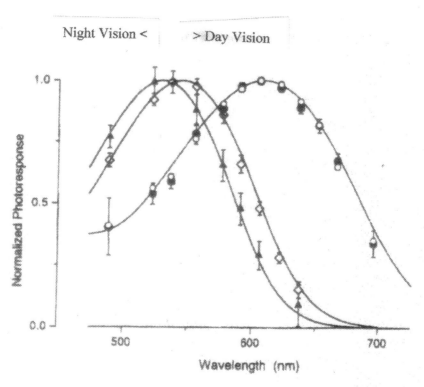

Fig. 5. Action spectra of the photocurrent of rods (▲), single cones (◇), common twin cones (●), and fast twin cones (○). The photosensitivity at each wavelength was normalized by the maximum photosensitivity. Points are the average (±s.d.) of data from 7 rod clusters, 8 single cones, 10 common twin, and 4 fast twins. The continuous line is an optimized fit to the data of a polynomial nomogram that describes the absorption spectrum of vitamin A2-based visual pigments (Dawis, 1981). The λ_{max} in the nomograms that best fit the data were: rods, 528 nm ±4.3; single cones, 542 nm ±3.2; common twins, 605 nm ±4.8; and fast twins, 606 nm ±6.5.

11
Striped Bass Basics
Inshore and Near- Shore

Morone Saxatilis

Known as: striped bass, rockfish, linesider, roller, squid hound, green head, striper, basse, quwnammag, bar-fish, missuckeke-kequock.

Found: Canada to Florida to Louisiana in open and near costal waters of the Atlantic Ocean and vicinity and the West Coast. Also found beyond 3-miles from the shore although illegal to catch.

Markings: Green, olive, steel blue, brown, black with seven or eight continuous lines on their sides from gills to tail.

Size: To over 100 pounds. Males 20-30 lbs. Females over 100 lbs. A Bass over 60 pounds is rare.

Life Cycle: Movement from ocean in the summer to bays and rivers in the winter. Spawns in estuaries of the Chesapeake Bay, Hudson River and in many other similar smaller estuaries along the East and similar waters in the West Coast.

Increase in water temperature in the spring: Starts the spawning cycle. Usually March to June in water temperatures of 59 to 65 degrees F. Females may spawn as early as four years old. Males two to three years old.

Spawning fish: Return to the costal waters depending on age, about 2-4 years.

Fertilized roe: Hatch in 29 to 80 hours.

Foods: Estuary fish feed on crustaceans while adult fish on anchovy, menhaden, spot, croaker, herring, small flounder, alewives, sand flea, clam, eel, lobster, sand worm and other small fish inhabiting the costal areas.

Active feeding: Starts at about 50 degrees Fahrenheit but fish will feed in waters less than 40 degrees. Resident coastal and estuaries fish feed year around in the local waters and at the local water temperatures.

Age: Can be estimated by counting the annual rings on its scales.

By the Numbers:

In 2008 the US 13 million recreational saltwater anglers, Maine to Texas, made 89 million fishing trips and caught 475 million fish of all kinds. That amounted to almost 7 trips per year per angler and caught almost 37 fish per year. Per the US Marine Fisheries, 55% of the fish were released alive. See Figure 3: Number of Fishing Trips per State.

2007

US Marine Trips by Recreational Anglers

M= million

Conn	_Maine_	_MD_	_Mass_	_NJ_	_NY_	_NC_	_VA_	_RI_
1.68M	--	4.05M	4.71M	7.43M	6.21M	6.98M	3.72M	1.55M

Fig. 3

Only 10 % of the anglers, 1.3 million, fish in Federal waters (3-200 miles out). This left 11.7 million anglers to fish from the shore or near shore (0-3 miles).

Along the Northern and Mid- Atlantic States anglers fishing from the shore or near shore were slightly less in numbers than fishing from private, rental or charter boats. As you move to the Gulf States, the majority of fishing was from all forms of boats. This amounted to about 30% more boat activity than the North-Mid-Atlantic States. In the far West about 70 % of fishing was from the shore.

Of the 13 million anglers mentioned above, about 2 –3 million are considered striped bass fishermen and women.

By Region: Numbers-Pounds

For 2007, 19.1 million striped bass were caught in the saltwater Atlantic Region. This number was generated by <u>observation</u>, <u>reported</u> and <u>released</u> data: estimated error about 9 %.

In the North, Mid-Atlantic and South Atlantic Region (Maine to Florida), 153,000 individual striped bass were observed and reported caught from the shore (error about 20%). The boats accounted for 1,200,000 fish hence about 1 % were caught from the shore and 8 % from the boats. The data indicated about 17,900,000 were released alive. The release-catch ratio from the shore was 124:1; for boats it was 16:1. See Figure 1 that shows the number of striped bass observed and reported caught from the shore and boats. Obviously there were considerable errors in gathering the observation, reported and released data as highlighted by the catch release ratios.

In the same Atlantic Region- north-mid-south- 22.7 million pounds of striped bass were <u>observed and reported and some released</u>. Those observed and reported harvested were 1.7 million pounds from shore and 9.2 million pounds from boats.

See Figure 2 that shows by State the pounds of striped bass observed and reported by shore and boat.

2007

Number of Striped Bass Caught by States

M=million   K= thousand

	Conn.	Maine	Md.	Mass.	NJ	NY	NC	VA.	RI
Shore	2.4K	13K	19K	39K	43K	26K	2.3K	4.2K	6.4K
Boats	1.06M	0.06M	0.66M	0.31M	0.16M	0.35M	0.05M	0.24M	0.09M

Fig.1

Weight of Striped Bass Caught by State- Lbs.

M= million K=thousand

Shore	30K	60K	62K	515K	514K	410K	61K	37K	73K
Boats	1.68M	0.26M	3.12M	4.27M	1.93M	5.36M	0.13M	1.96M	1.34M

Fig.2

The average weight of striped bass <u>observed and reported</u> from *shore* and from all the above States was 11.1 pounds and from the *boats* it was 8.7 pounds.

The Marine Recreational Fisheries Statistical Survey agreed there are errors in their methodology.

License, Dollars, Etc.

The National Marine Fisheries Service estimate 13 million recreational saltwater anglers fished 127.7 million days in coastal states in 2006. They spent $5.8 billion on fishing trips plus $25.6 billion in fishing gear. The total value to the US economy was $82.3 billion in sales and created 534,000 jobs. Even with this information from US Government agencies, the theory that the US saltwater angler needs representation in Washington, D.C. in order to establish a "foot print" is false. They already know the contribution to the GNP. The call for a Federal Saltwater License is merely to force the balance of the states not having one to help fund the State's Fish and Game Departments hence direct previous allocated dollars to other programs. It's like a tax to release other tax monies. The states must forward to NOAA certain catch data as requested. Has Congress taken away *state's rights* in this matter?

Since information is critical to the effectiveness of the Fisheries Department in Washington, D.C., the saltwater registry will also be used as a basis to follow saltwater anglers' activities as they prepare the National Marine Fisheries Statistical Survey. Such information gathered from phone calls, mail questionnaires, fax queries and emails will hopefully contribute to more accurate data on the health of the striped bass species in the marine environment. *Almost all species of desirable fish are over harvested as best the feds can estimate.*

It is interesting to note that Florida, which has a saltwater license, estimated the data error date (PSE) for the common weakfish is around 50%. This is for observed and reported (harvested) weakfish (spotted sea trout) using saltwater license money. Other states have similar error rates. It seems the use of a saltwater license fees has not provided the management and reporting accuracy that was anticipated

According to the Saltwater Sportsman Magazine, Jan. 23, 2009, Jim Balsiger, NOAA acting Assistant Administrator for NOAA's Fisheries Service, " The Registry will help us gather comprehensive data to ensure sustainable fisheries built on the best available science." In 1998 they stated the need to establish a core set of data elements that must be collected for all fisheries by all partners for all commercial and recreational fisheries. The State of Florida, using in part its saltwater license dollars, seems to indicate there is plenty of inaccurate data gathered following their popular weakfish. If you can't track this common local fish, how much more dollars will it take to track their uncommon fish. If we ask too many questions we may find Federal agents patrolling each beach and each vessel or have a local fisherman act as a deputy along each beach. Yes there are cheaters fishing from the shore and at the tiller but thank God I have not met one. To have an army of spies to catch the 2% cheaters is a waste of license dollars. Most recreational fishermen and women fish for the sport and not for a living. It may have been different in the past although some states still allow the sale of striped bass to licensed dealers and by licensed recreational anglers with commercial paper.

Obviously states will probably require licenses for fishing the shoreline (0-3miles), if they don't the imposed Federal license fee will go to Washington. Even spear fishermen require a license. This is a requirement in order to provide NOAA, under the Magnuson-Stevens Fishery Conservation and

Management Act, sufficient information in order to end over fishing of all species. Those recreational anglers, who fish for striped bass inland of tidal waters (rivers, estuaries), need not register i.e.; freshwater state licenses control, otherwise fishing tidal waters for migrating fish requires registration.

New Jersey has declared it will be a "free" saltwater recreational fishing State as of 2010. No license, no fees. They claim "States rights."

Registration starts in January 2010, fees start in 2011. Fees about $15 to $ 25 per saltwater angler except those on party or charter boats. Minimum information the Feds want are; name, telephone number and date of birth. The only exemption will be i.e.; senior citizens, handicap, youth and others. If a state already has a saltwater license, 17 of 25 do, there is no additional federal saltwater license fee. The feds can get the names, telephone number and date of birth from the state. If the state does not issue a saltwater license fee, the feds will require a registration and fee and they will deposit the monies in the U.S. Treasury not in a saltwater conservation program. The state can offer a lower saltwater license fee than the Feds if they care to.

In summary, the whole idea of the federal program is to gather data from up to 16 million saltwater anglers and commercial fishing boats of the "catch." Obviously they will not contact 16 million anglers or thousands of commercial fishing boats. When they or their agents have your name, telephone number, etc, they have the ability to communicate with you about your "catch" or anything and everything else. Statistical analysis is a valid scientific tool used to analyze <u>a population</u> of a species by randomly query of a segment of that population. The <u>population</u> in this case is the <u>saltwater anglers</u>. The key to the whole statistical program is that *every angler randomly selected must be queried* and *their answers accounted for,* else the survey is theoretically invalid. Even if all of the answers of randomly selected anglers were collected and total count was correct, the best accuracy one might expect is at a confidence level of around 90 %.

If you get a call from NOAA or their agents, they will need to have you answer all their questions in order to make the survey valid. Managing the saltwater fish stock or biomass successfully with this scientific information may prevent over fishing of the species providing the data collected is truthful. That's the math.

The Federal Government employs NOAA and the Commerce Department under Billing Code 3510-22-5, Docket   071001548-81392-02 to acquire information from the recreational anglers because, they claim not to know their "catch" yet they published the following:

In 2006 the recreational anglers caught this percentage of the following species:

Striped Bass	82%
Bluefish	71%
Fluke	46%
Dolphin	94%
Atlantic Croaker	32%
King Mackerel	57%
Sheephead	82%
Black Drum	49%
Spanish Mackerel	43%
Tautog	92%
Red Snapper	42%
Scup	24%

plus others.

There are some clever ways to come up with these figures if you don't know the answer to the question, " how much do the recreational anglers catch." Why not just say we really don't know the total catch and the license fees will help pay to obtain the data. In the November issue of the National Fisherman Journal (focus on commercial fishing) Jim Balsiger of NOAA, said that 10 years ago 98 species were thought to be over- fished. Last year it was reduced to 46 species over- fished. Further more 75% of the 230 important commercial stocks were not over- fished. Finally in the most important statement, he said, NOAA's plan to manage over 531 species of fish. You think you have a management headache when an army of commercial and recreation anglers are upset just when he said ¾ of the <u>money</u> fish stock is sufficiently managed and now you want to manage the whole 531 species. Just fix the problem with the over- fished species and leave the rest alone else you will bankrupt the NOAA budget on managing the "who cares" fish. This may be a moot point if NOAA is in the "empire building mode."

The fees, now collected by the states that already have a saltwater license fee, for years have previously designated this money to certain programs within the state. Now having to comply with NOAA for recreational "catch" data clearly means additional expenses to the state. States without a license fee will probably require one and use some of the fee to gather the information requested by NOAA.

Economics plus:

As a summary of the US fishing industry, NOAA states in their "Fish News", 2009 Economic Report, that $185 billion in sales was generated by the commercial and recreational fishermen who had these two (2) million jobs: Commercial accounted for $103 billion in sales, $ 44 billion in income and 1.5 million jobs. Recreational generated $ 82 billion in sales, $24 billion in income and 534 thousand jobs.

Prices: With the recent indication that the striped bass have toxins in them, the price per pound at the Boston docks has dropped from $4.00 in September of '08 to $2.00 in July '09. Contrary to this fact was the wholesale sellers at the dock said it's a supply-demand function not about toxins. Too little supply at the dock leads to higher prices and visa versa. Everyday at the docks is different. This particular day the porgies brought higher prices than the bass. In any case you could expect the bass to sell about $10.00 per pound in the retail fish markets.

Hybrid striped bass, farm raised, sold for around $2.50 to $2.85 per pound in Kentucky and $3.05 in Maryland, in July '09.

By the Numbers:

The Atlantic States Marine Fisheries Committee estimates that 76 percent of the striped bass caught by the recreational anglers were in the 4 to 8 year age group or 6 to 10 pounds each. The other 24 percent were heavier in 2007.

From the same 2007 data the weight of striped bass caught from the shore in the North Atlantic to Mid-Atlantic Region was 1,733,000 pounds with an estimated error of around 25%. The charter-private-party boat catch was about 9,211,000 pounds with an estimated error around 12%. The data for this catch was from observed and by various communication methods.

For 2007 the shore catch in number was 15% of the total and the charter-private-party boat it was 85%. The shore catch in weight was 18% of the total and the charter-private-part boat 82%. The data for this information was from observed and by various communication methods

Digging deeper into the data, it was estimated that the shore angler released about 1,752,000 fish in 2007 while having kept 153,000 fish. A release –keep ratio of more than 11:1. The charter-private –party boat released about 18,000,000 fish while having kept 1,055,000 fish. A release-keep ratio of 18:1. This applies for the same Regions above.

Keep in mind that all of this data is subjected to errors based on incomplete and inaccurate data. The Marine Recreational Fisheries Statistics Survey calls it, PSE (proportional standard error). It expresses; "The standard error of an estimate as a percentage of the estimate and is a measurement of precision."

12
Striped Bass Math and More

The first book highlighted the quantity of striped bass fishermen along with the quality of their catch. What may have changed is that the figure of two (2) million anglers fishing for the bass may be off by one (1) million. Some insiders says it's three (3) million men and women fishing for this species with rod and reel. No one can say with certainty the exact number but if you attended the numerous "Surf Days, Flea Markets, Plug Day, Surf Seminars, etc." during the late winter and early spring, surely there's both quantity and quality of anglers in attendance. Highly experienced fishermen freely give advice in all aspects of fishing from the shoreline to inland bogs. The boater's seminars tend to focus on the big game opportunities in the 3-to75 mile area offshore.

Both the novice retirees and novice youngsters want to hear from that fishing guru who doesn't spend too much time behind a desk. The questions are focused on each one's particular situation and the answers proclaimed to the satisfaction of the whole group.

The speakers, based on their years of extensive and successful experience, give excellent advice about equipment generally regardless of commercial commitments. Standing room only is often due to the anticipation of the talk by well-known authorities. With a keen ear and a focused eye you will hear and see improvements in the art of striped bass fishing; don't just do a walk through like I see too many do. They think they have seen it all but there is always something interesting and different which may help you be as successful as others in attendance. Can you imagine how many total years of fishing for the striped bass are housed in one of these events? Don't leave for home without some of this knowledge.

Two (2) to three (3) million striped bass fishermen and women fish the surf, jetties, groins and by boat. They average 8 trips per year and probably a few 60+ pound striped bass were caught each year. Assuming that very few more were caught but not weighed anywhere (keeping fishing secrets), we still can have a rough idea on the odds of catching such a trophy bass.

If only one (1) striped bass is caught per year and two (2) million anglers make eight (8) trips per year, that means that one (1) 60 pound bass was caught after 16 million attempts.

Double the trips per year and you have 32 million to 1 chance. Half the number of trips and you are still at the blue-sky number of 8 million to 1. It is quite possible that none may be caught that year or likewise more than one may be caught. In any case, catching a 60+ pound striped bass is a very rare event as indicated by these figures.

In December 2007 to January 2008 an event of gigantic proportions occurred out of Virginia Beach, VA. More than 10 striped bass over 60 pounds were caught during their annual striped bass tournament. All were caught by boat and many used eels as bait; by using a bobber to hang the eel. The 1880s may hold antidotal stories about big bass but nowhere can I find written where so many big bass were ever caught in such a short time. Not in a decade, not in a year, not in a tournament. This may go down as an historical event in the history of striped bass rod and reel fishing. To date, January 20, 2009 no bass of 60 pounds has been registered in the tournament. Read more about this event in other areas of the book.

It is estimated that about 50 striped bass weighing 50 to 59 pounds are caught each year. About 10 to 15 % are caught from the surf while the remainder were caught from a boat. Each season you can expect five to seven bass in the 50-pound range by surf fishermen and 35 to 40 from a boat. Whether by surf or boat you are looking at 1 chance out of 300,000 even for a 50-pound bass.

The striped bass **is not** among the top 5 saltwater sporting fish caught in numbers but ranks number 1 in pounds at 29.8 million pounds in 2008. Spotted trout is rated number 1 in numbers caught followed by croaker, spot, bluefish, and mackerel. It is interesting that the number one species ranked in quantity and value is the Pollock followed by the Menhaden.

The 60 pound and 70 pound class reigns by itself. There is no season for these fish whether in the surf or from a boat. It is a lifetime goal to catch one of these big bass. A very, very few anglers have caught more than one. Their names are known by a limited number of close friends in the same fraternity. Their favorite fishing grounds cannot be found on any map. Ask them for a GPS location and you'll be fishing off the coast of China or in the craters of the moon or coded names that have no meaning except for the members of the fraternity. This is truly an exclusive club. You can't buy your way into the club, you can't talk your way into the club, and you can only earn your way into the club.

Do you know of any? If you do, lucky you.

If a world record striped bass is caught sometime in the future, it will probably be a fisherman or woman **from a boat**. The historical data supports it but..........

PS: I have uncovered several stories that if the big, big bass were weighed soon after the catch, it would have broken Al Mc Reynolds World Record Striped Bass at 78 lbs. 8 oz.

Don't make the same mistake. I will hear your faint wailings, decades later.

13

Striped Bass Controversy
and Problems and More

Many fishing groups throughout the Northeast region are actively concerned about the condition of the striped bass especially in New Jersey where there is no commercial fishing for striped bass and the bass cannot be sold by recreational anglers.

New Jersey Coast Anglers Association, Toms River, NJ, is an association of 75 saltwater fishing clubs. They protect the right of fishermen while concerned with the quality of the saltwater environment. They work with other saltwater fishing clubs along the East Coast and may be considered one of the effective organizations of its kind.

Other clubs that do a similar service in each coastal state are: Rhode Island Saltwater Anglers Association (RISAA), Peninsula Salt Water Sport Fisherman's Association, Newport News, VA, Stripers Forever, South Portland, Maine, Massachusetts Striped Bass Association, Montauk Surfcasters Association, N.Y., NC Saltwater Fishing Club, North Carolina, The Asbury Park Fishing Club, Asbury Park, N.J. (oldest club, founded 1888.), Connecticut Surfcasters Association and there are also others.

Stripers Forever has a project underway to target the striped bass as a national game fish.

New Jersey in 2010 declared itself a free recreational saltwater fishing state in order to counter NOAA's request to require a saltwater license for the recreational anglers otherwise NOAA would impose the fee. This fee would not go to NOAA but to the federal national budget. New Jersey believes zero to 3 miles is state waters hence "state rights" rein supreme.

A previous Governor of New Jersey signed a bill to make the striped bass a game fish. There is no commercial fishing for striped bass in New Jersey waters. They continue to pursue this effort at the federal level for inshore and ocean fishing including   0 to 3 miles. In a similar fashion they have laws concerning the harvesting of menhaden, the most important food for the striped bass.

The Atlantic States Marine Fisheries Commission (ASMFC) is responsible for the determination of the overall health of the population of saltwater fish, including the striped bass along the Atlantic coast. Their technical committees make this determination.

The Atlantic Striped Bass Technical Committee is represented by the following States: NJ, CT, NC, NH, MD, DE, NY, RI, PA, MA, ME.

In 1984 the striped bass was a focus of the ASMFC (Atlantic States Marine Fisheries Commission) and the Atlantic Striped Bass Conservation Act was passed. The striped bass was highly managed for the next 11 years and was declared, "fully recovered" in 1995.

Statistical Analysis is the foundation on which technical then practical decisions are made for most all endangered fish whether for recreational or commercial activity. It is not practical to try to know everything about the entire population of a species. If a random sample is taken from a group that can be considered homogeneous in its distribution, a high degree of confidence can be given to the data when it represents the entire population. This method is used for all kinds of estimates where one cannot gather data from each and every member of the population i.e.; estimate winners and losers of elections, preferences and attributes of classes of people, weather forecasts, drug interactions in human beings, risk/reward in investments etc.

Recently it has been evident that the Atlantic population of striped bass is in deep trouble again, greater than in 1984 when Congress passed the Atlantic Striped Bass Conservation Act. At government managing levels it can take more than five years of scientific data for them to decide on a plan of action in order to save any species as they did for cod, haddock, marlin, swordfish, snapper, snook redfish weakfish, fluke etc. Until a crash of the species is indisputable, the ASMFC will wait. Their record indicates they like to skate on thin ice, very thin ice. *Managing for protein on the dock seems to be their charter.*

The 2008 statistics for recreational striper catch may question the goal of the ASMFC charter. Atlantic coast-wide anglers landed (killed or released) 14,107, 835 fish; the worst year since 2000- Maine down about 50%, New Hampshire down about 11%, Massachusetts down about 40%, Virginia down about 53% and North Carolina down about 21%.

The stock assessment of the striped bass is based on the landings by the recreational anglers not commercial fishing. One can say the data is biased because it can easily be explained that the fish were somewhere else hence the decline of harvested stripers by the recreational angler. This can be observed by noting the reduced catch along much of Atlantic coastal states. There are figures to prove this case and none to prove where the fish may have gone. In addition, each year the U.S. Fish and Wildlife Service work with the winter trawlers to catch striped bass and tag them. Since 1990 the best catch was 6,275 fish in 2000. The worst was 147 in 2009. The average for 1987 to 2008 was 2,212 but only 516 in the last six years.

Even with the 109,020 metric ton catch of menhaden in the Chesapeake Bay, the striped bass are starving. Malnourished bass are common in the Bay that produces 75% of the coastal population. The Omega Protein Company, the prime enterprise Company in the Bay, can only catch an average of 70% of their quota using their spotter planes and fleet of naval ships. Tough! Tagged and captured fish in the spring spawning grounds in Maryland and Virginia indicate that by autumn they are indistinguishable from fish starved in the lab for two months. This is a stress- related problem with mycobacterium, which affects about 60% of the Bay's striped bass. This bacteria is now associated with humans who handle affected fish, now known as fish handlers disease; swollen lymph-nodes, joint stiffness and bacterial infection. This could be an excuse to do something about the problem and benefit both man and fish.

Some experienced striper guides from Maine to North Carolina are in concert when they claim striped bass fishing is in dramatic decline due to poor numbers of fish in every year class. The ASMFC cannot dispute that the biomass and year-class distribution have been declining for the past five years. Crash levels of the species may not have been reached for the striped bass but the ASMFC is known for slow response in other species while looking for the "**crash level.**" Their system allows for fishing the biomass down. It is difficult to manage from behind an executive walnut desk, hand-weaved oriental floor rugs, oak paneled walls in Washington, D.C. The answers lie in the coastal waters; zero to three (3) miles out and beyond. Be there, work there and find the truth there.

Small errors in mathematical estimates of allowable biomass reduction can lead to big surprises after several years of accumulated errors. Currently a reduction of 27% of the population is considered safe. If the difference between safe bass extraction and crash levels is small, you cannot afford to make continuous small errors each year. Another mandatory moratorium is waiting. Playing around with estimates is part of the fisheries business but playing around with the livelihood of people who run the bait and tackle shops, marine boat and repair shops, guide services, sports retail centers, manufacturers of all kinds of fishing products from hooks to trawlers, catalogue mail centers, etc. is not allowed as you roll the dice looking for winning 7-11 numbers.

Monitoring all the recreational and commercial harvest may concur with the mathematical model but the illegal kill of striped bass is a guess at best. Physical evidence consists of thousand of pounds of illegal bass from Massachusetts, Rhode Island, New York, Delaware, Maryland, Virginia and North Carolina. With about 3,000 square miles of eastern coastal water from Maine to N. Carolina to patrol, catching striped bass harvested illegally in the daytime or night time consist of odds of astronomical proportions. The state's coastal area to patrol from Maine to North Carolina is about 2700 square miles. Trying to roll a 7 or an 11 is much better, day or night, full or quartering moon, good or bad weather, and much better if done indoors. But in February 2009 a five- year undercover sting operation caught a gang that sold 600,000 striped bass from illegal poaching in the Chesapeake Bay and the Potomac River. The fish were sold to wholesalers who conspired with the gang.

Massachusetts charges $65 to obtain a license to catch and sell striped bass at 34 inches minimum. The commercial striper season is a charade where the recreational angler buying a $65 commercial license can sell up to 30 fish per day at the minimum length. These semi-commercial recreational anglers have been referred to as "recremerical" fishermen. While the "recremerical" fishermen in 2008 landed 1,157,814 pounds of stripers (104.5% of the quota) but the 3,599, who purchased the licenses, only 1,207 reported at least one fish caught. The remaining 2,392, who may have also been fishing and catching up to 30 bass per day, may not have reported their catch. Massachusetts, the honor State, expects their licensees to use the honor system. If there is no report hence no income hence no State tax and no Federal tax. Rhode Island allows only 5 fish per day. This is all legal and has been going on for many years. You will find the very best bass fishermen in this group.

The idea of making the striped bass a game fish is not a new concept and already is in six (6) states under ASMFC management. Catchers and sellers in Massachusetts say it is a bad idea.

It has been estimated that 20% of the global fish catch was IUU; illegal, unreported or unregulated in 2002. More than 1200 industrial vessels fly FOC or Flags of Convenience and more than 1400 large –scale fishing vessels operate under unknown flags. This may lead to the estimate that 1/3 of all seafood in the US is mislabeled and the US imports over 80 % of its seafood. The species of the fish can be identified within 24 hours by testing its DNA at a cost of only $24. This is very important if the wholesaler ordered a million pounds of a particular fish. Under the US Food and Drug Administration only   **0.59%** of the imported seafood is tested. Because the competition for seafood worldwide has caused over-fishing for several species by one of the most effective fishing techniques "**long lining**" (catching anything that swims), USDA requested a reduction from 500 vessels to about 100. These vessels put out around 25 to 100 miles of lines with baited hooks at various depths hoping to attract only tuna and swordfish. A recent worldwide study has concluded that 63% of the fish species that are harvested are below what is considered "abundant" levels. Recently the BBC broadcast noted that the worldwide fishing fleet is 2 ½ times bigger than what is needed to catch a sustainable amount of fish but it's difficult to tie up the Bearing Sea fishing boats when the average wage is $700 per day.

A ground-fish trawler seining for herring, bunker, flounder, or other bait or fish considered table-fare might not have a license to catch striped bass. If the striped bass gets caught in their nets they will be discarded less a fine is imposed if brought to the dock. Striped bass feed on mostly any baitfish and "table fare" fish hence are part of the commercial haul aimed not at them but their food supply. Some estimates put this at 300,000 pounds per year of striped bass hauled in with a mortality rate of 100%. At 10 pounds each you have 30,000 bass and at 20 pounds each you have 15,000 bass discarded.

Presently the 3 to 200 mile off shore –no fishing zone for striped bass- also known as the EEZ zone in all states- protect the striped bass from the commercial fleets as well as recreational anglers. There is pressure by the commercial fishing industry to open up this area. If done, large spawning females will be legal to catch, to the detriment to all parties now and in the future.

You can check on the status of this proposal as well as others at www. asmfc.org (Atlantic States Marine Fisheries Commission) website.

The UN has drawn up a comprehensive law of the seas: Coastal countries have territorial waters up to **12 miles** from land, which they have total control, except for the right of innocent passage. The next **12 miles up to 24 miles** they have fewer rights but control of customs, immigration and taxation. Up to **200 miles** they have an economic zone (EEZ) with control over various maritime activities and the right to exploit natural resources under the seabed, on it and in it.

Saltwater License:

The PEW Oceans Commission and the US Commission on Ocean Policy have made similar recommendations to improve marine resource management. They both recommend selling licenses to recreational fishermen. **Congress has already developed a comprehensive ocean management bill.**

Comprehensive means "nearly all inclusive." That means control of all fish and fisheries at the federal level if Congress passes such legislation. If we cannot fix our problems ourselves, the feds will do it for us.

Today 14 of the 23 coastal states have some kind of recreational saltwater license fee to fish their waters. These recreational licenses may have to be modified or eliminated if a federal bill is passed. Data collection claims to be the main theme for a federal license. Anglers want to know who will benefit from the gathering of the data. Will it be the federal and state bureaucracies, commercial fishing industry (who now already pays for permits in each state) or the weekend angler? The license fees from the weekend anglers may add additional dollars to the federal and state pockets. They look for a benefit.

Without coordination between states to make their regulations nearly identical, the fate of these migratory fish will wind up being decided in Washington where influence depends less on data that on dollars.

The state license fees are to be used to gather data hence support the recreational angler's influence in Washington, DC but Government license fees have a tendency to find various pockets for other activities once they find their way to Washington.

Effective 1 January 2010 all saltwater anglers fishing in federal waters (3 miles to 200 miles) or fishing for fish, which migrate to inland waters, must register. The federal program will exempt anglers from federal registration if their state has license/ registration programs that satisfy the feds. Interesting, some states charge for parking at or near the beach which adds to the city's coffers, charge to access the beach in order to pay for beach clean up, lifeguards, rescue equipment, during the Fall, charge to drive on the same beach with your 4 x 4 and likely more fees if you transit another beach. This 4 x 4 fee I guess is to cover the tire tracks in case the ocean fails to do the same. Now the Feds want their share of this taxable activity by selling licenses. The licenses fees are intended to give the saltwater sportsmen a "presence" in Washington, DC.

Fresh water fishing licenses have been a benefit to the fresh water fishermen but they are state regulated and state collected. States perform data collection, water management as well as restocking from their hatcheries, mostly trout. Would water management and hatchery stock be a part of the salt-water license fee? Probably not since the charter is to collect data. It would be less expensive to hire a non –federal, non-political organization to collect the data. Transparency of cost would be clearer. Competing companies could give the better 'bang for the buck.' The spending of the fees would have a clearer trail to follow because in their quotes there will be a cost associated with each data gathering function. There will not be the goal "to spend until we get enough data." In statistics the highest confidence can be placed when 100 % of the population is surveyed. No one can afford to gather 100 % of the data, thereby getting to that 100 % confidence level where the data suggests what action to take. Statistics is an estimate that the sample data taken represents the total population at some confidence level, usually 90%. There is that 10 % we can worry about or spend more dollars to get to that magic 100% confidence level. Even as we approach the 100 % level there are statistical errors that cannot be avoided.

In Florida their saltwater license fees are distributed as follows: Less than 10 % for administration and the balance roughly divided evenly between research/management, fish enhancement and law enforcement. They collected $17 million in fees and permits in 2005. The number of licenses alone amounted to a little more than 1 million, which did not include special permits fees for other sport fish as snook, etc.

If 3 million East Coast striped bass fishermen (est.) have to buy a federal fishing license at $15.00 each (as Florida), they would contribute $45 million. With nearly 7 million saltwater fishermen on the East Coast, the total license fees would amount to $105 million. This means the striped bass fishermen, devoted to only fishing for striped bass, would account for nearly 30% of the total fees collected. Will 30% of the fees be directed to solve the striped bass problem? When solved will the 30 % be available to improve the striped bass situation? Who will monitor the changes in the problem and situation? There are many details for a just solution that must be addressed before the federal; state, commercial and recreational participants can feel their interest have been successfully addressed.

It seems like this idea of a federal saltwater license was generated mainly because of the striped bass question, especially in the northeastern States where they are heavily fished. I didn't hear much about a heightened battle between commercial and recreational forums for a license for blackfish, weakfish, flounder, porgy, cod, ling etc. Battles, yes but not to the point where a federal license would help solve the problem yet it is generally understood that the world faces serious consequences if the entire ocean eco system is not addressed. Many species are in trouble as countries greedily fish to satisfy themselves regardless of the biomass of reproductive fish to sustain reproduction.

What it probably amounts to is economics. What do the commercial fisheries contribute to state coffers and the national GDP (Gross Domestic Product); likewise for the recreational fishermen? Will license fees improve these figures so often estimated by the experts on both sides, especially for the recreational fishermen? Will the statistical data be skewed to favor one side or the other? *Do we have a GDP contest pending?*

It is a zero sum game. Whatever side loses some of its rights, the other side will pick up. Will the Government have the nerve to reduce commercial fishing for any or all species if the data indicates it is necessary? Jobs will be lost, boats idle or sold, equipment auctioned.

If the recreational angler has his catch reduced will this discourage his efforts to pursue his pastime? Tackle shops will be closed, party boats idle or sold, equipment stored, vacations spent on sand with family instead of on boats or jetties.

Like Florida, it is likely each state will have the opportunity to add permit fees for species of fish they deem needs further management. The striped bass is right on top of the list with 2-3 million anglers along the East Coast.

In Rhode Island, which just passed a saltwater license program, based on one proposed on 1 Jan 2010, it is interesting to summarize their understanding of the aim of the Federal program- Magnuson-Stevenson Fishery Conservation and Management Act.

A state-based licensing program will provide Rhode Island recreational fishermen, residence and non-resident, an opportunity to support and contribute more accurate state-based fishing resource assessments and effective management programs to optimize benefits and other opportunities for Rhode Island fishermen. Sounds impressive. The cost to the angler is $7.00 for residents and $10.00 for non -residents. No cost for residents if 65 or older, same for under16 years old, permanently disabled, on- leave from active military service and passengers on a party boat (boat has a all inclusive license) or fishing under a valid commercial license.

License issuance will be by authorized agents who will keep a part of the license fee as a commission. These agents will be required to develop a web –based application, collect fees and transmit it to others. All fees, less commissions, are to be deposited in the general treasury and appropriated to the department of environmental management. Its use will be for the administration, enforcement and managing Rhode Island marine recreational fisheries.

It appears that the essence of the program i.e.; gathering data on the fish caught, is not the state's prime responsibility. The state-based stock assessment will be left to the Government who claims to need this data. Aside for one or two public meetings of fishermen and state management, the exchange of information is limited and catch data is probably voluntary. There is lots of room for the count data to be skewed.

It looks like a program with questions except for the catch of the party boat anglers. I guess we may have a federal agent at the dock to count your fish by species and by numbers or have the party boat captain swear on a Bible before he released the count numbers. Counting fish caught, released and by species may be a difficult task from the bridge by the captain and the deck mate. A pin board could be mounted on the boat where one would have to stick a pin in the appropriate line each time the anglers caught or released a fish. Also we may need a beach patrol with - four wheel " Sand Rovers" to check the surf fisherman's catch and release. Of course, surf fishing allowed only when the "Sand Rovers" are active. *Can you believe this is possible?*

The Lord Gives and the Government Takes

NOAA is thinking of evaluating the usefulness of "**catch shares**" for the recreational anglers. This concept may be similar to commercial fishing that is based on days to fish in a season, sizes of fish and a quota. The recreational anglers could be subjected to number of anglers allowed to fish for a species in a season or share with others for part of a season, part of a catch and divide a time slot.

Since the recreational anglers catch is harder to estimate because of the quantity of anglers fishing for a great variety of fish, the amount of biomass permitted to be harvested is always a statistical computation based on unconfirmed data. The commercial catch due to a known amount of fishing vessels and fees and permits offer NOAA some comfort in their estimates, less poachers, by-catch, illegally fished areas and others.

If such a "catch share" program is used in the recreational fishing business, then time slots to trade or sell, days to fish to trade and sell, quota by species to trade and sell by 13,000,000 plus saltwater anglers nationwide becomes a viable option. A new business has sprung up. Can you imagine the government staff and equipment required to monitor, control and enforce the program on 13,000,000 plus saltwater anglers with multi species quotas, size limits and time slots. Insane except for the fact we now create a new government agency with more powers that need more tax dollars. Does any one believe these anglers are going to report the catch and placate the system they feel is taking their God given fishing rights away? The requirement to register in 2010 all the states saltwater anglers seems to bring into question other possible plans. Some one with a master's degree in chess has thought this a few moves ahead. This is only step one of many more.

Along with NOAA the Environmental Defense Fund and the Pew Environment Group apparently aim to make the national fisheries' *natural free gift*, a commonly held resource that can be a negotiated commodity with the dispenser in Washington, DC. It smells fishy and sounds like a socialistic system where the government owns everything and issues rights to the citizens to use the commodity. The concept is not new. Ten years ago NOAA introduced a similar system in order to limit the recreational participation by a method similar to the commercial fishing fleet. Today, Jane Lubchenco, head of NOAA, leads the effort to impose such a system on the recreational anglers. Her background is steeped in environmental issues. Congress, without much discussion, has by defacto made this a national policy.

The Chesapeake Bay

The present state of the striped bass from our most important hatchery, the Chesapeake Bay, is an interesting story. See: www.drn.state.md.us or www. asmfe.org.

Spawning success in late 2005 was high and well above the 52 year average and the mortality rate was below a set threshold value. Along with good news, the basic stock of the Chesapeake Bay fish remained at 65.3 million pounds some 10% higher than the average for the past 5 years. Along with this statistical good news we found out that up to 70 % of the Striped Bass in the Chesapeake Bay estuary have lesions caused by mycobacteriosis . It is fatal to a small percentage of native fish, more so with younger fish. Scientists at the Virginia Institute of Marine Science said they conclusively link mycobacteriosis to the death of rockfish. Although the disease was first detected among the Chesapeake rockfish in 1977, its virulence was not immediately apparent because the fish weren't dying in large numbers. The technical study was printed in the October 2008 issue of Ecological Applications and credited to Virginia Institute of Marine Science, Coastal Carolina University and the U.S. Geological Survey's National Wildlife Center.

Mycobacteriosis eats away at the fish's scales, scarring its streamline body. The disease is usually harmless to humans providing they wash their hands after handling the fish. These fish are safe to eat if thoroughly cooked.

It is not clear how the disease spreads or why it has increased sharply in recent years but historically it has been found in farmed fish. It is a "stress related" bacterial infection that may be caused by a low oxygen environment and a low food supply. It is not usually found in wild populations of ocean roaming fish.

The striped bass main food supply is the menhaden or better known by the surf and boat jockey as "bunker." These bunker tend to clean up waters where they swim by eating microscopic pant and food matter by filtering through their system 2 million gallons of water per year per fish. Without them vegetation matter in the bays and similar waters will be deprived of oxygen due to the explosive growth of algae. They are our ocean's environmentalists.

If the Feds do get their saltwater license dollars in order to gather data, which in turn will lead to better management of the saltwater species, maybe it would be wise to gather scientific data on the food supply for these fish. Up the license fee too, of course.

In the Chesapeake Bay area you will find Omega Protein with its 11 battleship- like fleet, 140 to 200 feet long being directed by the Company's 7 spotter planes seeking the menhaden. With a two- boat spread and their 1800-foot long seine nets, they can make quite a haul of the menhaden and whatever else gets in the way. If the striped bass are feeding on the menhaden, too bad, they will be also in the catch. What happens if they have to be thrown back or discarded due to a lack of proper permits by the netters, or the striped bass season is closed or the fish are too short or the quota has already been filled? It is left up to the reader to decide. According to the IGFA this by-catch per year amounts to over 2 billion pounds of other fish not intended to be caught. The Gulf of Mexico's shrimpers account for 4.5 pounds of by-catch for each pound of shrimp caught. The northeast multi-species ground fishing boats account for 1.7 pounds of by-catch for each pound of desired fish. It's like throwing 1.7 pounds of bait out to catch a one-pound fish. It should be at least the other way around.

The Omega Protein 17 million dollar new menhaden oil refining plant in the Chesapeake Bay area should or may have already been completed at this time. It will be able to process 100 metric tons of fish per day, which is 3 times the present capacity. They also have a fishing site in Houston, Texas and a processing plant in Louisiana.

Omega Protein is a 100 to 200 million-dollar business production with 40,000 tons of meal and 20,000 tons of oil per year. With the State of Maryland banning the seining of menhaden about 50 years ago, the Omega Protein boats and planes hover around the Virginia part of the Chesapeake Bay region for their catch. This catch amounted to 488 millions pounds in 2001 and 375 million pounds in 2003. In 2005 the whole Atlantic region gave up about 294 million pounds of which the Omega Protein catch was approximately 196 million pounds. The volume has been going down. I wonder why?

The Company still has the option to seek the menhaden from other northern coastal states although they spend most of their netting operations in the Virginia waters. They will seek further fertile waters but when? Some Eastern coastal states have already banned the commercial catch of menhaden.

The owner of Omega Protein is Zapata Oil owned by Palm Beach's Malcolm Glazer, son of Aviam Glazer, Chairman of Omega Protein and Zapata Oil. He also owns The Tampa Bay Buccaneers football team and has tried to buy Harley Davidson. L. A. Dodgers, Contrail and the British soccer team Manchester United. The $32,000 political contributions they have made in Virginia have probably not hurt their business. He sold the Omega Protein Company in 2006 for $76,000,000.

As recently as February 25, 2006 the Menhaden Board of the Atlantic States Marine Fisheries Committee put a cap of approximately 243 million pounds for the 2005-6 menhaden-netting season. The Company is trying to raise the quota. There is trouble in Seine City.

If Omega Protein produces 40,000 tons of meal and 20,000 tons of oil from about 175,000 tons of menhaden what, happened to the approximately 115,000 tons of waste?

Where has all the 'waste' gone? Is the waste the by-catch?

The commercial news in the "National Fisherman Journal" estimates that in 2002 the Chesapeake Bay produced 500 millions pounds of seafood. With the menhaden catch of around 250 million pounds, you can realize the significance of this catch. In the background lurks the soybean crop, which can provide as much protein as needed without the environmental, political and striped bass problems currently in Washington, DC and in each Eastern Coastal States. Protein is protein and apparently less of a headache if it comes from the ground than the sea, or bay in this case.

If it were not for the omega 3 oil that is used as an essential "good fat" in our foods, the menhaden crop would become a soybean crop. The processing of soybean into a protein source looks less expensive than a 10-ship navy with scout planes plus a multi million-dollar process plant. Unfortunately you cannot separate the oil from the fish without having the fish and there are no menhaden fish farms around here.

There is a more efficient omega –3 sources in development. It is made from the algae that the menhaden as well as other fish eat. Markek, a biotech Company, has developed a variety of algae stains rich in the benefits like the omega –3 oils. Interesting dilemma. If you take the menhaden food away; you take the menhaden away. Take the striped bass food away and you take the bass away. Take the bass away then close up the commercial and recreational business including tackle shops, boats, fishing equipment etc and then produce clog bays, rivers and oceans full of algae waiting to be harvested for its omega-3. It appears to be a zero sum game. What one loses, the others gains.

Looking at the saltwater fishing regulations-recreational and commercial, enforced in the East Coast States, indicates diversity, much diversity. Size, quantity, length of season, number of hours fishing per day, fishing days per week, number of nets, kind of nets, quotas for commercial harvesting, etc. The striped bass best decision would be to choose carefully the places where it wants to work for food and where it needs to vacate.

Here is the catch for 2008 in pounds and dollars of the leading ports in the US. Notice Virginia where much of the catch must have been menhaden.

Million of Pounds *		Million of Dollars *	
Dutch Harbor, Alaska	612	New Bedford, MA.	241
Intracostal City, LA.	254	Dutch Harbor, Alaska	195
Reedville, VA.	345	Kodiak, Alaska	99
Kodiak, Alaska	251	Hampton Roads, VA.	72
Empire-Venice, LA.	353	Cape May-Wildwood, NJ	74
Cameron, LA.	172	Honolulu	73
Pascagoula-Moss Pt., MS.	216	Empire- Venice, LA.	63
New Bedford, MA.	146	Naknek-K Salmon, Alaska	65
Los Angeles, CA.	124	Gloucester MA.	54
Gloucester, MA.	120	Cordova, Alaska	50

From the 'National Fisherman Journal' * 8/09

US overall landings worth $4.4 billion in 2009.

I would not anticipate much help from the costal states during their seasonal journeys. With regulations that serve the states' narrow vision, it seems unlikely federal license monies from a Federal saltwater license as well as additional monies from the state permit fees per species to effectively resolve the migratory striped bass problems. What is left is a "Sport Fish" classification if the states cannot themselves resolve the striped bass problems and its food supply. Washington is already involved heavily in the management of most all other saltwater "desirable" fish.

An international team of researches reported in the Journal of Science that more than 40 percent of the world's oceans have been degraded. The impact varies from place to place and includes water quality, disappearance in species, dying coral and receding mangroves. Fifty years ago man couldn't get to many ocean areas but today from the surface to miles below, man has a presence. His presence has been harmful in many areas. From the University of Canada we have a report that suggests that the global oceans have lost more than 90 % of large predatory fish as cod, grouper, salmon, and tuna. Hence the world produced 48 billion tons of farmed fish in 2005 worth 71 billion dollars with China having 70% of the total.

With the relentless harvest of large sharks, rays, skates and cow nose rays, smaller sharks are growing at a rate of 8 % per year along the East Coast. These rays devastate the scallops, oyster and clam population along the coastline providing less food for other game fish such as the Striped Bass.

NOAA (National Oceanographic Atmospheric Association) has identified **531 species of fish** for management. Currently less than 200 species are covered by 48 active fisheries management plans. NOAA will write new guidelines for all of the above. An ACL (Annual Catch Limit) will be in effect by 2011 for the 11 fisheries where over- fishing has occurred per James W. Balsiger of the NMF. Management, management and over management means more dollars are necessary to manage the management. Licenses, permits etc….. Have we brought this upon ourselves?

Even if a "sport fish," classification is attained; the management of their food supply must be addressed. If more striped bass will swim the costal waters after the commercial nets and rods are removed, what will this increased population eat? Bread and water?

14
Tools of the Trade

Rod, reel, line are not the weapons, they are tools used to launch weapons. Recreational anglers use nearly an infinite variety of man- made and natural products, all attached to rod, reel and line, to launch their weapons. While recreational fishing is concerned with the tools of the trade, the commercial fishing industry can choose their vessels, planes, nets and lines from improved electronics and mechanical products with assistance from satellites. It is a new set of tools of the trade with different weapons.

Claudius Aelianus, a Roman who lived during the third century A.D., wrote about fly-fishing for trout and other kinds of sport fish. He made lures of feathers, lead, bronze, wild boar's bristles, and horsehair. His fishing line was made of twisted flax. There is no written evidence of much improvement until in 1653, when Izaak Walton wrote his famous fishing book, " The Compleat Angler." He discussed fishing line, hooks, flies and the appropriate attitude required for the sport.

By the 1830s in England and the US the making of fishing tackle changed from the monopoly of individual craftsmen to commercial manufacturing of fishing products. Early in the 1900s Heddon and Pflueger developed the business of making lures for the fishermen but rods and reels were handmade by jewelers and watchmakers. In the late 1870s these technical products were commercially available. After WWII braided nylon and monofilament fishing line were the successors to cotton, twine and silk. The combination of commercially available fishing products and leisure time after a 40-hour week of work caused the recreational fishing industry to take off.

The manufacturers of lures were not in the hook, wire ring, plastic, forestry and metal business, hence most them bought the necessary components and produced the final product. As competition in the US increased work moved off- shore to Central America, Southeast Asia, Taiwan, Haiti and Mexico for components as well as the final product.

As fishing tackle improved over the years, new problems arose with these improvements. Pound for pound braided fishing line was claimed to be 100 times stronger than steel. Power Pro fishing line is waxed coated; others as Calcutta and Tufline have a coating around them, which offer some abrasion resistance in order to help with tying knots. Braided is about ¼ the diameter as monofilament for the same tensile strength. It has essentially no stretch, which makes it ideal for deep- sea bottom fishing. Sensitivity to bite is assured. Mono would stretch in the area of 15-20% but not braided. Surf jockeys can cast whatever they are using like a missile but may be subjected to the weak point of braided, low abrasion resistance. Sand, gravel, clamshells etc will wear on the braided material.

Many party boats have voided the use of braided line if the boat is made of fiberglass or plastic. The braided line especially in the greater strength, 60 lbs or more, can cut the boats hull if the braided gets hung up on the bottom or even with an angler's line. It's not a good idea to motor home with half a boat and half the fare. Never wrap your hand or fingers around the braided line in hope of loosing a snag. The braided line will cut flesh and can remove fingers.

The Weapons:

A: Bucktails

I'm sure there are bass and bluefish swimming the local coastal shores with a piece of metal and fiber hanging from its jaws. If you could trace the fishes' route, most likely it obtained its bucktail somewhere along New York's Long Island coast. It's a tradition to initiate your Long Island coastal fishing trip by choosing your initial weapon, a bucktail.

The bucktail is a shaped lead head torpedo or fish head plus a trailing stream of feathers, synthetics or natural fibers surrounding a barbed hook atop the head. The hook is molded into the metal head with an eye- loop atop the head or nose. The loop atop the head permits the bucktail to maintain a horizontal position moving through the water at a depth mostly governed by the speed of the retrieve.

Skipping it over the bottom, steady retrieve, drop and lift or trolling are typical ways anglers can use this weapon. The bucktail will not impart action by itself. The motion of the rod and the speed of the retrieve cause its action in the water. The angler is in control of the results. Colors and materials used for the head and bushy tail vary across the visible light spectrum of synthetics and natural textiles. Adding a wiggly tail of 4 to 6 inches to the hook, adds further action to the bucktail.

The most important and most effective location of the bucktail is at or very near the bottom of the water column. The only exception to this is in bridge fishing where the bucktail is more effective near the surface near the light- shadow region. At the bottom of the water column a color contrast between the color of the bottom and the bucktail is as important as the silhouette of a surface plug against the moonlit sky. A bright bucktail against the sandy or rocky bottom gives a good contrast of colors and makes it easier for the game fish to identify the difference.

The use of bucktails is not a modern invention but has roots in the fishing fraternities in other locations of the world especially in the Polynesian Islands. It would not survive its introduction in the states unless it was successful.

The bait tail is an American invention and a spin –off of the bucktail. Lou Palma in 1960 made the lure that looks like a small eel attached to a lead head. Previous to this application Ed Sens's bucktails set the basis for most all of today's version of bait tails of all sizes and shapes. Although the live eel may assume the place of honor in striped bass fishing, the bucktail with its spin-offs ranks next.

Bucktails can be repaired using natural or synthetics fibers, heavy- duty thread, fast drying glue and oil base touch-up paint. With the phase out of oil base house paint, you will have to get your touch-up colors in the craft section of the hobby store. Remember to touch-up the eyes with **red** oil base paint.

As an alternate with greater options, you can purchase at the local craft store, sequins in packages that contain many colored "circle" dots of various sizes. They are perfectly round with a small hole in the center to represent the fish's eye. Glue them to your bucktails and you may have a better product than the original painted eye. They are highly reflective of light and might make the difference between fishing and catching.

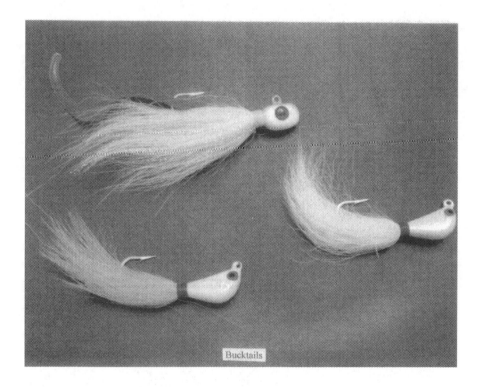

Bucktails

B: Plugs

Balsa, cedar, rare exotics woods and conventional plastics are used to float, dive or sink an infinite variety of plugs. They can be loaded with lead shot or water, swim with metal lips and dive with plastic or metal spoons in their mouth.

The woods are crafted by hand or machine so that they represent baitfish or something similar. The striped bass may not be too fussy if the plug does not swim like the real prey since the bass vision is not as acute as the angler. We have now moved from the basic plug whittling stage to the semi- tech modern plug manufacturing state with the introduction of added noise and oils.

Plugs are made to pop, wiggle, dart, dive and sink with noise and odors. Colors are carefully chosen to attract fishermen as well as fish. Knowledge about the color sensitivity of the fish's eyes as well as the psyche of the angler will permit the best selection. Read the chapter, " Striped Bass Vision, Revisited" for the right choice.

Wood needs annual maintenance more so than plastics. A dab of paint to cover chipped areas or wood filler to cover the teeth marks of that bluefish attack last Fall will be necessary. Plastics are not immune to the saltwater environment. Stainless steel accessories of hooks, rings and wire will surface rust if not properly cared for whether on wood or plastic. There are chemicals available to avoid surface rust but you will not find them in the local grocery store nor do you want to carry them around with you. A good rinse in fresh water will be sufficient.

Many fishermen will modify their plugs during the doldrums of the winter by adding weights or modifying the lip of the plugs. Doing either or both will affect the action of the plug. Modern plugs are tested before a production run (for large quantities) is committed. Changing items by adding or subtracting means you will impart a different action. Once modified it will be difficult to return the plug to its initial condition.

If you intend to add weight be sure to initially find the center of the plug via balancing it on the edge of a knife. Add weights forward and backward but keep the same balance point.

Shaving off part of the lip of the plug will cause it to reduce its action and swim less than the prescribed depth. Some plug gurus say that snap swivels interfere with the action of the plug. Others say the ability to change lures easily and quickly is an advantage that is necessary especially in adverse weather where tying anything to your line may be nearly impossible. As a compromise you may choose one of the modern, small high strength ball bearing snap swivels that offer small size with less interference to the action of the plug.

C: Eels, Sand Eels, Needle Fish

If there is a grand bait for the striped bass, it has to be the eel. It was used by C.B. Church in 1913 to catch his 73.0-pound striped bass. It was considered the World Record although it was unofficial for about 27 years until the IGFA took the responsibility to monitor and acknowledge past and present records of game fish. The eel hasn't lost its number one position since that time; in fact it may have improved itself by turning itself into plastic. The angler can place it in his surf or boat bag of tricks and not be concerned if the saltwater soaked seaweed doesn't have a sultry eel in its salty seabed for the night.

With the progress of science it has been discovered there are two major species of eels; the European and the American. In fact until 1777 the eel was believed to be an earthworm. Whether European or American, they both spent time in the Sargasso Sea south of Bermuda. After spawning the larvae of the European eel travel with the Gulf Stream for one to three years until they reach the coast of Europe. At this point they are nearly transparent and make great table food from England to Spain. If not eaten by man or other fish, they arrive in the rivers and grassy creeks in northern and southern Europe. It takes 10 to 14 years for the eels to grow to about 2 feet. Eels can have a life span over 100 years.

In the month of July some of them leave the fresh water rivers and creeks and make a 4000-mile open sea crossing back to their spawning grounds in the vicinity of the Sargasso Sea. Before they swim this long distant route, their gut dissolves preventing them from eating anything; hence they swim on stored energy for 4000 miles. Their body goes through some physical changes in route. We also know they are eaten by various marine creatures during the trek, including whales.

In Europe about 55 million pounds of eels are consumed each year but in Japan over 202 million pounds are eaten. The European eel population has been devastated by a nematode parasite. Thirty to one hundred percent of the European eels are infected and some of the American eels have the same problem. The nematode parasite affects the swim bladder, which stores the energy for the eels' swim to the spawning grounds. It has been estimated that their population is down to 2 % of what it was 30 years ago. Over- fishing is a major problem because their popular use as table fare and now the parasite has further affected their decline. After spawning they die.

The American eel uses the same spawning grounds although it is believed the Yucatan Peninsula off the Gulf of Mexico is also available. From here they swim up the East Coast in February and April to various rivers and streams where they make their home. In about a year they reach about 2 feet long.

A third species of eels is the Japanese eel found in the Suruga Seamount.

The north equatorial current moves them west towards East Asia where they are caught and served as food. The demand has increased so there are eel farms that raise this commercial product.

— Bass Application:

To use eels as bait somewhere between 10 and 20 inches seems to be the most available size. It's not like casting your favorite 2 oz plug or trolling a 16 oz bunker blade. The bait shop has what is available at the time. If you want a half dozen, be prepared to accept some smaller and some larger ones. He can't give you all the 12.25-inch eels you asked for.

Once you have them be sure to put them in some wet seaweed in your tackle box or very damp non- toxic paper bag or rag. They will live in the air very well but not in a little pool of water which the eels will extract all the oxygen and then die. Just keep them moist for max life.

In a boat you can place them anywhere you feel you will need them for a hook up, probably near the rods. On the beach a mesh bag hanging from your waders is a good place and gives easy access. Deep pockets on waders may also harbor your eels for the night. The bib pouch in front of the full- length waders is also a convenient place to keep them secure and handy.

Eels can be live- lined from the boat. They will swim to the bottom therefore you must keep them from finding a place to hide. Movement of the rod will force them to move along. A very, very slow retrieve should keep the eel in the camera's eyes of the bass. Recently in Virginia Beach, VA boaters were using bobbers to hang the eels and they were very successful. Who said fishing for bass was not much different than fishing for carp? Apparently they were right, indicated by the bobbling bobber's booty that attracted rockfish over 60 pounds. No trolling, no chum line, no hand- held rod, just stick it in the rod holder and have a drink; like fishing for carp.

Fishing from the surf also requires keeping the eel moving. A very, very slow retrieve is necessary, with rod in hand of course. Both from the boat or the surf hooking the eel is most often done with a 6/0 to 8/0 Gamakatus hook. It is either from the upper lip through the eye, lower lip down through the lower lip, through both lower and upper lips and out one eye or any other way you feel may be better. A 16-24 inch, 30-60 line strength mono line leader is necessary in order to keep the bass abrasion mouth from weakening the line when the bass swallows it into the gut.

There are plenty of books about how to rig a dead eel. If you are in New England, they may or may not rig the eel with a small weight at the head, a hook in the head either facing up or down and another hook mid-way down the length and tied down before the eye of the hook and at the curve of the shank. All the materials to make a dead eel lure such as hooks, Dacron line, bullet- shaped head weight are readily available except the long needle required to go from the head of the eel to its mid section. Two manufacturers of the long doll needles are: Prym-Dritz Corp. Spartanburg, S.C. 29304, www.dritz.com and Havels Inc., Cincinnati, Oh. 1-800-638- 4770.

Cut up dead eels are good bait along with cut up menhaden, herring, mullet, clams, crabs etc. Remember eels feed at night and hide in the rocks in the daylight. Adjust your schedule.

Last info about eels: keep the reel on live- line or free spool and wait longer than you think before setting the hook.

The New Jersey style of mounting a dead eel is by the use of a metal jig. A narrow one will run deeper than a Hopkins. Using the same materials as above, put the hook through the head, tie it down on the metal, using the needle string the Dacron to mid- way and attach hook and tie it down as noted above. The metal jig should be made containing some tin so you can shape it to ride in the water naturally. Pictures and details can be found in any striped bass handbook.

– Sand Eels (Sand Lance)

Sand eels are a major food source for the striped bass as well other numerous fish including whales. They tend to congregate in large schools near sandy bottoms of tidal flats and will hide by burying themselves in the sand. You will find them also in deeper tidal water that they use as an escape. As the tide drops the terns will dive to get them. Bass will root them out with their mouths until their noses are scraped. They are much longer in length (9 inches is a good size) than their width. Dark green and peacock make up their typical colors.

They can be found from Cape Cod to the Gulf of Mexico and along the Scandinavian coast and are easy to spot in shallow coastal flats. They swim like eels but look much smaller and have pointed snouts. They will bury themselves above the lower watermark and wait for the next tide to return to the water. If threatened they have been known to flee their predators and strand themselves on the shallow flats. Spawning takes place in deeper waters probably over 50 feet in sandy bottoms. Their eggs cling fast to the sand grains awaiting development. More is known about the European sand eel than the US species.

– Needlefish

The sand eel and needlefish could be mistaken for each other except that the needlefish snout contains a row of sharp teeth. Much of their time is spent in shallow waters preferring to hover near the surface where they prey on smaller fish. They also are found in fresh and saltwater and also form in large schools. Different species are found in the North and Eastern Atlantic, Mediterranean Sea and Black Sea.

A 12-inch needlefish is a good size but some species grow to over 4 feet. Its silver-green color make-up also can confuse it with its sand eel shallow swimming companion. Again striped bass find these easy pickings when they catch them in shallow water near the coast. Both Sand Eel lures and Needlefish lures can be used as "one is like the other." The striped bass like both species and will accept whatever is the vicinity.

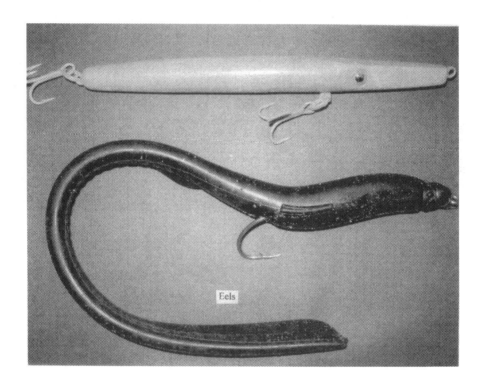

Eels

D: Menhaden

Food for fish or fish for food or both? For less than $0.20 per pound, it can clean up 2 million gallons of sea water per year while populating the ocean with itself by the millions to do the same. Sounds like there should be a deal for the stock market under a low cost IPO as an environmental cleaning processor for oceans, rivers and bays.

What is it? It's the menhaden fish also known as bunker, mossbunker and by other various names going back to the 1600s. The Indians knew its value not so much as edible fish food but helped unproductive land produce edible crops such as corn. This low- tech fertilizer was used in the 1600s-1700s-1800s-1900s and it was not high- tech chemicals but the menhaden. When grandfather put the fish heads in the ground by his vegetable garden, he was repeating what the Indian lore taught the Pilgrims. There was no side effect from this enriching fertilizing method but only harmony between Mother Nature and man. No toxic runoff to pollute the rivers, bays and creeks. Organic materials for organic plants, good for the environment and good for the crops.

The Atlantic Ocean and the Gulf of Mexico has produced an enormous quantity of menhaden, once deemed unlimited. With 61 sea -worthy reduction ships, 32 spotter planes, 5 land- based reduction plants, the Omega Protein Corporation guaranteed it would be the most harvested fish of all others along the coast, and so it is. More so than cod, tuna, haddock, mackerel, bluefish, weakfish, striped bass, swordfish, king mackerel, summer flounder, drum plus others combined.

The inexhaustible supply seemed guaranteed because the menhaden spawned as they swam the coastline, bays and estuaries. A 3- year old fish could deposit millions of eggs that hatched in 48 hours. These little fish as well as the adults only eat phytoplankton, the vegetation in the oceans, bays and rivers, which clog the waters and deplete its oxygen. In 10-18 months these juveniles are ready to do their clean sweep in the Atlantic Ocean and the Gulf of Mexico. They only need to survive for 3 years before they can reproduce. Indiscriminate harvesting of the small "peanut" bunker and the larger 2-pound adults can prevent the unlimited supply of the menhaden from being unlimited. The fish cannot be identified by age hence segregation is not possible nor cost effective for the menhaden fleet with purse seine dragging nets and spotter planes. Adult spawning fish are now down to about 13 percent of a school. These fish always travel in schools hence are an easy target for the netters.

Purse seine nets essentially capture the whole school both young and adults therefore limiting reproduction. As soon as the planes spot the school, ships launch the capture boats with seine nets, one to the left and one to the right. As they close the circle, the school gets trapped from the bottom up with no escape possible. A larger ship arrives to vacuum up the menhaden into the refrigerated holding holes. Since these fish cannot be caught by baited hook, nets are required but the purse seine net permits an efficiency of 100 percent – no fish escapes. Even mid- west farmers leave some rows of crops so the local animals, birds etc can survive the winter. The seine net does not leave any fish to survive and to reproduce itself. It's a one way net; once in, you're taken out of the ocean, bay, river etc. The use of these types of nets has disseminated the salmon, shad, and alewives population and the results are still felt today. The environmental ecology circle is complete. Reduce fin food for the food fish and you reduce the food fish. Reduce the food fish for the game fish and you cause them to feed on other marine foods especially crabs. It has been found that the striped bass have had as many as 87 to 113 tiny crabs in its gut. Now the crabbers can crab about their business. The Chesapeake Bay crab industry is well established but always at the mercy of the direct ebb and flow of the available food supply for its most important game fish, the menhaden. So it is with the other game fish. Bluefish will eat summer flounder, weakfish, croaker, kingfish as well as any small game fish therefore reducing their population. It is quite common to find small summer flounders in the stomach of striped bass. Steve Petri of Long Island developed a lure that imitated the summer flounder (fluke) and used it with such success that he was made an offer for sale of the product line. If you want crabs, give the Striped Bass menhaden; you can't have both. In the 1950s evidence shows that the gut of the striped bass was 98 % menhaden and 2 % crab. Things have reversed.

Many years ago the menhaden reduction industry was established along the East Coast with over 450 ships equipped to net menhaden from Maine, Massachusetts, New York to North Carolina. Menhaden hubs were where the fish were ground into fertilizer, animal food and materials for industrial process. The new purse seine nets were a boom to the industry. In 1956 the entire Atlantic coast produced over 700 metric tons or over 1,500,000,000 pounds of menhaden but by 1967 there was over a 70% reduction of the catch to only around 400,000,000 pounds. More pronounced was that the North Atlantic coast went from 200,000,000 pounds to 3,000,000 pounds. The seine nets were very effective. The nets were just as effective in trapping table food and game fish, which fed on the menhaden. This is known as by-catch, something more and more concerning to scientists. The menhaden land based reduction factories reduced all species trapped into one indistinguishable mass. No need to report on the mix of the catch, they were only interested in the menhaden, the rest was a gift. Where the menhaden catch had no limit (for decades), the other fish may have had quotas that would not be reported.

Why report on something you had no legal right to catch. The ACMFC of course must factor this unaccounted catch by species and by area when allocating quotas for the other commercial fishermen. What's in the right hand, the left hand has to guess at it. Most coastal fish will eat menhaden whole or in part, if they can find them.

Since 1880s Congress has subsidized and aided the menhaden reduction industry from the days of the "Bureau of Commercial Fisheries." With uncountable numbers of menhaden in the ocean, bays and rivers, there was no need to limit the catch. When the numbers of the Omega Protein reduction factories went from 14 to 4 in the Gulf area, their working ships dropped from 98 to 50 in 1998. Landings in the Gulf dropped from about 2,000,000,000 pounds to nearly half; the Department of Commerce ruled that after 1998 the catch data was not to be released. What the right hand has, the left hand can't look at. Members of the Omega Protein Corporation dominated the Gulf States Marine Fisheries Commission. Although this industry claims to be a job maker and should be encouraged and protected for the benefit of the employees, it employs less than 300 full time and less than 900 seasonal workers. There are more Christmas tree cutters, shippers, and sellers than all workers at the Omega Protein Corporation. The Christmas tree cutters, shippers, sellers should apply for representation on the GSMFC; they may obtain certain benefits.

Since WWII the US Navy has used their aircraft to report to the menhaden ships the location and size of the schools of the menhaden on the East Coast and the same for the sardines on the West Coast. The U.S. Bureau of Fisheries and the Department Commerce supported the seaplane patrols and reports. This helped peak the catch in the Atlantic region in 1956. Since 1963 the Gulf of Mexico catch has surpassed the Atlantic catch. Gradually private aircraft were used to spot the schools and soon Omega Protein developed their own air force.

Many, many small companies sought and caught menhaden in the 1700s but they were gradually bought out as the menhaden stock declined. Since 1964 names as The Brunswick Navigation Company, Standard Products, Zapata Corp. disappeared and finally Omega Protein has the ocean to itself. The Omega Protein Corporation may be doing more harm to the rest of the other commercial industry as its business is sinking. They now must take a greater percentage of a reduced catch in order to keep in business. The Government has kept throwing the industry a life jacket for the last two centuries. Why? Following political contributions from any organizations nearly always leads to favorable considerations. The menhaden could also use some favorable consideration. For the clean –up work they do in the ocean, rivers and bays the Government should give them a certificate of merit as the most efficient marine organization instead of a DOA certificate.

With the total reduction in menhaden harvested by the Omega Protein reduction industry, we also have the problem of striped bass being undernourished and exhibiting a mycobacterium disease. About 70+% of the Striped bass or rockfish of the Chesapeake Bay area are infected because of lack of adequate nourishment. Because of the lack of numbers of menhaden to clean up the river and bay region, the area south of the Potomac River to the Bay Bridge below 26 feet deep is now dead of life needing oxygen. The dead vegetation was once food for the menhaden but they are now there in limited numbers. In the Gulf of Mexico the same thing is being repeated which now amounts to 1000 square miles or 30 by 30 miles. Drive North in your boat for an hour at 30 mph, then East, then South, then West. It's a four- hour trip where fish cannot live in the total enclosed volume.

Of the 150 known dead zones around the world, the Gulf of Mexico is rated number two (2). It is also where Omega Protein nets more menhaden than in the Atlantic region. The Chesapeake Bay region of Virginia is where 75% of their Atlantic catch is made. All other states less Virginia and North Carolina have banned commercial catch of menhaden. Apparently these two states have not seen the light as the others because the waters may be too green ($).

As the catch of menhaden decreased with the use of ships, planes, seine nets, high tech communications, the scientist started to realize an association between fish, food, ecology and the environment. These entities were interdependent. Like an electric current flow, the quantity of amperes can be designed only when each component is known and their relationships understood. Similar each state can disrupt the balance between fish, food, ecology and environment if they are unaware of the relationship between the components of the natural system or ignore it. The states are responsible to 0-3 miles from the shore as well as the rivers, bays and other waterways that make up their circuit. History has shown that the industrialization of fisheries reduce the biomass by 80% after 15 years of exploitation by mechanization of fishing i.e.; tuna, swordfish, marlin, shark as well as ground fish, cod, halibut, flounder etc. This has united the usually uncooperative forces of commercial and recreational associations. Although one can point to the depletion by mechanization of the ground fish, over- fishing of the menhaden affected both fishing parties. The Coastal Conservation Association, Recreational Fishing Alliance, Stripers Forever plus many others have spoken up about the destructive commercial practices as: bottom trawling, long lines up to 100 miles, drift nets, gill nets to 40 miles long and purse seine nets. Yet it's the menhaden problem that is uniting these contestants.

The 13 million or so recreational anglers and their organizations have combined with 10 million concerned environmental organizations to speak with one voice in protecting the marine environment. The menhaden reduction industry has existed because its product is cheap. It is challenged on all levels by its substitute, the soybean.

In economics of scale large entities can reduce the unit cost, yet without sufficient supply of raw materials, the unit cost increases. The menhaden fleet no longer seeks menhaden north of the Chesapeake Bay because the states have banned it and the quantity of menhaden is limited due to over fishing for decades. Reports filter in that a return of the menhaden has been noted in the Northeastern States. It is small but they are there. The menhaden amount to the third biggest American fisheries product with probably the most impact on the marine environment acting as an algae vacuum cleaner.

Across the Country 430 dams have been removed from rivers in order to permit spawning alewives, herring and shad to reproduce. These forage fish are the food for larger fish and other marine life. In the Northeast these dams were once the power source for paper mills and are no longer needed with the advent of conventional electric power. The ASMFG, NOAA and the New England and Mid- Atlantic Fisheries Management Council have asked the states to reduce the herring by-catch in offshore trawl vessels in order to increase spawning in the local rivers.

– Menhaden Applications:

Use whole, as a chunk or as a head.

1: Live line the whole bunker with a 6/0 to 8/0 hook. 2: Cut the fresh bunker into 3 or 4 strips and attach to a 4/0 to 8/0 hook. 3: Take the head and put the hook through the toughest part you can. Don't believe you can't lose a bunker head without a bass taking it. Tidal action can do many things well with a heavy head. It will be thrown around. A large well -formed barb is a must.

In the 1850s the preferred method to use a bunker chuck was to fillet one side of the whole bunker, turn the flesh side to the outside and then but a hook through it. A rubber band helped keep the dinner on the hook.

If possible fresh bunker, especially live ones are best. Next, recently caught ones on ice, finally, frozen whole bunker cut into strips will do the job.

There isn't much more to say about this favorite bait of the bass. If you can't live -line one from the beach, try a bunker head. For some reason big bass take delight in gulping in the head, even the small ones will latch on and swim around probably hoping they will grow up soon in order to feast on this delight. Summer heat will quickly turn an iced or frozen bunker to near mush if you don't place in the sand 5-6 inched down. This also discourages the sea gulls from having a free meal at your expense. Be sure to remember where you dug the hole by placing a stick over it. It is embarrassing to move 50 yards down the beach, come back for a re-bait and can't find the bait hole. Check with the gulls, they probably know.

Menhaden

E: Surf Clams

The striped bass have several fish restaurants along the East Coast. One of the most prolific marine tidbits, especially close to the shoreline, the sea clam. The sea clam, one of 23 species in residence along the Mid Atlantic region, doesn't get its foot for burrowing until 18 days after fertilization. Prior to that time they drift along or swim along depending on the intensity of the current. Once the clam burrows in the sand, it is likely to stay to adulthood.

Where a 10+-year-old surf clam may be 5 inches along the New Jersey coast, an Ocean City, Maryland sea clam would be 5 inches in 5 years.

The New Jersey coast from Belmar to Cape May contains the highest abundance of sea clams from the shoreline to about 20 miles out although you can find them to about 200 miles. The surf clam can be found in moderate quantities from Maine to Cape Hatteras. The Long Island, New York coastline has a high abundance of sea clams especially towards Montauk Point.

The early methods of harvesting surf clams were by hand operated rakes. During the 1920s scraper type dredges towed behind power- boats were used. In the 1940s the water jet dredge was developed. This increased efficiency, decreased clam breakage and helped develop the modern surf clam industry. Today knife scrapers plus water jets further improved the gathering of the clams.

During WWII the commercial surf clam industry supplied about 3% of the US landings of clam meat. By the 1970s surf clam provided over 70% of all clam meats used in the US and in 1980 Virginia surpassed New Jersey in surf clam harvest. The 1976 Fisheries Management Plan required the surf clam harvested be 5.1 inches in diameter hence that saved the industry from depleting the biomass. No matter how many surf clams are harvested, the sex ratio of male to female remains 1:1.

Although the surf clam is a hearty species, pollutants affect its survival; i.e. human refuse, sludge and metals. A concentration of pollutants will severely impact the surf clams while outside the dumping area little effect can be noticed. In either case a lack of dissolved oxygen in the water means death to the clams.

It is a well-known fact that New Jersey anglers' favorite soft lure is the surf clam. With the greatest abundance of surf clams near shore, the surf caster has the "pier de resistance" no striper can resist. It's breakfast, lunch and dinner from   0 to 200 miles out. Although the boater may not troll with clams 20 feet off the New Jersey coast, the local surfcaster has no inhibitions to string two clams on a high low hook rig with 4-6 ounces to anchor the dinner plate. Dining on a clam on half shell or no shell is the preferred menu selection of the

New Jersey stripers. North to south the old salt with a 12- foot fiberglass surf rod and 200 yards of linen or mono line on his Penn 140 knows something you don't. You may find him from Maine to Cape Hatteras sitting on an old tin milk pail watching for the first twinge of the rod tip.

Atlantic surf clam

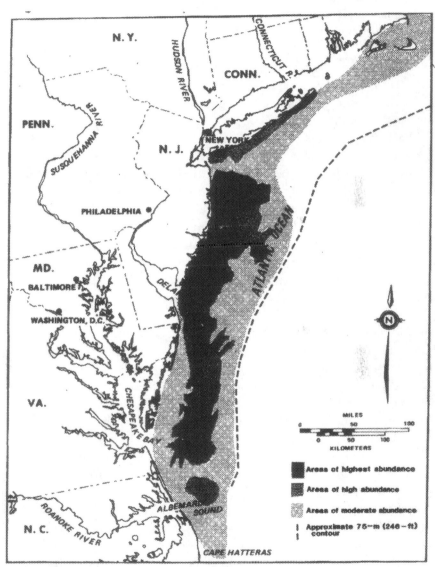

Figure 2. Mid-Atlantic distribution of the surf clam, with areas of relative abundance indicated.

F: Metal

There is an old golf saying that never bet an old, well- tanned golfer with a rusty two iron in his golf bag. You can be sure he has used it as his "money" stick. Likewise, if you hear the rattle of metal in the surf bag of another surf jockey, you ought to listen to him carefully about the use of these metal weapons.

Surf's up, winds up, currents up, give me a metal. You can choose among a near endless variety of shapes and weights. From a ½- ounce diamond jig to a 32- ounce-trolling spoon, the metal gets you where you have to be in nearly un -fishable conditions.

Various mold sizes and combinations of tin, zinc, copper and lead will give you the ability to match almost any baitfish. Bend the tins to simulate the spearing, mullet, herring, menhaden, and sand eel. With a mold that produces a keel on the metal you will be able to get deep into the water column. The diamond jig is a multi- keeled metal that mimics sand eels while other single keeled metals are molded to mimic spearing or thin finned fish.

The well-known Hopkins metal is a dupe for the menhaden. Its flat shape rides mid-way in the water column. Chromed with fish scale pattern embossed on its surface, it will swim and wobble with the prevailing current to present a reasonable representation of the common menhaden.

Almost all metals are chromed. Low light levels may compromise a dull tin clad metal but has less affect on the high gloss chrome. Metals cast like bullets from the surf or boat. With a single or gang hook with feathers, the mighty metal can challenge most winds up to a gale force. If you can stand erect against the gale, your metal will be the only weapon that will work; all others are second best options. Many surfcasters may not be concerned with the shape of a metal lure but are concerned with its weight. You'll find 1 to 4 ounce hunks of no- name chrome jiggling in their surf bag. Party boat captains load up on 3-4 ounce diamond jigs that are good for anything that swims 20 to 60 feet under the surface. They instruct their novice fishing fares, to keep it simple and keep it moving.

Trolling bunker spoons with its heavy weighted keel will get down to the mother load. The striped bass is a good fighter that would rather feed on the sandy bottom. Big bait for big fish is a truth that experienced captains learned many moons ago. These bunker spoons weighing 2 pounds may question the meaning of a "sporting battle" between man and fish. Add monel or wire line and you have a poor man's long liner rig. A parachute of bunker spoons near the bottom surely look like a pod of bunkers looking for some friendly places to hide.

A flash off the chromed metal may be all you need to get the attraction of a bass, blue, weakie, flounder etc especially if you move it along at a clip that gives these predators little time to say "no."

Others:

There may be another level of weapons which have useful purposes in certain seasons, in certain places, by certain anglers with certain local knowledge such as; sea worms, blood worms, mullet, squid, crabs, sand flees, herring. The readers probably know of others and it's their secret.

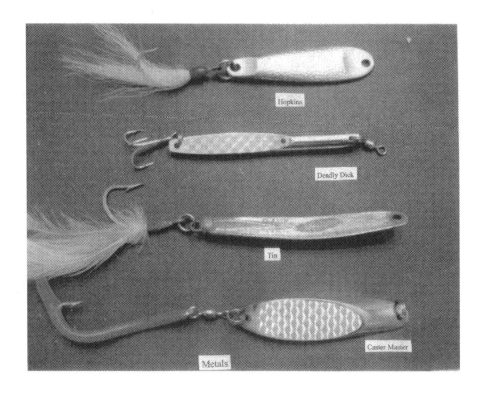

15
Plugging Away

Many fly rod fishermen avoid making their own flies. It is easier to purchase them and avoid the time to learn the techniques. Passionate fishermen would probably refrain from buying such an essential product that he could make himself. This would bring him closer to the imagery perfect angler in the presence of the reclusive trophy trout. Yes, the average trout angler will purchase an array of flies and avoid discovery of the inner secrets of tying flies. He will also not be able to experience the oneness of the spiritual world between angler and trout.

The same techniques in tying flies are known by today's striped bass fishermen and women. Some bait and tackle shops along the eastern shore cater to these anglers. It is comradeship between like fishermen with similar interests about the striped bass and tying the perfect fly. How well can one copy the shape, color and action of a menhaden, spearing, mackerel, porgy, croaker or the irregular action of a crab, lobster or similar shell dweller? It is a perfect pastime during the cold winter months when anxiety and anticipation are alive and well. It is not work but play where ones efforts may have a memorable outcome. Focusing one's talents, whether God given or acquired, is to choose the correct hairs, color, thread and hook. A surgeon- like sensitive hand lends itself to a successful job well done. A discerning eye admires the creation because it was instrumental in leading the hand to create the final product.

Within the spring, summer, fall seasons the freshwater fly- "tyers" have an expansive quantity of insects to copy. It is a dedicated fresh water "tyer" that takes seriously the real insect world with the make believe world of feathers, thread and fabric. Matching your knowledge about the world of insects with the seasons is a satisfying accomplishment. How can one attain sufficient knowledge of the variety of insects? Bring along your hand- held computer with Internet access in order to discover the insect world on your favorite trout stream. You can match the real insect world with a computer simulation. You'll be a better fisherman or woman.

Why cannot the saltwater brethren enjoy the same success tying together the materials that represent the local baitfish? Fly or plug? Both tying flies and plug making for salt-water species of baitfish have a narrow variety of fish to imitate. Where tying a fly is more of imagination and mixing materials in the proper order; plug construction requires a little more elbow grease. The science of tying a fly may be more art while the science of whittling a plug may be more science than art.

You can buy a plug kit where the wood has been shaped and the hooks, wire rings all supplied. What is left is the sanding, painting and installation of the hooks and wire. With a few tools you can assemble your own weapons. You can also enjoy the winter months designing and manufacturing your own plugs.

There are a few rules to follow in order to be successful in plug making. Rule number 1 is from Archimedes: Circa; B.C.

*The plug (any material) will only **float** if the water it displaces weighs more than the plug with hooks, rings, wire, paint and tail materials.*

Rule number 2 is also from Archimedes:

*The Plug (any material) will **sink** if the water it displaces weighs less than the plug with hooks, rings, wire, paint and tail materials.*

For instance: Get or make a shaped block of plug material including all the accessories (ignore the paint). Fill a bowl of freshwater with a pouring spout and fill it to the very brim of the spout. Immerse the plug and all the accessories that will be attached and save the water it displaces. You may have to push the plug under the water in order to make it displace the water. Drop the accessories in the water; they will displace their own volume of water (hooks, wire etc). If the plug material is wood you should spray it with a light coat of clear paint in order to prevent the absorption of water.

With the water that was displaced and saved, weigh it on a sensitive scale (grams or   0.1 ounces). Then weigh the plug material and accessories on the same scale; note the difference. Now follow Rule 1 or 2. Be aware that seawater weighs about 3½ % more than freshwater. That means you can have the plug and accessories weight nearly 3 1/2 % more than the captured and save water and still have a floating lure. Add more than 3 ½ % if you want a sinking lure. For instance; a 3-ounce plug could weigh 3.11 oz in saltwater and still float. If you use seawater as the test water, the 3-½ % addition or substation is not in use. In the finer points of plug making there is a difference between the saltwater density in the northern States and in Florida, with Florida having a gallon of saltwater weighing more than a gallon from i.e.; Cape Cod etc.

If you want to be creative forget the cedar or hard woods and use cork or balsa.

Did you know that Rapala made its first freshwater fishing plug out of cork in 1936?

With cork he would wrap it with the tinfoil from a chocolate bar after melting a photographic negative around the cork as a protective coating. With a proper size hook he perfected the wiggle's "wounded minnow action." This was the Original Floating Rapala. Being so light it easily wobbled with a left to right yaw. Today it does the same thing right out of the box but it's made out of balsa wood.

In 1965 the Rapala saltwater lures used the African Odum wood due to its ability resist warping and be adverse to the salt environment. This hard, heavy and high resistance to wear wood is also used for flooring, furniture and African spiritual ceremonies. It has a specific gravity of   0 . 6 7 , which means in its natural state it will float in fresh water since water has a specific gravity of 1.0. Since it's a hard wood, it would be difficult to work without mechanical equipment. Other woods used in saltwater fishing may be easier to obtain and work. Plastic are another option but usually restricted to manufacturers with special equipment.

You could still use cork for saltwater lures. By taking 3 or 4 corks from empty wine bottles, a little sandpaper to smooth the end surfaces, you can then epoxy the corks together. Now you have the bases of a floating saltwater plug. After the hardening of the epoxy, take a fine- edged saw blade and cut a line the length of the entire corks to half its depth. Next take a wire coat hanger or similar stiff wire and place it in the sawed grove. Find the center of the plug by balancing it on the edge of a knife. Then bend a U joint for the front hook and locate it in front of the balance point. Attach the hooks to the U -joint and extend the wire to the end of the plug. Slip the tail hook on the end of the plug, find the balance point of the plug using the edge of a knife and twist the ends of the wire to secure the tail hook and the front where the line will be attached. You now have a front hook and a rear hook separated enough so that the plug balances at about the mid-point of the plug. Then mix a two- component epoxy and pour in the grove holding the wire. The coat hanger wire or similar strength wire will withstand the pull of any bass. What is left is to add wood or cork to fill the void if necessary. Sand to a smooth finish, paint or use as is. Add a flat piece of aluminum to the front cork as a popper, if necessary. Now even a bluefish will have a difficult time to cut cork.

An identical approach can be used to make a balsa lure. Shape the balsa, cut the grove, place in the wire after forming, and epoxy in the wire. Buck shot bbs can be used to add weight and level the balsa and cork plug, if necessary. Put the hooks on and find the center of the plug by balancing it on a knife's edge. Add equal bbs to each side of the center point to get to the desired weight. Beware of Rule 1 and 2. Balsa wood, if weighted properly, can function as a floater (it natural state) or a sinker. For cork or balsa (specific gravity 0.16) it will be difficult to make it as a sinker. In either case you are the creator of the shape, size, balance and color.

See Figures; 30-33.

Urethane paint will add abrasion resistance and toughness to plugs the salt environment. Did you know golf balls are painted with multi-component polyurethane? Aircrafts are also painted with polyurethane because of the environment of speed and altitude. Urethane is long lasting, abrasive resistant and has a high gloss finish.

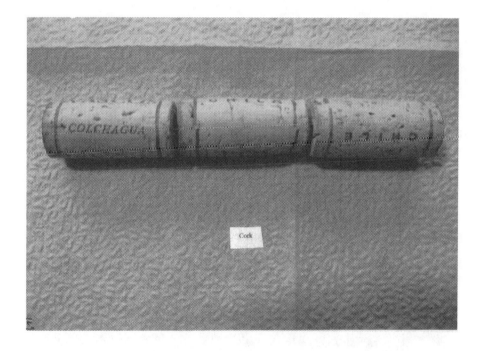

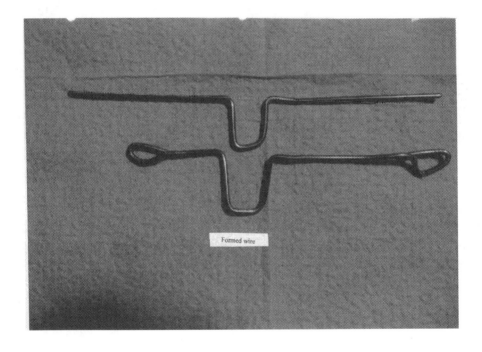

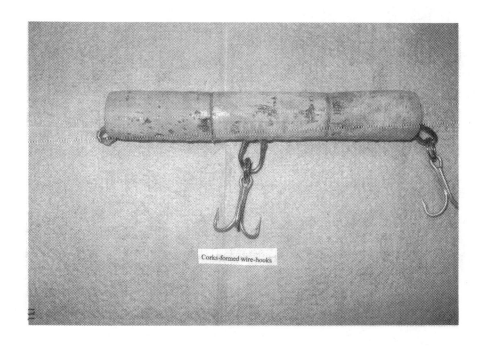

Corks-formed wire-hooks

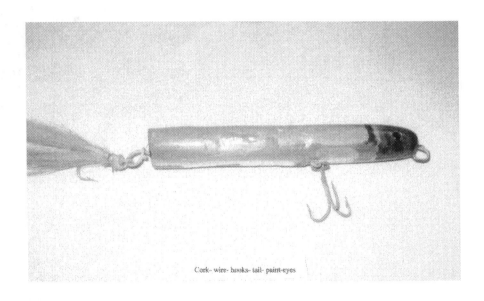

Cork- wire- hooks- tail- paint-eyes

16
Surveys

The IGFA* has compiled over many years data on the most popular fishing equipment used in fresh and saltwater. The information was not segregated between uses in fresh or saltwater because some equipment might be used in both arenas. For the saltwater only application of the equipment some judgment has to be made because the IGFA data included the equipment used to catch over 230 species of fresh and saltwater fish. From the great deep-water monsters to the tiny trout, the fishing equipment would be quite different but if there were many anglers after tiny trout and only a few after deep water monsters, the data would have little benefit to the Striped Bass anglers.

The data is revised each year based on new applications for record fish.

When this application is submitted to the IGFA, the rod, reel, line, lure/bait manufacturers as well as sample of the terminal tackle are required. Pictures of the catch are also necessary. Applications are received from around the world. The 300 plus IGFA representatives are found in over 90 countries and are an essential part of the sportsmen/fish- recognition process. They monitor compliance of the catch to the rules and regulation of the IGFA.

The IGFA comply records of 112 fresh and 122 saltwater species of fish. Within each species they issue; All Tackle Records (worldwide) certificates for each species, record fish for each species in 11-line class (line strength) as well as 7 line classes for fly rod anglers. There is also a Junior and Small Fry class for all species in 2 line classes.

State records (USA) are recognized for each species in each line class and also for the fly rod anglers. Some species have no fish/anglers listed. You can get your name in the record book by catching some species of any weight in any line class via a submission of an application.

They similarly approve and certify weighing scales at IGFA official weigh stations worldwide, approve IGFA boat captains, educate and train IGFA observes who represent the IGFA in IGFA fishing tournaments. Other non-IGFA tournaments may use these trained observes at no charge. Most of the 693 observers live in the USA.

*IGFA-International Game and Fish Association

Most Popular Tackle Equipment

The information collected in the survey was not separated by use It is plausible that the data, although representing a small group of anglers, may represent the preference of the entire population of fishermen.

I tried to eliminate the names of products probably used by anglers fishing for other than the Striped Bass.

Equipment use by small fish saltwater anglers

Rods:	Reels:
Shimano by 3x more popular, others	Shimano by 2x more popular, others
Penn, St, Croix	Penn, Daiwa, Van Staal, Abu Garcia

Lines:	Lures:
Berkley, Power Pro,	Rapala by 4x more popular, others
Suffix, all almost equal	Storm, Yo-Zuri, Zoom, Rebel

The data is revised each year based on new information from new record holders.

Survey of Striped Bass Fishermen 2008

Stripers Forever is an organization who's aim is to have the striped bass designated as a game fish both in Federal waters (3-200 miles already accomplished) as well in state waters (0 to 3 miles out). Their efforts stem from the furthest northern state visited by the striped bass during their annual migration; Maine. Since 2003 they have surveyed striped bass anglers from Maine to South Carolina concerning a variety of fishing related topics.

It has been estimated that there are several million striped bass anglers along the eastern coast. It may be said that any fisherman can claim to be a striped bass angler if he once attempted to fish for the bass with clams or worms or something similar.

There is no data separating the casual bass angler from the devotee. The 2008 survey received a total of 636 returns from 14,000 emails. Although conducted in unscientific methods the data illustrates the opinions and preferences from those who wanted to express their desires and knowledge. These opinions may or may not represent the estimated 2 - 3 million striped bass anglers along the East Coast but it is worth reading.

Both New Jersey and Massachusetts amounted to 50 % of the returns followed by Maine, New York, Connecticut, Maryland, Rhode Island, Virginia, Delaware, North Carolina, New Hampshire.

About 70 % of the returns were from those fishing mostly from boats and 30 % from the shore. Nearly 80 % had more than 10 years experience fishing for the striped bass.

About 30% of the anglers thought fishing was worse but more thought it was the same or better. It was the same percentages for those who thought the bass were smaller but more thought the fish were the same or larger. The National Marine Fisheries Service through the Marine Recreational Informational Program is responsible for keeping statistics on the number of striped bass caught. In year 2009 the decline has continued since 2006. In 2006 there was 28.6 million bass caught but in 2009 only 6.9 million. The minimum decline from 2006 to 2009 was -27% but by 2009 it was -50%. The data seems to indicate knowledge of where and when to find the Bass is essential for a successful trip especially with a smaller population of numbers and weights.

Both New Jersey and Massachusetts anglers claim they caught as many bass this year as last year; followed by those in the same States claiming the catch was less than the previous year. Hardly any State claimed many more bass were caught. Overall the survey indicated that almost 50% of the anglers claimed they caught fewer or many fewer per hour in 2007.

All anglers led by Massachusetts would like to keep one school striper per day at 18 to 28 inches. This would be in addition to the State's legal limit. Add a "slot fish" and it should be somewhere between 20-30 inches and would be in addition to the legal limit.

If the bass were claimed as a game fish, the anglers would like to see between 50-100% of the previous commercial quota used to increase the bass population biomass.

Around 80% of the anglers thought a $10 to $25 striped bass stamp would be acceptable to buy -out the commercial quota and be used for use in the management the species.

Fifty-six (56) fishing guides also answered the questionnaire and in general said their client were interested in catching more and bigger fish.

General summary of responses from 2003 to 2008 (my opinion reading the graphs):

1. The Quality of fishing has degraded since 2004 and is accelerating through 2008

2. The size of fish caught has been getting smaller

3. Less fish were caught per hour

4. Fishing from boats was probably more productive

In the 2009 they again issued a survey and they used the same questions in order to compare results from previous years.

Again most of the answers were from boaters. Of the 902 returns 819 were from boaters yet 34% of the 902 anglers also fished from shore. Over 50 % of the boaters spent more than 75% of their fishing time from their boat

1. The quality of fishing continues to degrade during 2009

2. The quantity of the fish caught has gotten smaller but larger fish were caught

3. Catch per hour was way down

4. Top States responding were: MA, NJ, RI, ME.

The Best of the Best

In Book I " The Striped Bass 60+ Pound Club," I had a chapter about Best Places, Best Times, Best Locations. I merely added and subtracted data from the actual results where these big bass were caught. Higher the number, better the choice. No statistical calculations about future probabilities and trend lines but what has already happened in these places, times and locations.

Concerning the best State to fish for 60+ pound Striped Bass remains Massachusetts with New York and Rhode Island second and third. More anglers with 60+ pound bass have been found hence the total landings have changed but not the best State to fish for them.

By State:	+ Book **I**	++ Book **II**
Mass.	19	39
NY	15	26
RI	8	19

With more bass registered since the first book was published, the month of June has taken first place with Nov and July following up. The warm weather may have caused the increase numbers during the summer season although Nov numbers seem consistent over the last few years.

By Time:		
June	9	28
Nov.	14	18
July	6	14

By location has not changed at all. The anglers still go where the action is or hope it will be as in past years. What is surprising is the emergence of Virginia Beach into the special home of the Striped Bass. A few years ago it was not on a list to be considered. Is there a shift in the bass preferences? Block Island may be inhibited in its ability to produce more big bass due to restricted access to its many productive beaches. More seaside homes less surfcasters?

By Location:		
Nr. Truro- Nauset	7	14
Cuttyhunk	7	14
Montauk Pt.	7	13
Virginia Beach	-	11
Block Island	6	7

Research has indicated that it was possible to put a plug, bait, eel, lure with some of the big bass fishermen and their fish.

1. 22% of the big bass were caught on eels
2. 19% were caught on various lures
3. 9% were caught on plugs
4. 7% were caught on bait

Of the 60+ pound bass caught records show 24% were caught from a boat and 16% from the surf. It seems to indicate the big ones don't show a decided preference for the boat or the surf; they swim the entire pool. See further data on striped bass in the Chapter " Striped Bass Basics."

17
Striped Bass-Length-Weight-Age

Length Inches	Weight Av. Lbs	Age Years	Length Inches	Weight Av. Lbs	Age Years
12	1	1	36	19.5	10
13	1.5	1	37	20.7	11
14	2.3	2	38	22	12
15	2.5	2	39	24.4	12
16	3	2	40	26	13
17	3.5	3	41	27.3	13
18	4	3	42	29.7	14
19	4.3	3	43	32	14
20	4.9	3	44	34	15
21	5	4	45	36	15
22	5.8	4	46	38.7	16
23	6.3	4	47	42	16
24	7	5	48	44	17
25	7.8	5	49	47.1	17
26	8.5	6	50	50	18
27	9.8	6	51	55	18
28	10.3	6	52	58	19
29	11	7	53	60	19
30	12.3	7	54	64	20
31	13	8	55	70	20
32	14.5	8			
33	15.9	9			
34	16.5	9			
35	18	10			

Max-Min differences in weight is about plus 0.2 to minus 0.2 lbs for small fish to plus 10 to minus 10 lbs for larger fish.

Heavy fish can be over 30 years old. and 60 inches long.

18
IGFA rules and regulations

Equipment: Saltwater

Line: Monofilament-multi filament-lead core. Wire line not permitted.

Backing: No restrictions but maximum of 130 lbs. strength. Line will be rated at backing strength if it exceeds the other line on the reel.

Double line: *To 20 lb test:*
From a double line to end of leader 20ft (15 feet double leader, 5 feet leader).

Over 20 lb. Test:
From the double line to end of leader not to exceed 40 ft. (30 feet double line, 10 feet leader).

Leader: Not required, if used see above.

Rod: Rod must be sporting type but if it gives an unfair advantage to the angler, it will be disqualified.

Rod tip minimum length-40 in., if less than 40 in. remaining when rod tip is broken- disqualification.

Butt maximum length: 27 in. (surf casting rod excluded)

Reel: Complied with sporting ethics and customs. Not motor driven or two handles to be cranked at the same time or ratcheted reels.

Hooks: Bait fishing:
1. Maximum of two single hooks in the bait and no more than 18 in apart.

2. Double and treble hooks prohibited.

3. Two-hook rig consisting of two single hooks with its own separate bait, must not allow one hook to foul hook the fish if attached to the other baited hook.

4. Sketch of hook arrangements must be part of the record application for item 3.

Hooks and lures:

1. Two hooks maximum allowed with lures plus a skirt or trailing materials.

2. Gang hooks on plugs or other artificials must be free swinging and a maximum of three locations on the lure.

3. No bait attached to the lure and a sketch is needed with the record application.

The IGFA Basic Requirements:

1. From the time the fish strikes, the angler must hook, fight and land or boat the fish without the aid of others rod, reel and line must not be touched by others except during gaffing of the fish.

2. More than one gaffer is permitted.

3. No resting of rod, reel or line on the gunwale of the boat or any object.

Note:

Imagine your trophy size striped bass failed to be recognized by the IGFA because of your rod, reel, line, hook set up, lure adjustments or inadvertently help from others.

Although breaking the striped bass record is becoming less and less a possibility for all the previous reasons mentioned, the disqualification of the catch would be a personal tragedy. One that would haunt you for a lifetime.

Yes, you may want to mount your record bass on the wall of your den, but missing would be the plaque that identifies it as the IGFA world record line class or IGFA world record all classes.

Present records: Striped Bass

Line Class: *Men*

Weight	Line Class	Angler	Location	Date
66 lbs 12 oz.	M-06 kg (12 lb)	Steve Thomas,	Bradley Beach, NJ,	11/1/1979
69 lbs. 0 oz.	M-08 kg (16 lb)	Thomas Russell,	Sandy Hook, NJ,	11/18/1982
78 lbs. 8 oz.	M-10 kg (20 lb)	Albert McReynolds,	Atlantic City, NJ	9/21/1982
71 lbs.0 oz	M-15 kg (30 lb)	John Baldino,	Norwalk, Conn.,	7/14/1980
76 lbs. 0 oz.	M-24 kg (50 lb)	Robert Rocchetta,	Montauk Pt. NY,	7/17/1981
70 lbs. 0 oz.	M-37 kg (80 lb)	Chester Berry,	Orient Pt., NY,	9/5/87

Women

| 64 lbs 8 oz. | W-15 kg (30 lb) | Rosa Webb, | North Truro, MA. | 8/14/1960 |
| 64 lbs. 0 oz. | W-24 kg (50 lb) | Asie Espenak, | Sea Bright, NJ, | 6/27/1971 |

If you want your name listed above, spend more time on the beach or in the boat with rod and reel in hand. Time spent fishing is the biggest factor in catching fish and with a little luck you will catch the big one. It happened to those listed above and it may happen to you. Whether being successful or not, it is an old proverb saying that the Lord above excuses all fisherman for the time they spend fishing. This is a win-win situation. *Apparently, in heaven fishing must be regarded as an approved option as it is on earth.*

Reference by Numbers:

1-4: Author's notes

5: Record Striped Bass Registration
   2009 World Rated Game Fish, IGFA.

   The Striped Bass 60 Pound Club book- Book 1.

   Striped Bass, Nick Karas, The Lyons Press, 2000.

   Field and Stream Magazine, 1950-1970.

6: State Record Striped Bass
   "2009 State Record Striped Bass", IGFA.

7: The Battleground
   Eastertide: A Surfcaster's Life, Frank Daignault, Globe Press, 1992.

   The Trophy Striper, Frank Daignault, Globe Press, 1993.

   The Complete Book of Striped Bass Fishing, Henry Lyman, Frank Woolner, Winchester Press, 1983.

   Bass From the Beach, Volume II, Tim Coleman, Surf Casting Rhode Island, 2008.

8: The Stories
   Bill Gavitt, Alfred Anuzewski, George Cheshire, Peter Vican, Ten Nimiroski Joe Szabo, Ray Jobin, Richard Colagiovanni, Sherwood Lincoln, Al Mc Reynolds

9: Tips from the 60+ Pound Club Members
Alfred Anuzewski, Ted Nimiroski, Richard Colagiovanni, Sherwood Lincoln, other club members.

Striped Bass Seminar, Frank Daignault, Tom River, N.J. Feb. 2005, notes.

10: A Southern Shift
Virginia Striped Bass '07-'08 Tournament.

Lee Tolliver @pilotonline.com, consultant.

11: Striped Bass Vision Revisited
"Photo transduction and Adaptation in rods, single cones and twin cones of the Striped Bass retinas: A Comparative Study, James I. Miller and Juan Korennrot of Medicine, University of California at San Francisco, 9/16/1992.

Colour in the Fishes Eyes, Maac Garth, 1990.

Keith Jones PhD, Berkley Fishing Products: Dir. of Fishing Resources. " Biggest change in technology is in fishing line and the chemistry in fish attraction."

12: Striped Bass Basics
Massachusetts Division of Marine Fisheries- Striped Bass Species.

Recreational Fishing Alliance, Winter 2006.

Wildlife Agencies, NWTF Partners, www.nwtf.org.

Chesapeakebay.net, Striped Bass, 4/9/2006.

13: Striped Bass math and More
Marine Recreational Fishing Statistical Query, 2009.

"NewsLines, Stock Report, Angling's Scorecard", Saltwater Sportsman, Feb. '06.

Striped Bass Seminar, Frank Daignault, Toms River, N.J., Feb. 2005.

14: Striped Bass Controversy and Problems and More
Striper Wars, Dick Russell, Island Press, 2005.

Jersey Coast Anglers Association, Jan. '06 Newsletter.

Saltwater Sport Fishing Partners Meeting, St. Petersburg, Fl. April 13-14 '05.

"Did You Know," International Angler, IGFA, Vol.68, No, S, Sept/Oct, 2006.

Biennial Report to Congress by NMFS, National Fisherman Journal, Pg.9.

"US Must Support Sustainable Fisheries," '09.

"Part of the Problem", Rip Cunningham, Saltwater Sportsman, 3/10, Pg.34.

"The Trouble with Fish Oil," Time Magazine, 1/25/10.

Rhode Island, Bill H626, 7/23/09.

Blue Ribbon Fish Company, Boston, MA. 7-08. Telephone call.

"Fish News," NOAA Fisheries Service, 7/30/09.

"Saving the Sea Bounty," National Geographic, 4/07.

"Top Down Strategy," Rip Cunningham, Saltwater Sportsman, Pg. 22, '09.

"Striper Signals," Ted Williams, Conservation, July-Sept, 2009.

15: Tools of the Trade

www.Answere.com/topicfishing-lures-1.

The Most Important Fish of the Sea, H. Bruce Franklin, Inland Press, 2007.

Striper Strategies, D.J. Muller, Burford Books, 2008.

Fishing Diamond Jigs and Bucktails, Tom Mugdalski, Burford Books, 2008.

Bait Tail Fishing, Al Reinfelder, A.S. Barnes and Company, 1969.

" The Mystery of the Eels Marathons' Swim," Philadelphia Inquirer, 9/09.

16: Plugging Away

Physics Books.

Odum wood reference.

17: Surveys
　　IGFA 2009 Annual Book.

　　Striper Forever Survey 2003-2009.

　　NMF Marine Recreational Catch Statistics 1995-2008, 2008.

18: Bass-Age-Weight Chart
　　Mass. Division of Marine Fisheries: Striped Bass Profile.

19: IGFA Regulations
　　IGFA Annual Yearbook-2009.

Minor reference material in book, "The Striped Bass 60+ Pound Club" may have also been used.

Index